THE HISTORY OF CRIME AND CRIMINAL JUSTICE SERIES

THE RULE
OF JUSTICE

The People of Chicago
versus Zephyr Davis

Elizabeth Dale

OHIO STATE UNIVERSITY PRESS
Columbus

Illustrations: On pp. 15, 18, *Chicago Tribune*, February 28, 1888;
on p. 28, *Chicago Daily News*, March 2, 1888; on p. 55, *Chicago Herald*, March 29, 1888;
on p. 58, *Chicago Daily News*, December 18, 1888; on p. 67, *Chicago Herald*, March 29, 1888; on
pp. 95, 97, *Chicago Herald*, May 13, 1888.

Library of Congress Cataloging-in-Publication Data

Dale, Elizabeth.
The rule of justice : the people of Chicago versus Zephyr Davis / Elizabeth Dale.
p. cm. — (The history of crime and criminal justice series)
Includes bibliographical references and index.
ISBN 0-8142-0867-3 (cloth : alk. paper) — ISBN 0-8142-5068-8 (pbk. : alk. paper)
1. Davis, Zephyr, d. 1888. 2. Criminal justice, Administration of—Illinois—Chicago—History—
Case studies. 3. Criminal justice, Administration of—Illinois—Chicago—Public opinion—
History. 4. Trials (Murder)—Illinois—Chicago—History—Case studies. 5. Mass media and
crime—Illinois—Chicago—History—Case studies. 6. Mass media and public opinion—Illinois—
Chicago—History—Case studies.   I. Title. II. Series.
HV9956.C47 D35 2001
364.15'23'0977311—dc21
00-012145

Text and jacket design by Gary Gore.
Type set in Electra by Graphic Composition, Inc., Athens, Georgia.
Printed by Sheridan Books.

9 8 7 6 5 4 3 2 1

CONTENTS

ACKNOWLEDGMENTS

Several groups and individuals helped make this book possible. The Interlibrary Loan staff at Clemson University did a wonderful job of finding me materials. Charles L. Cali at the Illinois State Archive and Phil Costello of the Cook County Court Archives helped my research by responding promptly to my requests for materials. The staffs at the Newberry Library in Chicago, the Chicago Historical Society, and the Joseph M. Regenstein Library at the University of Chicago also helped me find information I needed when I needed it. Some of the research was paid for by a Clemson University Research Grant that I was awarded in 1997–98. I finished this book while on a one-month fellowship at the Newberry Library in 1999.

A variety of people helped me focus my thoughts by reading and commenting on various stages of my work. I gave an early paper on this case at the Social Science History Conference in October 1996, the Law and Society Conference in May 1997, and the American Society for Legal History conference in November of 1997. In each case, the panelists, commentators, and audience provided helpful remarks. I gave a second paper on this case at the Social Science History Conference in November 1998, and once again received helpful comments.

Some of those papers turned into an article that set out some of my preliminary conclusions about this case and about law and justice in Chicago that ultimately appeared in the *Law and History Review*. The comments of the journal's anonymous reviewers, as well as those made by the editor, Chris Tomlins, helped me make my arguments stronger. Mike Grossberg read parts of the book at several stages and helped me refine my thinking in the process.

David Tanenhaus and Jeffrey Adler both provided additional help, answering my questions about what they had found during their research and setting me on the track of materials. Jeff, David Johnson, and the other people at the Ohio State University Press have also been a delight to work with in other ways as well.

INTRODUCTION

The Rule of Law in
Late Nineteenth-Century Chicago

Shortly after 3 P.M. on February 27, 1888, Eddie Dwyer, one of the young employees at Greene's Boot Heel Factory in Chicago, discovered a body in the
closet at the rear of the factory. Investigation established that it was another employee, Maggie Gaughan, a fourteen-year-old Irish American who had been
missing all day and apparently had been hacked to death sometime before work
started that morning. Suspicions quickly centered on the factory foreman, a seventeen-year-old African American named Zephyr Davis, who was away on an errand when Eddie found the body. When Davis failed to return to the factory, suspicion became certainty.[1]

Local papers reported the crime in their evening editions and continued to
follow the story over the next several days, as Davis was hunted and then captured
in Forest, Illinois. The case remained front-page news while he was returned to
Chicago, swiftly indicted, tried at the end of March, sentenced in the beginning
of April, and executed on Saturday, May 12. In the days after Davis was sentenced, several Chicago newspapers commented approvingly on his conviction
and the speed with which it had occurred.[2]

It seems a familiar story and hardly remarkable that papers in late nineteenth-
century Chicago would celebrate the verdict against Zephyr Davis. His was a
horrid crime, made all the worse by his marginal status as a young, working-class,
African American male, and by the fact he had killed a young white girl. At best,
the story offers the minor consolation that he was tried according to law, not
lynched in a cornfield in Forest, Illinois.

As an instance of the exercise of law rather than popular justice, the case
appears to fit neatly into the standard account of criminal law at the end of the
nineteenth century. When that century began, criminal law was a wide-open
affair. Legal processes and rules were often only one aspect of a larger system of

1

popular justice in which extralegal efforts sometimes complemented formal law, at other times replaced it entirely. As the century progressed, some in the urban North concluded that such fluidity was a problem. So long as criminal law rested on a popular base, subject to loosely defined, changeable norms, it could not effectively counter the instabilities seemingly inherent in the fast-moving, heterogeneous cities of the nineteenth-century United States. Fear of disorder led to calls for reform, and from mid-century on, as anxiety about labor and its potential for destruction was added to the mix, those demands led to changes. By century's end, law in the North became more formal, while the older, extralegal tradition carried on only in the South and West.[3]

Those reforms were not simply markers of regional difference. The transformation of criminal law from subject of popular will to instrument of popular control was a major undertaking, which occurred at all layers of the legal system. At the most mundane level of police courts and misdemeanor arrests, institutional changes put an end to the use of those courts for private prosecutions, on the theory that such private actions functioned too much as personal vendettas. The police court's new role was to maintain public order, and to do so its judges relied on laws that criminalized behaviors that had been permissible, if not acceptable, before. Other reforms gave law enforcement greater power to arrest and prosecute those perceived to threaten public order. Few of these petty cases and fewer cases generally were tried before a jury, limiting popular influence on law still further. Even in the felony courts, where juries remained integral to the process, judicial authority increased at the expense of the jury, as jurors were restricted to judging the facts, never the law. Other laws reformed punishment as well, providing for sanctions that disciplined the individual and separated wrongdoers from society. Executions, previously treated as public spectacles, were closed off within prison yards. By the last half of the nineteenth century, criminal law in the North had become the monopoly of the State, so that wrongdoers like Zephyr Davis received their punishment from institutions, rather than popular hands.[4]

That transformation of criminal law, while an immediate reaction to urban disorder, was part of a larger, systemic reform. As Charles Sellers has demonstrated, wholesale alterations made to the common law in the first half of the century permitted the rise of capitalism. During that market revolution, judges rewrote laws, freeing up capitalist ventures, while lawyers acted as the revolution's "shock troops," litigating and manipulating the new laws to help those ventures take off. Once the revolution's aims had been achieved, the common law underwent a second reform. In place of the interpretive flexibility they had favored previously, judges embraced legal formalism, freezing into place the earlier changes in the law and blocking further expansion with an insistence on precedent. Lawyers helped those who had prospered prevent others from taking their profits or market share. By the final decades of the nineteenth century, legal formalism guaranteed the discipline capitalism demanded, and an institutionalized legal system was in place wherever the market held sway.[5]

Sellers's interpretation, which emphasized the extent to which civil law began to control people, built on the earlier work of the legal historians J. Willard Hurst, William Nelson, and Morton Horwitz. By tying the transformation of the common law to the market revolution, Sellers made a point that had only been implicit in those other works: law became a powerful institutional agent of control only because of a larger, cultural shift. People did not give up their tradition of popular justice, or embrace the discipline of the market, simply because lawyers and judges changed some rules. The transformation depended on popular works such as self-help manuals, novels, and news reports to train people in the new ideology, reshaping their reactions and providing them with a new value system.[6]

Others have argued that popular culture played a particularly significant role in reframing attitudes about criminal law. Accounts of crimes educated the reading public about the increased need for order through law. The memoirs of police officers and detectives reinforced the idea that order was possible; mysteries and detective novels fulfilled a similar function. Books and pamphlets based on trials emphasized the degree to which criminals were alien from normal society, justifying decisions to isolate them from society through execution or imprisonment.[7]

This message about criminal law spread to its widest audience through news reports of the sort written on the Davis case. Stories about important felony cases—show trials, to borrow Lawrence Friedman's phrase—taught people "about rights, about due process. They learned that there were many safeguards; that America left no stone unturned to protect the rights of people accused of crime. They saw that judges and juries were fair and impartial. They saw the wicked (sometimes) punished, the innocent (usually) vindicated. These were important, vital, essential things to learn."[8]

By describing protections and rights, these stories introduced people to a new theory of justice, one based on the rule of law, the principle that justice came from the "impartial administration of fixed rules, not uncontrolled judicial discretion, empathy, or whim." Community norms no longer played a role; in exchange for relinquishing the popular-based system of justice that had failed to control those who violated the public peace, people received the protection of the rule of law. That rule provided for prompt punishment of wrongdoers and, as the stories of the show trials demonstrated, also controlled the State, by guaranteeing that government and individual would be held to the same standards.[9]

According to this model, popular accounts of trials helped the transition from ad hoc, community-based justice to institutionalized justice resting on the rule of law. But while it sounds like the traditional description of the role of law in the self-limiting State, that is not the final picture that emerges. Instead, the basic model of criminal law in the late nineteenth century asserts that the transformation stripped people of power and rested on a fraud. Popular accounts of trials concealed far more than they disclosed, downplaying the extent to which popular authority had been lost and exaggerating the scope of the rule of law by implying it governed even the pettiest of cases. Stories of trials made the reforms of criminal law palatable, precisely because they concealed their cost.[10]

Viewed from that perspective, any sort of relief, no matter how tempered, at the manner of Zephyr Davis's conviction seems inappropriate. Davis was spared an execution by a mob only to be sacrificed to the more devious power of the State. The history of his case appears to be just one more example of State power, made the more sordid by its background of racism.

But the actual situation Zephyr Davis faced was more complicated. As a young, working-class, African American male living in Chicago in the decades before the Great Migration, he was not subject to the degree of prejudice his peers would suffer a decade later, although Chicago in the 1880s was still no racial paradise. Its small African American population was not yet segregated from the larger city community; whites and blacks mingled, or at least shared public spaces, most often without incident. But when African Americans excluded from public accommodations stood on their rights and sued, they found their legal victories rarely translated into actual change. Although crime statistics for working-class African Americans resembled those of their white counterparts and did not yet reflect a particularly racist backlash, most African Americans bought peace by avoiding places they might find trouble.[11]

Racism had not yet solidified in Chicago, but some residents of the city already had the sense that the law could be ignored when it came to blacks. Less than a week after a jury awarded significant damages to an African American woman who had been barred from a theater because of her race, another theater made an African American minister sit in segregated seating. Similar instances suggested that if some believed that the people, not the courts, should determine what justice required in race relations, not much could be done about it.

The reaction to the verdict against Davis echoed that sentiment. The Chicago papers that praised the outcome in his case did not celebrate law, they rejoiced in its absence. One, the *Chicago Times*, made the point explicitly. "Swiftness of justice," it wrote, "is a necessary element of justice." The courts, usually delayed by legalisms, had "avenged" Maggie Gaughan's murder with dispatch; justice had been done because law, in the form of legal rules, had been kept under control. Talk of vengeance on the streets of Chicago before the trial more than hinted that race played the major role in defining what justice required in the Davis case. But the idea that law and justice were at odds was not unique to the *Times*, confined to the streets of Chicago, or limited to cases of interracial crime. Several stories on late nineteenth-century criminal cases published in *Frank Leslie's Illustrated Newspaper*, a New York–based weekly with a national circulation, lamented trials that reflected "too much law and not enough justice." None of those cases involved an African American.[12]

Others worried that there was too much justice and not enough law in the legal system, though they were not always sure about who, or what, to blame. Several critics of criminal law writing at the turn of the century faulted the press, complaining that newspapers weakened respect for law by encouraging calls for vengeance, but usually they carried that criticism further. Arthur Train, a district attorney from New York, argued in one essay that newspapers undermined law by describing killers who committed crimes of vengeance sympathetically, but in other essays he indicated that law itself played a role in the problem. Train was torn between criticizing lawyers who undermined popular support for law by playing tricks in court (at times, Train seemed sympathetic to their tricks) and explaining the fault in terms of the technicalities law encouraged. But he was sure one or the other undermined the sense that the legal system was doing justice, in the process encouraging people to distrust the law and favor extralegal remedies.[13]

Train's occasional enthusiasm for the instances when one attorney pulled the wool over his opponent's eyes weakened his argument and seemed to endorse the very "sporting approach" to trials that law professor Roscoe Pound, an advocate of sociological reform of law, blamed for law's loss of respect. But Pound, like Train, did more than blame lawyers for law's failings, he also deplored the effect of law itself. Jurors who refused to follow their instructions, or entered verdicts consistent with their own sense of justice, did so, he claimed, because they perceived the law to be "an arbitrary mass of technicalities, having no basis in reason or justice." The problem was not "disrespect for justice" so much as a well-founded sense that law was unjust.[14]

One problem led to another. So long as law remained a collection of technical rules unrelated to contemporary circumstances, it inspired and rewarded legerdemain, not the pursuit of justice. By describing the problem in terms of legalisms, and law standing in the way of justice, Pound and Train resorted to language very similar to that used by the Chicago papers after the Davis trial to come to the opposite conclusion. Where the *Times* favored justice at the expense of law, Train and Pound worried about how the two could be reconciled. Nor was their fear that legal rules were losing out to popular notions of justice unrealistic. In cases involving crimes of revenge, juries did ignore instructions and impose their own standards of justice, permitting some defendants to go free under the so-called unwritten law. While the issue arose most sensationally in those cases, such results were not restricted to them, nor was the influence of popular justice limited to the occasional dubious verdict. One weekly magazine, the *National Police Gazette*, reported all sorts of instances of extralegal activity in the 1880s, describing mobs, vigilante groups, and public protests of verdicts. Taken together, these accounts indicate that popular notions of justice played a bigger role in the late nineteenth century than the familiar history of criminal law would credit. At the very least, they suggest a need to revisit the relationship between criminal law and popular justice in the late nineteenth century.[15]

This study uses the Davis case to reexamine law's relation to popular justice. There are several reasons why the case is a profitable site for such reconsideration, not the least that it arose in late nineteenth-century Chicago. At the end of that century, Chicago was firmly part of the capitalist economy and had modified its political practices accordingly. Government at the state level had consolidated its power, dismantling the community-based practices that had limited it in the earlier part of the century. At the level of city government, uniform, centralized taxing practices replaced special, neighborhood assessments; reforms of the increasingly professional police department separated the officers in local districts from the communities they served, undermining popular influence on law enforcement in that respect as well. In the same period, concern about crime and disorder increased. By the time of the Davis trial in 1888, Chicago was exactly the sort of place where criminal law should have been firmly in the control of the State.[16]

But it was not. Popular political activity—mob actions in public streets, debates in public forums, and indignation meetings held in churches and public halls—continued even after the Haymarket Riot in 1886. Writing about the period after Haymarket, Jane Addams noted the extent to which efforts were made to permit people to meet for debate and protest. Recent histories of nineteenth-century Chicago have confirmed her account, demonstrating that an active civil society existed in the last decades of the century. Activities in that realm provided Chicagoans with a mechanism outside the formal political system for challenging the authority of the State.[17]

Addams suggested that not all challenges to State power took the form of protest, and in the late nineteenth century, Chicago's civil society also included voluntary, or civic, associations of all sorts. Sometimes, these associations engaged the State for antidemocratic reasons, as was the case immediately after the Chicago Fire in 1871, when businessmen created associations in order to bypass city government, which they distrusted as too democratic and popular. But, as Jane Addams's account indicated, other reformers created associations with the intention of challenging the authority of the State. Nor were all associations paternalistic creations of elites; some were founded by workers or represented working-class or ethnic interests. These groups were often mocked for their efforts. The Trade and Labor Assembly's calls for an investigation into charges of neglect at Cook County Hospital were reported with scorn by local papers. Although many of these associations, elite and popular alike, failed in their aims, some succeeded in pushing through reforms, and many more managed to call attention to problems. At a minimum, their efforts inspired other civic associations to try to advance their interests. Their agitation also demonstrated that the State could be questioned.[18]

Chicago's newspapers, whether mainstream dailies or ethnic, racial, religious, or radical weeklies, played several roles in Chicago's civil society. Many of the weeklies offered a particular community's perspective on popular problems, and the mainstream daily papers reported many popular protests and expressions of public outrage. In that way, the papers helped spread different perspectives to a wide audience. At the same time, the papers themselves had different perspectives on issues, which meant their treatments of events differed enough to add another layer of dialogue to Chicago's civic culture. As was the case with the voluntary associations, the papers played a mixed role, trying to silence ideas they disapproved of as often as they encouraged debate. Even so, the very process of reporting ideas in order to attack them meant those ideas reached a broader audience than they otherwise might have.[19]

All this popular activity influenced the law. Just as Pound and Train feared, papers reported acts of popular justice, encouraging people to ignore the rule of law. The people seemed more than willing to do so, no matter how serious or formal the circumstances. Although the Chicago police department's record *Homicides and Other Events* indicates that roughly half the homicides in Chicago involved an immediate arrest at the scene, Jeffrey Adler's study of conviction rates indicates that no more than 25 to 30 percent of homicides resulted in a conviction. That low rate suggests that many juries deliberately chose not to convict individuals who had probably committed the crime, a conclusion supported by newspaper anecdotes about trials.[20]

Zephyr Davis's case is a suitable site for investigating the entire phenomenon of popular influence on law. It fits within that general story: Mobs and groups reacted to his crime almost from the moment it occurred, bringing that aspect of popular justice into play. Newspapers exhaustively reported the case, debating the issues it raised and providing a forum for expressions of opinion. But while all these popular forces were brought to bear on the Davis case, the ultimate result—his conviction and execution—was at odds with the tendency to acquit. All of this means that the case offers a chance to read actual practice in Chicago against the grain, providing a means of questioning how law and justice impinged upon one another and fit together within Chicago's civil society.[21]

To unpack the relationship between law, justice, and Chicago's civil society, this study breaks the Davis case into stages. The chapters of the book proceed chronologically; each corresponds to a particular stage and permits examination of a specific aspect of popular justice. Beginning with the discovery of the murder in late February, chapter 1 considers the intersecting roles of the mob and press. Even before Davis was captured, mobs formed to look for him with lynching on their mind. Nor was this mere talk. A mob ultimately caught Davis in Forest and was barely restrained from stringing him up on the spot.

News coverage of the mob action that marked the case's first days was surprisingly sympathetic. The press did not simply record popular outrage, it fanned it, exaggerating the details of the murder and portraying Zephyr in as unappealing a light as possible. But although they framed the crime in terms that guaranteed popular outrage and provoked the mob, press reactions were not uniform. The various papers differed about when, where, and to what extent mob violence was permissible. They also offered very different views about whether mob actions were extralegal or illegal.[22]

The second chapter covers the pretrial period and another aspect of Chicago's civil society. As Davis waited for trial, a variety of groups, some formally organized, some spontaneous, addressed themselves to a variety of legal issues arising out of the case. They represented the softer, more civilized aspect of popular justice, but even so, they reflected the sense that public opinion mattered and demonstrated it had a well-established role. These protests even occurred within the formal legal system. At the start of the Davis case, the coroner's jury used its official meeting as a forum from which to issue a statement denouncing labor practices in the city. The local papers played a role at this stage as well, mocking or dismissing those views they did not agree with and emphasizing those they felt worthwhile. While the papers reduced the impact of some voices, and other factors limited them still more, this period demonstrates the extent to which even the marginalized tried to direct opinion.[23]

In the pretrial stage various civil associations concerned themselves with trying to advance a particular view of what justice required. The trial was an official moment when popular justice actively engaged the formal law. Chapter 3, which covers the trial, demonstrates how ironic that interaction could be. The prosecution tried to exploit popular outrage by urging the jury to use the verdict to ratify public opinion, while the defense tried to counter that argument with a theory of justice based on the rule of law. Popular justice prevailed, but not exactly in the co-opted sense urged by the prosecution. Rather than ratify the instructions of the judge, the jury consciously ignored the law, imposing a verdict based on its own sense of what was right.

The execution on May 12 provided a final setting for a public debate about justice. Treating the execution as the type of edifying moment Mary Ryan has dubbed a civic ceremony, ministers from local African American churches challenged the popular forces that had played such a significant role in Davis's arrest and trial. In the process, they raised the possibility that justice in the hands of the people could be as oppressive as law in the hands of the State. While chapter 3 ended with the triumph of the popular, the final chapter closes with contemporary criticisms of popular will, criticisms that raised the question whether it could be truly just.[24]

Several points emerge from this history. The most basic is that in late nineteenth-century Chicago popular forces limited the rule of law. The case demonstrated how, and to what extent, popular forces could counter the authority of the State, making sure that criminal law conformed to popular will. By demonstrating that as the nineteenth century came to a close, popular justice continued to play a determining factor in criminal law in a city like Chicago, the case invites consideration of the possibility that the same was true in other parts of the country.[25]

With its argument that popular influence limited the role of law and the authority of the State, this study also questions the ideological determinism assumed by histories of nineteenth-century criminal law. But it does not replace that idea of ideological hegemony, the sense that ideological "meanings are so embedded that representational and institutional power is invisible," with an open, democratic public sphere. Civil society in Chicago challenged the State, but while it brought popular notions of justice to bear on the criminal law, those popular forces were not always the products of reason or dictated by equitable principles. Nor was Chicago's civil society equally available to all. Popular actions were contentious and often violent. Newspapers reprinted debates and described protests to a broad audience, but they also silenced dissent or tried to advance the narrow interests of particular groups. Far too often, popular action reflected prejudice or an unreflective demand for vengeance.[26]

Ultimately, that means that the Davis case is a story about justice, and not a particularly happy one at that. The best that may be said about late nineteenth-century Chicago is that justice did not have a single meaning but many. It encompassed the rule of law, and the lynch mob; it encouraged people to call for more legal protections, and to demand that laws be ignored. It justified challenges to the power of the State, and acts of oppression. Its capacious nature made justice a handy tool for nearly everyone; its flexibility meant that it could, and did, excuse nearly anything. To borrow a phrase from Bryant Garth and Austin Sarat, the case demonstrates that "justice disciplines power, but it also legitimates power."[27]

1

Murder and Capture,
February 27 and February 28, 1888

Shortly after 3 P.M. on February 27, 1888, a coal truck pulled up at the two-story frame building at 1319 State Street in Chicago. The building housed Greene's Boot Heel Factory, and when the truck stopped outside, John Greene, manager of the factory, told Eddie Dwyer, his newest employee, to clear space for the coal in a back closet. Minutes after he started, Eddie called out that something seemed wrong. When he insisted there was a problem, Greene went back to investigate and discovered that Eddie had found the body of another employee, fourteen-year-old Maggie Gaughan, who had been missing all day. She had been hacked to death and hidden beneath some sacks.[1]

The murder apparently happened that morning, sometime between 7:00 and 8:00 A.M. About 7:00 Maggie said goodbye to her mother and left the house to walk to her job as a heel cutter at Greene's. At roughly the same time, seventeen-year-old Zephyr Davis dashed out of the two-room apartment that he shared with his family. He was also on his way to the factory, where he was foreman. Both lived roughly a mile from the factory, and neither walk can have been pleasant, or quick, that particular morning. A stiff wind was blowing in from Lake Michigan, it was sleeting, and the temperature was well below freezing.[2]

Close to 8:00 A.M., Zephyr opened the door of the factory and let the other workers inside. An hour or so later, John Greene arrived. He noticed Maggie was missing; when he asked where she was, the others said she had been absent all morning. Work at the factory's benches went on uneventfully until early afternoon, when the stove that heated the shop began to smoke. After he found the leak, Greene handed Zephyr some money and sent him to buy stovepipe at the Fair, a department store a mile to the north. No sooner had Davis put on his coat and left for the Loop than the coal truck appeared; shortly thereafter Maggie's body was discovered.[3]

Even in the factory's bad light, it was clear she was dead. After shooing the others back to their work, John Greene sent Eddie to find the police. On his way to the nearest police call box, Eddie ran into James M. Swift, a patrol officer. He stopped Swift, told him what had happened, and led him back to the factory, where they met up with Greene, who had raced to the corner drugstore to phone the Harrison Street Police Station. Within minutes, Swift was joined at the factory by two more officers, then a squad of detectives, and finally a lieutenant and the captain of police. Reporters from the various local papers followed close behind.[4]

In hindsight, the story seems newsworthy as a troubling case from a troubled time and place. Maggie Gaughan was a young, white woman, Zephyr Davis a young, black man. The factory where the murder occurred, a branch of a Massachusetts firm that had opened its Chicago location around the first of the year, was, more significantly, a sweatshop, exclusively employing boys and girls, black and white, under eighteen. Like many another dubious enterprise, it sat at the edge of Chicago's vice district, known as the Levee, between a poolroom that took nickel and dime bets and a cobbler's shop. All around were struggling businesses, tenements, and rooming houses for the railroad workers, intermixed with saloons, gambling dens, variety theaters, and houses of prostitution. The Levee, and its denizens, represented the threat of disorder within Chicago, even as Chicago played that role on a grander scale. By the late 1870s and early 1880s, a sizable immigrant population, the presence of vocal radicals, and ongoing problems with political corruption (to say nothing of its gamblers and vice areas) cemented Chicago's reputation for lawlessness.[5]

Yet the situation is not so straightforward. Race, though an important aspect of the case, was a variable, not a constant, in this period. So too, in the late nineteenth century Chicago's lawless image, strong as it was, lacked the edge it would have in the twentieth century. The Levee was disreputable and vice-ridden, but it was fear of labor unrest threatening property and economic stability, far more than fear of murder, that lay beneath the anxiety expressed by the *Chicago Tribune* when it railed against the rise of violent crime. That is not to say that murder was unheard of in late nineteenth-century Chicago, merely that in the 1880s it was not a daily or even a weekly event. According to the Chicago police department's *Homicides and Other Events*, there were fewer than fifty homicides in 1888.[6]

Relative novelty, far more than paralyzing fear, gave murder its éclat, and killings of all types were the subject of rapt attention. A case in point was the mysterious slaying, a few weeks before Maggie's murder, of Amos Snell. Snell, a wealthy resident of the city, was discovered early one morning on a stairway in his home, shot to death, apparently in the act of surprising a burglar. His killer was never captured, though for months afterward the police issued statements that claimed they were on the trail of the chief suspect, the ne'er-do-well son of another Chicago industrialist. The papers exhaustively reported every step in that singularly fruitless investigation.[7]

From the perspective of popular fascination with homicide, February 1888 was a banner month. Between the Snell murder at its start and Maggie Gaughan's death at month's end, readers of Chicago's daily papers could get their fill of stories about murders in various stages of investigation. Next to accounts of the hunt for Snell's murderer were stories about Mathias Busch, a beer peddler arrested for slashing his wife to death in their home. Reports of the discovery of Maggie's body shared the same pages as accounts of the trial of August Heitzke, charged with beating his young stepson to death with a belt. As domestic crimes, the Busch and Heitzke cases were more typical than the Snell and Gaughan murders. But for all they were routine, neither was slighted by the press.[8]

So the reporters swarming into the factory on the heels of the police were not unusual. Once there, everyone had to wait for the coroner, out on another job. Taking advantage of the delay, the police and reporters questioned Maggie's co-workers, who graphically recounted the way sacks had been pulled out of the closet to reveal Maggie's disfigured and bloody corpse. John Greene offered predictably polite recollections of his former worker, emphasizing how quickly Maggie had learned her job. He reminded everyone he had noted her absence that morning with particular regret, since he wanted to introduce her to his brother, G. M. Greene, in town to do an inspection at the factory. There was one unexpected moment amid the gore and platitudes. According to the *Chicago Times*, Eddie Dwyer, who lived with Maggie's family, claimed that when he went home for lunch he had mentioned Maggie's absence to her mother and that she seemed unconcerned by the news.[9]

Because Eddie's recollection raised some doubts about Maggie and her family, it did not fit the prevailing mood, so it was quickly lost in the shuffle. In contrast, another casual comment led to an important clue. Confirming the general sense that the day started badly, another factory worker, Lizzie Lemke, said that when she arrived at the factory not long after 7:00 A.M. she found the front door unexpectedly locked. As a result, she had to stand outside in the sleet with some of the others for over forty-five minutes, banging on the door. Davis did not let them into the building until nearly 8:00, when he came out of the back of the factory to unlock the door. Prompted by her story, several police officers and

reporters went to the businesses nearby to see if anyone noticed something suspicious at the back of the factory that morning. Next door, in the house behind
John Conlon's cobbler shop, they found what they were looking for. Conlon's
wife, the washerwoman Mary Johnson, and a boarder named Henry Meyers all
recalled that Zephyr came to the back door with a basin around 7:30 that morning, asking for hot water. They agreed they saw blood on his hand when he
poured the water, and that, when one of them asked about it, Zephyr said he had
cut himself.[10]

Within the factory, other, increasingly inconsistent memories tumbled out.
Greene claimed that Zephyr had acted strangely all day, refusing to leave for
lunch and agreeing to run his errand that afternoon with great reluctance. Others told a different tale, remembering that he had gone out on several errands
during the day, and recalling that Greene had pointed out to his brother how
well Zephyr did his work during the inspection. But Greene's brother confirmed
that Davis seemed preoccupied, and clinched the point by recollecting that he
refused to accept the cigar he was offered when the inspection was done. The debate ended when Cook County Coroner Henry Hertz, and two other doctors, finally arrived, nearly two hours after the discovery of the body. Someone cleared
off a workbench, and Maggie's corpse was removed from the closet to be hoisted
onto the makeshift table for a preliminary examination. When she was lifted off
the floor, a small, blood-stained hatchet was found beneath her body.[11]

An hour after the coroner arrived, her corpse was carried out of the factory
and put on a police carriage to be taken to the morgue. When, at roughly that
same moment, Zephyr's younger brother Marvin arrived at the factory looking
for his brother, he was seized and taken to the nearby police station for questioning. A few detectives went from the factory to the Fair, to try to trace Davis's
movements there. Others went to interview drivers of State Street cable cars, to
find out if any remembered giving him a ride. The other workers went home,
and slowly the people gathered outside the factory left as well. Some went home
themselves, to dazzle neighbors and family with what they had seen. Others, em-
boldened by a combination of whisky and descriptions of Maggie's mangled
body, needed more excitement, and went prowling the city for Davis.[12]

When setting the scene of the crime for their readers, the daily papers competed
to present images of carnage. One described the way the fingers of Maggie's
hands had been nearly chopped off and the gashes on her face and head, including one so deep that it almost removed her "staring eye" from her skull. Others emphasized the blood-stained walls of the closet and the gore that covered
the floor and sacks near where her body was found.

THE CLOSET.

A close look at those accounts suggests how much the papers chose to emphasize atmosphere at the expense of accuracy. The story the *Daily News* rushed out in its evening edition February 27 reported as fact that Maggie had been raped as well as murdered. But that was not all: According to that paper, she had been "hacked to pieces" and only found at 4:30 that afternoon "after a long search" that began when she was missed that morning. Moreover, it reported that "the alleged assailant [was] a negro employed in the neighborhood," a statement that was both literally true and so recklessly broad that it amounted to a virtual declaration that any black man seen within miles of State Street should be seized on suspicion.[13]

The account the *Daily News* published the next morning, Tuesday, February 28, was more thorough but still fraught with imagined drama. It re-created the moment Maggie entered the factory. "No one but the porter [i.e., Davis] knew that Maggie came as early as seven o'clock in order to be on time. No one saw him building the fire at the back of the stove, as the little girl tripped in at the front door and ran back to warm her fingers." The sight of her, face "glowing from the nipping air," was too much. Davis "had daily seen the innocent face of the half child, half woman, as she bent over her work. He doubtless made some careless reply to her remarks, not knowing what he said." When he saw her step into the closet, he followed, hatchet in hand. "She had just hung her hat on a peg. That is the last sign of any act of Miss Gaughan." The paper scrupulously reminded its readers that no one knew what motivated Zephyr to do what he did. But its emphasis on Maggie's appearance, and its suggestion of his unspoken desire for "the half child, half woman," made his purpose all too clear.[14]

The feverish speculations in the *Daily News* were matched by the other papers. In the story on the murder in its morning edition for Tuesday, February 28, the *Chicago Times* described the scene when John Greene first noticed that Maggie was not at work and was told that she had been missing all day. "Davis was standing a few feet away," the article continued. "He made no remark, but his face expressed such anxiety and there was such a troubled look in his eyes, that the employer asked him what ailed him. He muttered some explanation and moved away. All day long, he was absent minded and nervous." Nor was the *Times* content with that. It also supplied its readers with a graphically inaccurate description of the damage done to Maggie's body, noting that as she was carried out of the closet, "part of [her] brain fell to the floor."[15]

The *Tribune* was not noticeably more restrained. Its first article on the crime, published on the morning of February 28, described the discovery of the murder weapon in the pool of "blood and brains" under Maggie's body. It also offered its readers a dramatic moment involving Zephyr and the people in Conlon's shop next door. According to the *Tribune*, when they asked Zephyr why there was blood on his hand, his "face paled." Each account cast the murder in the most horrific possible light in an effort to stir up reaction to the case. More to the point, each was written so that anyone who read even partway through the story would know that Davis had committed the crime.[16]

A tension surfaced even in those earliest stories, which became more marked as coverage of the crime continued. The first reports focused chiefly on Maggie and on what befell her, but within twelve hours the attention of the papers began to shift. By the day after the discovery of her body, the stories were no longer about the murder of Maggie Gaughan so much as they were about the Zephyr Davis case.

The shift began the very night of her murder. That evening, after her body was removed from the factory, some of the curious milled around the worker's cottage near Twentieth and Indiana that was the Gaughan home, or gathered with the neighborhood men in nearby saloons. Inside the Gaughan house, Maggie's mother, aunt, and uncle sat talking to reporters and police officers as they waited for her father to return home from his job as a teamster. Accounts of that interview published the next day in the local papers emphasized different bits of information, offering the first hints of the different perspectives of the daily papers.[17]

The Democratic and vaguely populist *Chicago Times*, which ran a series on "white slavery" (an ambiguous term that referred to both prostitution and the wage labor of white women) in the summer of 1888, cast Maggie as a working-class victim. It emphasized her youth and the fact that until recently she had gone to the nearby Harrison school. But, the paper went on, "her parents are poor and she turned out bravely to earn a few dollars a week for them. First, she went to work at a downtown notion store." Unfortunately, at the end of "the holiday rush, she lost her place there"; tragically, she quickly found another job at Greene's.[18]

Another Chicago daily, the Republican *Inter-Ocean*, which had run its own series on working women in 1887, depicted Maggie as a worker-saint, rather than a martyr. It emphasized her mother's description of Maggie as a model child who told her parents everything, always came straight home from work except for the evenings she took music lessons, had no boyfriends, socialized with no one from Greene's, and never complained about the factory. The *Inter-Ocean* reinforced this rather overpowering impression of responsibility by asserting that Maggie's mother knew nothing of her absence from work because Eddie Dwyer had been unable to get to the Gaughan home at lunch to let her know.[19]

That description was in deliberate contrast to the *Inter-Ocean*'s usual treatment of young working women. In its pages, young women who worked invariably died, though typically they became pregnant or prostitutes before they were corpses. Sometimes, their desire for adventure led to degradation; other times circumstance made the result inevitable. Poor wages forced them onto the streets; men they met while working corrupted them. Occasionally, their parents were to blame, setting their daughters to work at an early age or deliberately exposing them to vice. The *Inter-Ocean* clearly wanted to distinguish Maggie from those unfortunates. By emphasizing how responsible she was, it intended to squelch speculation about her or her relationship with Zephyr. Unfortunately, the very words it used to try to make that distinction echoed the phrases it employed when describing others who always went home at night, and never disobeyed their parents, until one fateful day. By invoking, even accidentally, its stories of those other girls, the paper made its picture of Maggie far more ambiguous than it intended, calling to mind the very questions about her murder that it had hoped to silence.[20]

In contrast to this emphasis on Maggie, the *Tribune* and *Herald* focused on her parents, and both papers attempted to characterize the family as middle-, rather than working-, class. Contrary to the *Times*'s suggestion that the Gaughans lived in "dingy rooms," the *Tribune* pointed out that her father owned the family home. The *Herald* went a step further, describing Owen Gaughan as economically comfortable. Here again, the characterization rested on something other

THE MURDERED GIRL.

than circumstance, as both papers tried to frame the case in a manner that would make their readers sympathize with the Gaughans and provoke outrage about their daughter's death. The vociferously probusiness *Tribune* only approved of workers who were hard-working, disinclined to strike, and respectable. Cast as a homeowner, Owen Gaughan fit that image far better than he did as a teamster, and became more sympathetic and palatable to the *Tribune's* readership. The *Herald*, marginally more liberal than the *Tribune*, occasionally ran stories that presented even radicals in a positive light. But its bourgeois readership also identified with stable homeowners far more than with working-class families who needed wages from their children to make ends meet.[21]

Not content with inflating their economic status, the *Tribune* made a concerted effort to present Owen and Mary Gaughan as sympathetic parents. It emphasized the way Mary Gaughan received the news of her daughter's death in the kitchen, surrounded by three younger children, a picture of domesticity. According to the paper, upon hearing the news, the "motherly" woman dragged its reporter by the hand around her kitchen "in her agony as if he were a child." She sobbed about her daughter's death, worrying about how she would break the news to her husband. Her intense, highly emotional reaction was mirrored by her spouse's. When he learned of Maggie's murder, Owen Gaughan "became frenzied with grief, and rushed from the house bareheaded, 'to bring his girl home.'" All the other reports agreed that Maggie's parents were upset by the news of their daughter's death, but none offered so dramatic a description of their despair. The *Tribune*, alone among the papers, presented the Gaughans as characters from a sentimental novel, perhaps because as an Irish American working-class family, they were otherwise too foreign to be of much interest to the *Tribune's* readers.[22]

These efforts to make Mary and Owen Gaughan attractive and sympathetic had unintended consequences, since they weakened the picture of Maggie as they bolstered her parents. According to the *Tribune,* Mary Gaughan was so worried when her daughter did not come home for lunch that she sent one of her sons to Greene's around noon to find out what had happened. He returned to report that she had been missing all day. After that, as the *Tribune* put it, Mary Gaughan "was prepared to hear bad news, but not such news." While that story was consistent with the image of a concerned mother that the paper was trying to present, the suggestion that she had managed to resign herself to bad news carried with it the implication that her daughter had skipped work or acted irresponsibly in the past. The evening edition of the *Daily News* added to the confusion about Maggie's relationship with her parents by reporting that although Owen and Mary Gaughan had been concerned when they learned that the foreman of the factory was "a colored boy," Maggie refused to agree when they asked her to quit her job. Instead, she talked them into letting her stay on at Greene's through St. Patrick's Day to make pocket money. There was a picture of a willful daughter that contradicted efforts to cast Maggie as a good girl and undermined the claim that she worked to help her family.[23]

As they revealed the different perspectives of the various papers, those stories marked the moment when coverage of the case shifted away from a focus on Maggie Gaughan. That transition raises the question of why it occurred. Part of the answer lies in the ambivalence that accompanied stories of young working women, but as Karen Halttunen's study of popular accounts of murder trials suggests, that is only the beginning of the problem.

Halttunen observed a distinction between works describing the murders of wives and mothers and those treating murders of women at the hands of strangers or acquaintances. The former emphasized the victim's virtue, casting the murderous husband as a destroyer of the family circle and domesticity. Accounts of women who died in other circumstances—murdered by lovers, abortionists, or persons not related by blood or marriage—tended to emphasize the sexual, physical nature of the crime. Victims in this second group were obviously the cause of their own downfall, their sexual allure leading men astray to the point of murder; but having identified that distinction, Halttunen demonstrated that it was a distinction without a difference. She concluded that all sorts of popular accounts blamed women for their deaths, and that the two, seemingly different, approaches to murdered women made up two sides of a single whole, much as the literary figures of the virtuous and seductive women were "two forms of a single image." In each case, one picture called to mind the other, just as the *Inter-Ocean*'s description of a respectable Maggie contained within it the images of working girls who died in disgrace. According to Halttunen, both types of account shifted "the guilt for [a woman's] violent death from her killer" to the victim by suggesting that women were so different from men that they inevitably inspired violence.[24]

The first day's coverage of Maggie Gaughan's murder, with its broad hints of a sex crime, fit into the general pattern Halttunen described; but by the next day, descriptions in the papers, with their shift in focus away from Maggie, began to deviate from her model. This shift was manifest in the emphasis the *Herald* and the *Tribune* gave to her parents, and in the *Times*'s descriptions of the reactions of her neighbors to her death. In the *Times*'s account, women from the neighborhood spoke of Maggie, emphasizing her virtues, some recalling how pretty she had been with her dark golden hair and blue eyes. Others pointed out how quiet she was, and thoughtful. In contrast to that emphasis on Maggie and her life, the *Times* reported that conversation among men in the local saloons and on neighborhood streets centered on her death. They called for revenge, not remembrance; as they did, they focused on Zephyr, demanding that he be found and burned alive. They made little mention of his victim.[25]

This shift in emphasis from victim to murderer was no accident; it reflected the pattern of murder coverage in Chicago. When Mathias Busch killed his wife in 1888, Katherine Busch received little attention in the reports of his crime or in accounts of her husband's trial. Instead, stories focused on Mathias and his odd behavior. In 1885, when Frank Mulkowski was arrested for the murder of a very young, very pregnant woman, the papers quickly dropped his victim, emphasizing instead Mulkowski's dubious past. Murder victims who were not women disappeared as quickly from stories about the crime. Account after account of August Heitzke's killing of his young stepson offered descriptions of the burly murderer but were sparing in their discussion of the boy. Amos Snell faded from the stories about his death within a day or two, as attention shifted to speculation about his suspected murderer and his whereabouts. Murder in Chicago was predominantly a tale of the criminal, not the victim, and accounts focused on the murderer's distinctive nature, not the victim's.[26]

Although the accounts in the Chicago papers resembled the stories Halttunen described, their purpose was different. By demonizing the criminals and demonstrating how different they were, the papers rallied the community against them.

This result was particularly necessary in Chicago, where papers feared that through ineptitude or indifference the Chicago police department would never capture criminals, an anxiety that was heightened in the Davis case because no one was sure where he was. At roughly the same time as the men in the saloons off Twentieth Street were talking about forming a lynch mob, and less than a mile away, the police ransacked the small apartment at the rear of 2129 Clark that Zephyr shared his mother and two younger brothers. Ignoring the protests of one brother that they needed a warrant, the officers questioned everyone about Zephyr and swept through the two rooms. Unable to find even a likeness of their suspect, they went back to the station and prepared a description, which read:[27]

> Please notify immediately all station agents and conductors on your line to look out for and arrest for murder Zefter [*sic*] Davis, a colored man, 20 years old, 5 feet 9 inches high; weighs about 165 pounds, slim build, square shouldered, dark brown skin, wore dark brown check suit and dark brown overcoat, with fur or astrachan [*sic*] cuffs and collar. He is supposed to have left the city late last evening or early this morning. Any expense incurred by you in telegraphing this information will be promptly paid. George W. Hubbard, Acting General Superintendent of Police.

The announcement reached rail stations in Chicago by 9:00 the night of February 27 and was then telegraphed out along each rail line. Other copies were hand carried to nearby suburban stations.[28]

While detectives, reporters, and the curious chased down rumors that variously placed him in pool halls, saloons, and African American homes near Greene's, Zephyr Davis sat ten miles away at a train station just outside the Chicago suburb of Hyde Park, waiting for a freight. He had seen the people gathered at Greene's when he returned from the Fair and, having spotted police in the crowd, decided not to get off the cable car. Instead, he rode past the factory to Fifteenth Street, where he jumped off (leaving the stovepipe behind), turned the corner, and sat in a doorway until dark and cold made him move on.[29]

His first stop was the switching yard a few blocks west on Sixteenth Street, where he caught a ride to the Chicago, Burlington and Quincy yard, just southwest of the city. There, he learned for the first time that a strike that morning had shut down the entire line. Trainmen sitting by the idled cars told him that if he wanted a ride out of town he would have to catch either an Illinois Central or a Wabash freight, so he walked south to the Wabash yard and sat, warming himself, until a train arrived. He then hopped on its caboose and rode south to the

Forty-Third Street station, where he jumped off to wait for a faster train. Several hours later, the Wabash freight going south slowed as it went through the station, and Davis scrambled aboard. A little past midnight, the train arrived at Forest, Illinois, a junction nearly ninety miles south of Chicago. As it pulled to a stop in the station, Zephyr climbed out of his hiding place, brushed off his clothes, and walked into the station's waiting room. Nodding a greeting to the telegraph operator, he settled down on a bench to wait and get some sleep until another train arrived.[30]

Around 11:00 A.M. the next morning, as Zephyr still dozed on a bench in the station, the description from the Chicago police department came over the wire at Forest. When he read it, O. F. Clark, the telegraph officer, remembered the young black man he had seen come into the station the night before. Once a quick glance confirmed that Davis was in the waiting room, Clark compared his appearance with the description in the circular and concluded he was the man it described. Just then, a train to Kansas City pulled up to a stop, and Zephyr got up from his bench, heading toward the train. Clark followed him out of the station, hurriedly attracting the attention of the train's conductor. The two stood by the tracks, discussing Clark's suspicions and keeping a weather eye on their suspect. When he noticed their serious discussion and stares, Davis turned from the train, walked a few steps, and then broke into a run, dashing north along the track. Men raced after him, while others ran back toward town to find the local constable, William Martin. After running two or three miles down the track, Davis veered off into a cornfield, crowd and constable following behind. In the middle of the field, they overtook him and he surrendered.[31]

Accounts provided by the Chicago papers the next day described the chase vividly, though they were circumspect in their discussion of what happened as Davis was captured. When he came out of the field, in the custody of crowd and constable, his coat was missing its cuffs and collar. Several papers suggested that he ripped them off as he ran, unwittingly permitting those following him to use the pieces of fur to track him (the *Tribune* even speculated that he tore them off to try to disguise himself). But none bothered to explain why Davis would wait until he was running for his life before trying to remove his cuffs and collar, or why he might think so minor an alteration would confuse anyone about who he was. No paper ever hinted that Davis was beaten in the field, although that seems the more plausible explanation of his torn coat and certainly would have been consistent with the prevailing ethos. Quite a few arrests in the late nineteenth century were accompanied by a beating.[32]

Beaten or not, Davis was hustled out of the field and back to the station, where he was locked in an office while word of his capture was telegraphed to

Chicago. As the constable and station officers waited for a train that could take Zephyr back to the city, the crowd grew outside, demanding that he be turned over to them. To make their intentions clear, they also sent for a rope. Although the constable refused to release Davis, the mob lingered, hoping for a chance when the train arrived. When it did, they rushed the train, grabbing at Davis as he was hustled on board. After a moment's confusion, Martin and Clark forced their way onto a car, with him in tow.

Four Chicago dailies, the *Times*, the *Tribune*, the *Inter-Ocean*, and the *Herald*, published lengthy articles about the capture in Forest. Although fundamentally the same, the stories offered different perspectives on the chase and capture. According to the *Tribune*, Davis was pursued into the cornfield by a posse of six men organized by Constable Martin. As he fell to the ground in the field and lay there panting, Martin came up and single-handedly placed him under arrest. When Davis demanded to see an arrest warrant, Martin responded by "producing a revolver" and saying, "Here it is." Confronted with a gun, Davis gave up, assuring Martin that he had intended to take himself back to Chicago and turn himself in.

Those few details carried a wealth of significance. The police, embodied by Martin, were in control throughout; he organized and led the chase, and he made the arrest. He loaned his authority, as an officer of the law, to the men he made part of his posse, and his authority was such that he was able to arrest Davis without resistance. The very act of pulling his gun on Davis symbolized his power, since it trumped Davis's legalistic demand for a warrant. The entire scene captured the *Tribune*'s interesting view of law enforcement. Although Martin was an officer of the law, the paper gave more weight to the power of his office, and his capacity for force, than to the law.

In contrast, the more populist *Times* emphasized the mob's role in the chase and capture. According to its account, a group of rail hands first noticed Davis and grew suspicious of his presence in the station, presumably because of his race. Just that moment, the description of the murderer came over the telegraph. The men, "noting the resemblance, started to ask" Davis questions. He fled, and they chased after him. It was not until later that Martin joined the pursuit. When they all caught up to Davis, Martin, "brandishing a big revolver" and backed up by the crowd, ordered their quarry to stop or be killed. At that point, Davis "turned, threw up his hands, and said: 'I quit.'" Where the *Tribune* emphasized the official nature of Martin's authority, the *Times* derived it from the power of the mob. In its version, the mob was always the initiator: it first noticed Davis looked suspicious, it began to question him, and it began the chase through the fields. Martin merely tagged along, giving official sanction to its actions; if the mob represented public opinion, bent on seeing Davis got his just deserts, Martin was the agent who carried out its will.[33]

That distinction between authority based on official status and authority derived from the community itself subtly shaped the two papers' description of the scene at the station. According to the *Tribune*, once Davis was taken back into Forest, "news spread far and wide, and in a short time there was a crowd of a hundred or more at the building." The article continued, "'Judge Lynch,' arrived with the first, and the depot officials hastily cleared the building and locked the door." As the crowd grew, "a committee started for a rope, and to all appearances the murderer's time was short." Fortunately, an express to Chicago pulled up to the station at just that point. "Word was taken to the conductor, and just as the engineer was opening the throttle Martin and Clark rushed their prisoner out of the back room past the edge of the crowd, and onto the train. The engineer pulled his throttle wide open, and the train shot away from the yelling and disappointed crowd of sturdy and determined farmers." There was a final moment of tension. As the train pulled out, "Davis opened the window and spit on one of the crowd. Quick as a flash, the farmer drew a wicked looking knife and made a desperate lunge at the Negro through the window. Davis drew back and Martin dropped the sash." The phrase "Judge Lynch" suggested the *Tribune*'s hostility to the mob, and the rest of the story reinforced Martin's authority against it. He rescued Davis from the mob not once but twice, preserving him first from its rage and then from his own stupidity. The moral was straightforward: law, in its official guise, was needed to prevent the resort to extralegal conduct, and thus prevent disorder.

The *Times* drew a very different moral from the scene at the station. In its version, Martin barely managed to keep Davis from being lynched. "'If I had kept him there till night,'" the paper quoted Martin, "'they'd have hanged him for sure. They were yelling for the rope even there.'" Having reminded its readers that the crowd which captured Davis thought he deserved to die for his crime, only to be thwarted by Martin, the *Times* warned that law might prevent Davis's rightful execution in a more final way. "He was old enough to strike down a helpless girl and hack her to death without one thought of mercy, but not old enough to die the way everybody who saw the mutilated body thinks he ought to die." This was true because the "law in Illinois says that capital punishment shall not be inflicted on a murderer who is less than 18 years old, and as Davis maintains that he is only 17, he is safe from any punishment worse than imprisonment." In fact, Illinois law said nothing of the sort; the only relevant statute appeared to indicate that a person under eighteen charged with murder, or some equally serious crime, could be punished as an adult. But accuracy was less important than the message. The people had spoken, indicating that Davis should pay for his crime with his life, and those sentiments reflected a popular sense of justice that no legal rule should be permitted to thwart.[34]

Rather than follow the *Times* or the *Tribune* by presenting accounts that suggested their reporters had been at the scene, the *Inter-Ocean* and the *Herald* offered stories about the capture at Forest supposedly based on interviews with Constable Martin. The *Inter-Ocean*'s version, which otherwise bore a distinct resemblance to the account in the *Tribune*, emphasized Martin's simple honesty and dogged determination, noting that he first learned of Davis's presence in Forest while he was at dinner. Upon being told that "the negro who murdered a little girl in Chicago was in town," he jumped from the table without finishing his meal. Arriving at the station, where he learned that Davis had fled half an hour before, Martin followed the trail of Davis's fur cuffs. He worked alone for a while, until he met up with several men on a handcar. No sooner had he joined forces with them than they spotted Davis. Martin got off the car and "marched up" to Davis, who "didn't try to run." "I want you," he said, and when Davis demanded to see an arrest warrant, Martin "pushed a cocked pistol under his nose" and said, "This is my warrant." Davis "weakened," admitted his guilt, and whined, "For God's sake, don't shoot me." Martin then led Davis back to the station, where he kept the mob at bay by threatening to shoot anyone who went near his prisoner.[35]

In contrast to the *Times*, and like the *Tribune*, the *Inter-Ocean* cast Martin as the hero, capturing Davis and holding back the mob that called for rough justice. The *Inter-Ocean* suggested its hostility to the extralegal action by noting that Martin used the same pistol to subdue both Zephyr and the crowd, a deft stroke equating the mob's lawlessness with that of a murderer. Consistent with its support of legal, as opposed to extralegal, judgment, the *Inter-Ocean* ended its story with the bald assertion that Davis would not escape execution because of his age. For the *Inter-Ocean*, it was important to remind people that the law would and could work, a noble sentiment that was more than a little tarnished by its hostility to Davis's demand to see a warrant.

There were actually two, mutually inconsistent, accounts of Davis's capture in the *Chicago Herald*. The first, based on an interview with Martin, resembled the account in the *Inter-Ocean*. In it, the *Herald*, like the *Inter-Ocean* and the *Tribune*, made the constable the prime mover. He received the bulletin from Chicago reporting Zephyr's crime, he began the chase alone, calling for assistance only after he was sure he was on the right track. He captured Davis in the cornfield and took him back to the station. Like the *Tribune*, the *Herald* reported the exchange in the field about the warrant, and in this version as well, it culminated with Martin pointing his gun at Davis and saying "this is my warrant" in such a way as to suggest that Martin's authority put him above the technical limitations of the law. In contrast, its account of what transpired at the station differed significantly from the versions offered in the *Tribune* and *Inter-Ocean*. Where those papers suggested that Martin kept the mob at bay single-handed, the *Herald* reported that he was only able to do so with the assistance of "his friends and the cooler heads of the wiser of the people."[36]

Immediately after the story about Martin's role, in the same column, the *Herald* offered an alternative account of the arrest. In this second version, W. H. Powley, a freight conductor on the Wabash line, received the description of Davis as his train pulled into the station, and just that moment he noticed someone who fit the description. Powley raced after the person, who happened to be Zephyr, and chased him down the tracks, ultimately commandeering a handcar to help keep pace with the younger criminal. After a while, he caught up, pointed his gun at Davis, and took him into custody. Once he had Davis subdued, he brought him back to the station.

Nothing in the *Herald* explains why it offered two inconsistent versions of the capture, but a third story, on the same page, provides a key for interpreting the other two accounts. The story concerns a mob that had gathered on the West Side of Chicago in the mistaken belief that Davis was inside a building. The crowd, encouraged by the irresponsible behavior of Chicago police on the scene, grew considerably, until it ultimately reached several thousand people. And at that size, the mob posed a serious threat. It seized, and hassled, all black men in the neighborhood, especially those wearing coats with fur collars and cuffs. Eventually, the police had to subdue the mob, which they only managed to do after a considerable effort.

Read as a whole, these three stories sum up the *Herald*'s attitude toward extralegal justice. It was not, as the story about Powley indicated, opposed to individuals taking law into their own hands, especially when there were no legal authorities in sight. Nor was the *Herald* as enthusiastic as the *Tribune* or *Inter-Ocean* about the authority of the police. The police appear more than a little inept in each of the *Herald*'s accounts: Martin needed help subduing the mob at Forest, and the police on Chicago's West Side made a bad situation worse. But while it was not opposed to private law enforcement, and was less than ecstatic about official law enforcement, the *Herald* had serious doubts about mobs. They could become unruly, uncontrolled, and unreasonable, like the one that relentlessly seized all black men who crossed its path on the West Side. The paper made a similar point in another story about a near lynching in Chicago published about this time. When a popular saloonkeeper was found dying one morning, the *Herald* reported that when he was asked who had attacked him, he gasped out the name of the police officer who patrolled the neighborhood. His outraged neighbors formed a mob and proceeded to track down the officer, only to learn at the last minute that he had not killed the saloonkeeper. In fact, the dying man's last words were nothing more than a request that the neighborhood tell the officer of his death. While the *Herald* presented its account of the neighborhood's reaction sympathetically, its story made it clear that mobs could, all too easily, make the wrong choice.[37]

Of all the papers, the *Daily News* offered the briefest account. It recorded in a single paragraph that an employee of the Wabash line had captured Davis in Forest. Two days later, however, the paper made its position plain. A large, three-column-wide cartoon on the front page explained "How Chicago Criminals Are Captured." In the center of the montage were Chicago police officers, sleepily writing out wanted posters. Along the bottom and left sides of the cartoon, a series of buffoonish county constables hunted for criminals, shotguns in hand, much as they might hunt game. Along the top and right sides of the cartoon, a mob gathered at night on the outskirts of Chicago, apparently primed to hunt down anyone who was wanted. The implication was that the Chicago police never captured criminals but relied instead on a ragtag band of others to do their work for them. Extralegal action was necessary, the cartoon suggested, because law enforcement was helpless.[38]

That contempt for, and hostility to, organized law enforcement indicated the degree to which the papers feared the police would not, or could not, put in the effort necessary to capture criminals. Most of the accounts of the mob action in Forest, diverse as they otherwise were, implied it had been a necessary part of the capture. One might think that each story also demonstrated the risks involved. Popular action in Forest may have made Davis's capture possible, but his near lynching also suggested that once unleashed, mob action was difficult, if not impossible, to control.

But the papers' attitudes toward extralegal conduct were too ambiguous for them to draw that second point. Officially the Chicago dailies condemned mob action and lynching. The *Chicago Daily News* in particular denounced extralegal acts done in the South by lawless whites, and was equally outraged when victims of lynch mobs were Chinese workers in western mining camps. But for all the indignation they could muster on the subject, the papers accepted lynching without blinking as often as not, and their ambivalence reflected the temper of the times. Less than twenty years before the Davis case, during the Chicago Fire of 1871, newspapers reported that gangs roamed the streets looting and start-

HOW CHICAGO CRIMINALS ARE CAPTURED.

ing more fires. Those same papers noted with approval the way groups of other citizens gathered to restore order, capturing and hanging looters or incendiaries to do so. Although apparently apocryphal, those accounts were repeated in histories of the Fire printed after the event. In those histories, as in the original versions, the lynch mob's role was unequivocally good, its purpose the restoration of order and the protection of society. A similar attitude prevailed during the labor unrest of the 1870s and 1880s. Then, papers enthusiastically reported efforts to lynch people believed to be anarchists, including, in one instance, Albert Parsons, who was later executed after his conviction in the Haymarket trial.[39]

The various papers continued to support lynchings throughout the 1880s, doing so for a variety of reasons. The *Daily News* typically failed to condemn any lynching that followed the murder of a young child or an elderly woman. Its sympathy for the victim justified other lynchings as well; one account noted with approval that it was quite likely several people in Kentucky would be lynched. There, an opponent of drinking was tricked into drinking himself into a stupor and then died as his companions laughed over his condition. The *Daily News* article ended with the thought that a "strong rope would help his slayers to realize the fiendishness of their treatment of him."[40]

When it was not excusing lynching on the basis of sympathy for the victim, the *Daily News* justified lynchings on the basis of popular sentiment. One story briefly noted that "[t]wo men at Fort Snelling, Dakota Territory, became enraged at the behavior of a drunken man and effectually suppressed him by chasing him from town and shooting him to death. This action was certainly effective, and, as the shooters were released on their own recognizance, it seems to meet with the approval of the great northwest."[41]

For the *Daily News*, lynching was a legitimate way the people could make sure that justice was done, and the paper also approved of less drastic examples of extralegal conduct. It praised vigilantes in West Virginia who whipped a man who beat his wife and children. The paper admitted that the "act, of course, is without sanction of the law, but it would be difficult to find a jury willing to convict men engaged in the administration of justice in this form." Nor was its approval limited to actions away from Chicago. When I. H. Cady attacked his wife outside a Chicago courtroom before a divorce proceeding, the *Daily News* blithely reported that he was chased down the street by a mob and escaped assault only because he ran into the arms of a police officer. Another time, when a man apparently beat up a five-year-old boy, the *Daily News* reported with satisfaction that he was captured and nearly killed by people from the neighborhood before the police arrived and took him into custody. In both cases, the *Daily News*, usually quick to condemn conduct it disapproved of, reported without a hint of censure these efforts to execute rough justice on Chicago streets.[42]

The *Daily News* set out its rationale for extralegal, popular justice in a story from 1886. When a man from the Chicago neighborhood of Irving Park was accused of taking indecent liberties with small girls, several "well to do citizens" gathered together to discuss the situation. Some wanted the suspect tarred and feathered, but the majority decided that he should be driven out of town, so a group of fifty "of the most substantial men" went to his house and convinced him to leave. The paper's story on the incident quoted the village postmaster as saying: "'The citizens thought it was best to take the law into [their] own hands. If [he] had been prosecuted criminally there would have been many things in the way of securing a conviction. Only the statement of the little girl could be used as evidence against him.'"[43]

These remarks revealed the several factors that the *Daily News* felt justified an extralegal response. The mob's action was legitimate when it reflected the decision of the community, or when the legal system could not be trusted to act. The *Daily News* made a similar point in 1885, when it ran a story approving of South Carolina regulators who whipped or otherwise tried to drive out of town couples involved in interracial marriages. The paper treated those actions as legitimate, community-based responses to a morals problem that the law could not reach, without bothering to explain what the underlying moral offense was.[44]

Extralegal actions undertaken in self-defense, or on behalf of family members, were also justified. In one article, the *Daily News* denounced a New Orleans lynch mob that went after an African American man suspected of killing a white man who had been part of a group of men who had severely beaten him. Although apparently days separated that beating and the murder, the account in the paper excused the killing as self-defense, which, in turn, meant the subsequent attempt at lynching was wrong. Another story in the paper called for lenient treatment of a young African American woman accused of killing her father; her defense was that her father had beaten her mother repeatedly. The paper's attitude toward those actions implied it was prepared to approve some murders as individual acts of justice.[45]

Similar thinking influenced its reaction to mob action in the Davis case. Although the paper made little mention of the capture, its brief description praised the act by a public-spirited citizen who had stepped forward where the law had failed. The cartoon it published shortly after the capture implied that for all its possible faults, mob action was necessary in Chicago, where the police could not be trusted to actively hunt for criminals. The paper also treated the calls for mob action by Maggie's family and friends sympathetically and offered no criticisms of mobs formed by other Chicagoans who thought they had found Davis.

The other dailies also publicized calls for mob action against Davis and likewise indicated that they supported some kinds of extralegal action so long as certain conditions were met. The *Chicago Times*, the most explicitly racist in its early treatment of the Davis case, suggested that Davis deserved to be lynched simply because he was black. The story it printed the day after the murder ended with the sentiment that if Davis "had appeared near Maggie Gaughan's home last night he would have met with treatment such as they give down south to criminals of his class." Mostly, the paper emphasized that extralegal reaction was a privilege reserved for Maggie's family, friends, and neighbors. The *Times* also advised its readers that many police officers "individually, proclaimed that they felt but little like offering any determined opposition to the wrath of the people." Nor did the paper express any outrage when the mob in Forest tried to lynch Davis, suggesting that it was not firmly wedded to the idea that the right to lynch was limited to those with a personal stake in the outcome.[46]

The *Times* did add occasional notes reminding people of the dangers of lynching; it recounted, for example, the narrow escape of one young black man who was mistaken for Davis and nearly captured by a mob hell-bent on hanging him on the spot. Typically, however, it reported the calls that he be lynched in a manner that sympathized with, rather than condemned, the sentiment. Its attitude toward tales of lynching from other states, particularly in the South, was uncritical; only rarely did it raise the possibility that extralegal conduct was wrong. Those few instances when it expressed hostility to mob action usually involved mob rule that interfered with politics or elections. The *Times*'s guiding principle seemed to have been that mob action undertaken to enforce a law, or express outrage about criminal conduct, was acceptable, even if it supplanted the legal system. By contrast, extralegal action that threatened the political system, or the democratic process, was not.[47]

Even the *Chicago Tribune*, a "pioneer" in keeping statistics on lynching from 1882 on, did not uniformly denounce extralegal conduct. The nature of its attitude is often hard to figure; it frequently reported lynchings, even of African Americans in the South, without comment or condemnation. One story, from July 1887, suggested that its ambivalence toward popular justice was more racially tinged than its reputation might indicate. The paper reported the near murder of an elderly white couple from Waukegan, attacked in their home by an African American from the area who was angered by their attempt to drive him out of the community. When the suspect was captured, the *Tribune* reported that there was "great indignation but the general sentiment is favorable to law rather than lynching." While it seemed relieved that the people left the perpetrator to law, the paper did not condemn the sentiment of the neighborhood. The *Tribune* may have become increasingly opposed to the lynching of blacks in the lawless, and not coincidentally Democratic, South, but it was not consistently hostile to extralegal justice in the North.[48]

Not surprisingly, the *Tribune*'s greatest enthusiasm for rough justice was for

that variation practiced by the police. In an era when other papers, and several
civic associations, complained about the brutal methods of the Chicago police
department, the *Tribune* denied there was a problem and ran editorials justifying the use of force. Just as Constable Martin could pull his gun on a prostrate
Zephyr Davis to remind him of his power, so too was brutality on the part of the
police a legitimate response to strikes and work stoppages. Yet while police officers could react violently, crowds could not. Consistent with that principle, the
Tribune deplored the hints of mob violence in the Davis case and was quick to
report that the police had mobs under control.[49]

Of all the daily papers, the *Chicago Inter-Ocean* took the dimmest view of
matters that interfered with law's formal workings. As did the others, it reported
many lynchings without a touch of reproof. At times, it excused the conduct of
vigilante groups, but whenever it did so, the support was tempered. In one editorial on the "Bald Knobbers," vigilantes from Missouri, the *Inter-Ocean* pointed
out that the group acted "with intent to remedy an older and generally greater
evil, namely the miscarriage of justice." In conditions where, as was true in Missouri, courts were feeble and few, any "law, even lynch law, is better than no law
at all." Although that sounded like the sort of rationale offered by the *Daily News*,
the *Inter-Ocean* refused to let the failings of the legal system excuse mob action.
It demanded that the legal system in Missouri improve and called to have the
Bald Knobbers suppressed.[50]

The paper was more sympathetic to mob action that stopped short of killing,
particularly when it was undertaken on behalf of women or children. It reported,
without disapproval, the story of a mob in Michigan that seized a man who had
beaten his wife and then left her to live with two other women. The mob tarred
and feathered the man and his two female companions and drove all three out
of town. In another case, it approvingly reported the action of a mob from Minnesota that removed a suspected wife beater from jail and threatened to hang
him if he did not mend his ways. In a third instance, the *Inter-Ocean* applauded
community action that forced the Chicago police department to arrest a man
suspected of molesting a young girl.[51]

As these examples suggest, even in cases where the extralegal action stopped
short of a lynching, the *Inter-Ocean* preferred popular justice that pressured the
formal legal system to work rather than supplanting it. On a few rare occasions
where victims were children harmed by people who were supposed to protect
them, the paper was prepared to go further. In March 1888, it reported a case
from Evansville, Indiana, where an African American schoolteacher was suspected of seducing several of his young, black, female students. When one of his
victims died as a result of a botched abortion, the African American community

in the city determined to track the man down and lynch him. The *Inter-Ocean* reported that sentiment without censure. On those rare occasions where it endorsed lynching, the paper did so only on behalf of those unable to use the law to protect themselves. But even then, the paper typically demanded that the legal system be permitted to work or be reformed so that it could do so.[52]

These stories, and others like them, demonstrated that while mobs appeared to act independently of the press, their acts were often supported by the newspapers. Papers encouraged mob action by reporting their behavior but also tried to set limits on their activities by drawing distinctions between good and bad mob action. Each time a paper supported a mob, it did so at the expense of the State and the formal law, either by encouraging mobs that replaced official action or by using the threat of a mob to provoke official action. Yet, if papers helped to call mobs up, like the monsters of fiction, mobs could escape from their authors' control, as the crowd threatened to do at Forest. And as they did so, they acted out of their own senses of justice. Mobs were as much a threat to the power of the press to define popular justice as they were a popular check on the State.

The papers' role in the Davis case took on another aspect after his capture. Twenty miles outside Chicago, the train carrying Davis stopped so that several reporters, accompanied by John Greene, could board it to interview the captive. The different accounts of this interview all reported that he admitted he had killed Maggie because she refused to follow his order to start work. Pressed further, he vehemently denied raping Maggie, grabbing her around the neck, or tearing her clothes.[53]

The stories in the papers also agreed that Davis elaborated on the details of his crime without hesitation. He explained that he had arrived at work shortly before 7:00 and let Maggie in when she knocked on the door a few minutes later. Still wearing her coat, she went to the fire to warm herself and stood there several minutes. When he told her to get to work, she refused; when he repeated his order, she laughed in his face. Angry, Zephyr grabbed the hatchet and threw it at her, hitting her. As she turned from the stove and ran back to the closet at the rear of the factory, he snatched up the hatchet and followed. At the closet, he struck her with the hatchet again and again until she fell to the floor. Leaving her there, he went next door to Conlon's for water to wash the blood off his hands. Once he had cleaned up, he returned to the factory, opened its doors, and let the others in to work.

Recounting that story for their readers, the newspapers emphasized Davis's lack of remorse and concern. The *Times* noted that when Davis denied sexually assaulting Maggie, he made the comment "much as if he would have said 'If the watermelons were ripe now we'd have some of them.'" The others did not play so explicitly to racist stereotypes but agreed that he appeared jaunty, defiant, and seemingly unaware of what he had done. In other ways, their descriptions began to put Davis beyond the pale. They debated whether he appeared "intelligent" for an African American, or simply looked like an "ordinary colored boy of no great intelligence." They wondered whether his skin color helped indicate whether he was dangerous or not, and quarreled over whether he was light skinned, had white features, was dark skinned, or looked "typically negroid." This emphasis on racial characteristics was not a simple reaction to the fact he was black. Several years before, accounts of suspected murderer Frank Mulkowski quickly turned him into a dangerous Pole. In the same way, stories about the "trunk murder" described the defendants, Ignazio Syvestri, Giovanni Azari, and Agostino Gelardi, as stupid Italians. In cases where the race of the defendant offered no convenient peg on which to hang hostility, the papers found other ways to demonize the defendant. William Tascott, the suspect in the Snell murder, was quickly revealed to be a spendthrift with all sorts of bad habits. Race was a means of making a suspect detestable, not the reason to do so.[54]

As it neared Chicago's Loop, the train stopped at the Archer Avenue station. There, Chicago police officers boarded, took Davis into custody, put him into one of the department's fastest wagons, and raced him to police headquarters. Their effort to avoid another mob seemed warranted. That same afternoon, as the train brought Davis back from Forest, other reporters went to the Gaughan house to tell Maggie's parents that he had been captured. They walked into her wake and a house full of women, some keening as others came to stare at Maggie's body. When the reporters arrived with the news, people at the house reacted with rage. Their anger was fanned by one elderly woman who challenged the neighborhood men who trooped into the house behind the reporters. If they were men, she taunted, they would meet the train and kill Davis then and there. Some raced out; a few stayed behind, muttering their plans to do something.[55]

Others had the same idea. At roughly the moment the police hustled Davis off at the Archer Avenue station, a crowd was gathering at the Polk Street station (which was closer to police headquarters), hoping to grab him off the train. Having avoided the mob one last time, Davis was pushed into Lieutenant Henry Henshaw's office and questioned in the presence of several officers, John Greene, and the ubiquitous reporters. If the papers are to be believed, Davis freely confessed his guilt once again, admitting that he killed Maggie when she refused to follow his orders. He was then locked in a cell for the night.[56]

All the stories suggesting that Davis confessed willingly are suspect. After his trial, in an interview with a *Tribune* reporter, Zephyr somewhat ambiguously denied ever making a confession. As the paper reported it, he said, "I didn't make no confession." Then, specifically referring to his alleged confession in the police station (the only one referred to at his trial), he went on, "The detective [Henshaw] lied. He took me, and threw me down, and then I might have confessed to anything." It bears noting that Davis never referred to a confession on the train, raising the possibility that there never was an interview on the train and that press reports were based on statements he made in the police station—possibly under duress, if he confessed at all. Significantly, the court file in the case contains no written statement or other form of confession.[57]

Coverage of the case over the first thirty-six hours had two basic, related, functions. The earliest stories were intended to ignite public outrage. Later stories of the chase and capture fanned that outrage, focusing popular hostility on Davis. In the process, the case was cast as a conflict between justice, which was associated with popular outrage and demanded that Maggie's death be avenged swiftly, and law, which was slow, cast up roadblocks in the way of prosecution, and seemed likely to protect Davis.

Although Chicago's dailies all presented the tension between justice and law in the same basic terms, they approached the events of the first day and a half from different perspectives. For the *Times*, the contrast was most stark. Justice reflected what the people wanted, and they had made their desires clear; law represented rules and pitfalls that might help Zephyr escape the punishment he deserved. The *Daily News*, always quick to denounce the legal system, also worried that the case might be an instance where law or its agents might prevent a just outcome. Even the *Tribune*, generally unwilling to support a popular mood or equate it with justice, went so far as to admit that legalistic niceties should not be allowed to interfere with the proper resolution of the case. Only the *Inter-Ocean*, which generally supported law, used the events of those first days to argue that law would secure a just outcome, and even it saw fit to mock Davis's demands for a warrant.[58]

2

Public Opinion,
March 1 to March 28, 1888

If the day and a half immediately following the discovery of Maggie's body were dominated by the dailies' efforts to engender public outrage, matters changed once Davis was captured. By Wednesday, anger gave way to argument as groups began to meet and demand consideration of issues they thought arose from the case. Those efforts, stemming from frustration with particular aspects of law, its substance and enforcement, dragged the case onto a larger stage, revealing in the process Chicago's civil society, its successes and its limitations.

The transition began fitfully, when the coroner's jury met in the basement of Cook County Hospital early Wednesday morning. Apparently still worried about the possibility of a lynching, the police raced Davis from his cell in the Harrison Street police station to the hearing. The decision to take him in the department's fastest wagon, surrounded by sixteen officers, smacked of self-dramatization, but perhaps not more than a bit. Both the *Daily News* and the *Chicago Times* reported that angry people lined the route, and a crowd met Davis and his escorts at the door to the hearing room.[1]

Nothing came of it. Although crowded with the curious, the hearing before the coroner was quiet and straightforward. Maggie's parents identified her body and established that she worked, although her father could not remember where she was employed. Eddie Dwyer and James Swift, the first Chicago police officer called to the scene, testified about the discovery of the body and identified the bloody hatchet found beneath it. Harold Moyer, the Cook County Physician, described the various blows to Maggie's head. Fascinating as those gruesome details doubtless were to everyone but Maggie's parents, the only real moment of excitement occurred when John Greene testified. He tried to minimize Zephyr's role at the factory, denying that he was much more than a janitor. At that point, according to several accounts, Zephyr audibly scoffed and Deputy Coroner W. E. Kent began a withering examination of Greene. When it was over, Greene had conceded that Zephyr "was virtually" his foreman, entrusted with the keys to the factory and permitted to fire other employees. Zephyr then testified, confirmed he held the power to fire, admitted he had killed Maggie, and, reiterating the point that would become his constant theme, denied he had raped or attempted to rape her.[2]

Predictably, the jury found that Maggie Gaughan "came to her death by blows inflicted on the head with a hatchet in the hands of Zeph Davis, employed as foreman by Greene Brothers," and recommended that he be held for the crime. Significantly, the verdict continued, "We further find that the system pursued by said Greene Brothers of employing negro and white labor, male and female, promiscuously, is pernicious to public morals and should be stopped."[3]

That additional point was no accident. In the course of his interrogation of Greene during the inquest, Kent remarked that he "found the habit" of employing a black "as the foreman over girls from 14 to 17" to be "very pernicious, and apt to bad results." Later, in his concluding remarks to the jury, he commented on the evil of having "colored" supervisors in "places where girls are employed." Kent clearly intended to inflame the jury and use the hearing to send a message to employers and the public at large, but he did not succeed in making the jury frame its verdict in his terms. Whereas he had objected to putting white women under the authority of a black man, the jurors denounced all employment settings that mixed races and sexes.[4]

The struggle over the verdict's message, and the underlying premise that the coroner's inquest might serve as a platform from which messages could be sent to the public at large, was consistent with general practice in late nineteenth-century Chicago. Procedurally, a coroner's jury was called after any sudden death. It was supposed to consist of six people, known as bystanders, called from the vicinity in which the death occurred, on the theory that they would have knowledge of the circumstances of the crime. As the Supreme Court of Illinois explained, the coroner's jury had two functions. It was to determine how anyone who died suddenly came to do so, and, in the process, it was to make an inquiry into "all things which occasioned" the death.[5]

Although its antecedents stretched back to English common law, by the end of the nineteenth century more than a few questioned the value of the coroner's jury. Only a few weeks before Davis's appearance before one, Cook County Coroner Henry Hertz expressed doubts about the jury, and in particular the people who hung "around his office and made their living as professional jurors." He accused some of "having access" to the coroner's books, which let them arrive at crime scenes before coroner's deputies, guaranteeing that they would be picked to serve on the jury investigating the matter.[6]

Hertz was not alone in his hostility: the *Daily News* endorsed his remarks and added a few of its own. As had Hertz, the paper criticized overly zealous would-be jurors for their ghoulish interest in death, but it also questioned their general intelligence. Of the two problems, the latter seemed the more significant. The paper offered as an example one Georgia jury that sat at a hearing on the death of a hermit. According to the *Daily News*, the jury first finished all the hermit's whiskey and then deliberated for two hours before returning a nonsensical verdict finding "the defendant guilty as charged." People of that sort, the paper made clear, did not serve justice and should not be on coroner's juries. This hostility reflected the *Daily News*'s occasional annoyance with juries that came down with verdicts the paper did not approve of, but it also hinted at a concern with juries that acted too much on their own.[7]

That anxiety came rather oddly from a paper as contemptuous of officials and supportive of popular outrage as the *Daily News*, but it was a reaction to an important phenomenon. In late nineteenth-century Chicago, it was not unusual for investigative juries (such as coroner's juries or grand juries) to act outside their specific charge or impose their own standards in reaching decisions. One grand jury sitting in 1888, for example, ended its term with a call for improvement in the air circulation in the Cook County Courthouse. Others proposed criminal sentencing reforms and denounced police corruption. Sometimes prosecutors or judges initiated these investigations, other times juries acted on their own. Papers and the public typically approved expressions of jury independence when they agreed with the result and opposed them when the call was for a reform they felt unnecessary.[8]

In the Davis case, both Kent and the jury wanted to use the verdict to send a message, but their respective messages were not terribly clear. That confusion did not arise as a result of their conflicting emphases so much as from the welter of concerns and assumptions that shaped possible interpretations of the two sets of comments. Either statement could be interpreted in different ways by different audiences, which meant neither could send a clear message.[9]

Taken at face value, Kent's remarks read as an assertion that black male supervisors posed a danger to young white women. His statement echoed the sentiment that the *Daily News* attributed to Maggie's parents, and immediate reaction to his comments suggested others shared the concern. In a column in the *Chicago Times* the next day, the editor, W. F. Storey, reiterated that a "colored boy of 17 was clearly not the proper person to place in authority over a force of white working girls." But Kent, the Gaughans, and Storey notwithstanding, for most people in Chicago in the 1880s, the possibility that a black man of any age would supervise anyone, let alone a white woman, was so remote as to be unimaginable.[10]

Racial distinctions, though significant, did not yet keep African Americans from working with, or for, whites (sometimes in predominantly white work-forces), or from having contact with whites outside the workplace. Housing seg-regation was not firmly in place, although interracial housing typically existed in poor or marginal neighborhoods. Amusements were not entirely segregated: blacks and whites shared parks, engaged in sports together, and watched every-thing from horse races to variety shows in each other's company. At the same time, blacks and whites did not always work or play side by side, even when they shared space. Businesses typically relegated blacks to jobs as porters, maids, or food servers, or hired them as strike replacements. African Americans who went to public amusements found themselves increasingly separated from whites, and as the decade went on, African Americans who applied for jobs at white-owned businesses did so without success.[11]

Implausible on its face, Kent's image evoked other, somewhat more credible fears. One was the wholly racist assumption that all black men posed a danger to young white women; the other, the apparently race-neutral claim that young working women were vulnerable to exploitation by their supervisors. Of the two, the first—now a familiar cliché of the black male rapist—was not a salient image in late nineteenth-century Chicago. News accounts from the South increasingly reported that black men who had been lynched had attacked white women, but they still relayed that information only in passing. The idea of unbridled African American male sexuality may have been an increasingly significant excuse in the segregating South, but in late nineteenth-century Chicago, African American men were rarely cast in that light. Far from being sexual predators, in popular ac-counts African American men seemed less sexually threatening than their Chi-nese counterparts, who were often accused of seducing or raping young white women. The dominant image of black men in Chicago in this period was effete. They hovered at the edges of vice, acting as doormen (literally and figuratively) into dens of sin, but while they often seemed depraved, they rarely appeared threatening or even particularly virile.[12]

In contrast to an interpretation that rested on the still mostly uncharted field of black male sexuality, the general idea that young women were vulnerable in the workplace was well mapped, with several points of reference all its own. A se-ries of letters to the editor of the *Chicago Tribune*, written in the 1870s, provided two perspectives on this issue. One group of writers argued that working women, although essentially virtuous, risked sexual exploitation by supervisors who would take advantage of their financial needs and lack of protection. Others were as certain that women who worked were inherently promiscuous and willingly put themselves in harm's way. While they reached very different conclusions about the causes of workplace sexuality, these letter writers agreed that work threatened female chastity.[13]

Concern about young women's vulnerability in the workplace was not just a matter of sexuality, as the series on working women published in the *Inter-Ocean* made clear. The first article in its series, published on August 21, 1887, took the position that sexual exploitation by male supervisors was only one risk faced by young working women. In the workplace, women faced the equally great danger that they would be overworked or injured. A second article in that series gave more credence to the issue of sexual exploitation, but again refused to limit its discussion to sexual concerns. It argued that young working women could be preyed on, sexually and economically, by supervisors because they had no one to turn to for protection. Their parents cared only about the income they produced; the legal system, and society more generally, refused to protect them in their parents' stead.[14]

If the *Tribune* defined workplace exploitation in terms of sexuality, and the *Inter-Ocean* set the issue in the larger context of the breakdown of families and the failures of society, the Democratic *Chicago Times* offered a third perspective. In *The White Slave Girls of Chicago*, an exposé of the condition of working women the paper published a few months after the Davis case, Nell Nelson elaborately documented the problems of young women in the workforce. Much in her account seemed to confirm the disparate fears of the *Tribune* and *Inter-Ocean*. She described women who were routinely coerced into working without wages during "training periods," or who signed one-sided contracts or were consistently overworked by supervisors, male and female alike. They were propositioned by middle-class men on the street, who assumed that their working status meant they were sexually available. Male supervisors and coworkers, when they were not trying to seduce them, subjected them to sexual remarks.[15]

Though far more exhaustive, Nelson's descriptions of workplace dynamics had a paternalistic tone much like that of the *Tribune* and *Inter-Ocean*. But the workers she interviewed challenged her assumption that working women were exploited or victimized by their jobs. Many, to be sure, expressed a wish to escape the circumstances Nelson described, but others had a different perspective. These young women found their work gave them chances they otherwise would not have had. While some told stories of abuse in the workplace, others reported quarreling with their parents and skipping work for an occasional day in the park. They de-

scribed camaraderie with their coworkers and flirting with the men they met on
the job. These young women took advantage of the opportunities and limited free-
doms work gave them, sometimes becoming, as a few stories hinted Maggie had,
daughters who were more independent and less dutiful because they had jobs.[16]

Kent's comments to the jury, unclear as they were, reflected one possible interpretation of the condition of young working women, but the young workers in
Nelson's study served as a reminder that there were other points of view. At the
same time, their understanding of their situation, although it provided a distinc-
tively working-class perspective, was not, obviously, the only one. Surprisingly,
given the emphasis on workplace issues at the coroner's inquest, most of Chicago's ethnic and working-class weeklies made no mention of the inquest or the
verdict, nor did they offer an alternative perspective on its assumptions. The *Irish
World and American Labor Intelligencer*, a New York paper with a national (and
Chicago-based) working-class readership, never referred to the verdict, or the
murder, in its weekly section on events in Illinois. That was not because the paper was above reporting murders; it described the search for Amos Snell's murderer every week for nearly two months after the crime. Its enthusiasm for the
Snell case made its failure even to mention Maggie's murder more striking, particularly given her Irish American background.[17]

The *Irish World*'s reticence may have reflected the ambivalence about working women within the Irish American community. While the Knights of Labor,
with whom the *Irish World* was affiliated (a tie that was particularly strong in Chicago, where the local correspondent was a member of the Knights), argued that
women should be treated equally in the workplace and respected for work they
did as homemakers, the *Irish World* emphasized female domesticity. As the paper
put it in an editorial written around the time of Maggie's death, "women of Irish
blood" made "the family circle, and all the social charms and occupations which
adorn and constitute home is their peculiar sphere." This sentiment illustrated
the association, prevalent in the Irish American community (as well as among
other marginalized groups), of stay-at-home wives and respectability. While
many single women of Irish ancestry worked, married Irish American women
typically did not. Alternatively, the paper's silence may have had another, uglier
basis. From the antebellum period on, many Irish Americans had struggled to
distinguish themselves from African Americans, often embracing exclusionary
and racist attitudes as a result. Consistent with the sentiment that apparently led
Maggie's parents to object when they learned that she was working in a shop with
a black man for a supervisor, the *Irish World* may have avoided reporting a crime
that raised awkward questions of race, particularly in the context of Maggie's relationship with Zephyr.[18]

Of course, the *Irish World*, for all its support of the Knights of Labor and protests against English misrule in Ireland, was hardly a radical workers' paper. Although some have argued that it only became moderate, even conservative, on many issues after the Haymarket case for fear of anti-Irish backlash, its attitude can be more easily explained. The paper praised the verdict in the Haymarket trial and supported the plan to build a monument to the Irish American police officers it believed were martyred in Haymarket Square. In Chicago, where a significant percentage of the police force had Irish ancestry, the *Irish World* was a proponent of law and law enforcement because they seemed respectable and for reasons of racial solidarity.[19]

While intra- and interethnic dynamics probably contributed to the *Irish World's* silence, they cannot explain the equally muted reactions of other, far more radical Chicago weeklies. To consider just one, obvious, example, the *Alarm* (the paper edited by several of the defendants in the Haymarket trial) never mentioned the crime or the coroner's inquest. That may have arisen from the paper's increased disengagement with Chicago after Haymarket. Having been temporarily closed down immediately after the Haymarket Riot in 1886, the paper resumed publication in 1887 but moved its base of operations to New York shortly thereafter. More likely, the paper's failure to discuss the case stemmed from its lack of interest in concrete labor issues after 1886. Before Haymarket, it published particular examples of workers' hardships, including several stories that described working women who were sexually assaulted by police officers and others with authority over them. It also offered accounts of young children whose families had to send them out to work. After the Haymarket trial, the paper became concerned with abstract issues of social justice and left concrete problems alone. Ethnic divisions within Chicago's working class, which tended to pit Irish Americans against workers of other European backgrounds, may also have contributed to the *Alarm's* lack of interest in the Davis case.[20]

Not every working-class paper in Chicago ignored the inquest verdict. The *Labor Enquirer*, a locally published socialist weekly, discussed it briefly, denouncing it for failing to go far enough. The jury should not have reproved just Greene's, the paper argued, it should have condemned the entire system that forced "a girl (white or black) of tender years to slave labor." By casting the problem in those terms, the *Labor Enquirer* altered the equation. No longer was the issue one of racial mixing or sexual danger; it became a question of how the workplace exploited young working women. Yet while that resembled the concerns of the *Inter-Ocean*, for the *Labor Enquirer's* readership—mostly working class men—the phrase "slave labor" had a double meaning it would not have had for

Inter-Ocean readers. It referred to the exploitation of young girls, but it also called to mind the threat their low wages posed to the more expensive labor done by men.[21]

Whereas Kent's comments could be read as the expression of a racist sentiment or as reflecting a host of anxieties about women in the workplace, the jury's restatement of his remarks seemed to rest on nothing more complex than a crudely obvious racism. Certainly, that was how one local African American weekly read it. The *Western Appeal* denounced the verdict and claimed it had been met with an outcry of public support, an exaggeration that was probably intended to spur Chicago's African American community into its own display of outrage.[22]

The *Western Appeal* notwithstanding, reactions to the verdict were hardly overwhelming. The *Tribune* dismissed the jury's concern about racial mixing, noting that while it might be "pernicious to public morals," it was not illegal. The crux of the matter, so far as the *Tribune* was concerned, was that Greene violated the law by employing children under the age of fifteen. Although the paper was correct about the relative legalities, this reaction did not do full justice to the problem. Racially mixed workforces existed; *White Slave Girls of Chicago* described several, as did the *Western Appeal* on more than one occasion, and they rarely engendered any obvious hostility.[23]

But while having blacks and whites working together did not routinely provoke anxiety, race in the broader, late nineteenth-century sense was a source of concern. Employers who were Jewish and foreign-born, considered members of separate races in this period, figured prominently in Nelson's account as sneaks and thieves who should be barred from employing young "American women," a category she used that sometimes included the native-born children of immigrants and sometimes not. Nelson's treatment of the racial tensions between workers of what we would consider different ethnic groups was more nuanced. She noted that some workers were hostile to fellow workers of other races (young Jewish women, in particular, were censured for driving down wages since they were willing to work for very little), but suggested that the stereotypes and prejudices did not go so deep that individuals refused to work in places employing women of different races. Even so, the different workforces she described seemed to be dominated by people of particular races, suggesting that a considerable degree of self-selection, exclusion, and outright avoidance was going on.[24]

That seemed to be the pattern of late nineteenth-century Chicago race relations, as demonstrated by a civil rights case tried the same year as the Davis case.

The defendant, a theater owner, argued that under a state civil rights law he was only obliged to give African Americans access to his theater, which meant he could establish segregated seating within it. He claimed that he had to separate his black and white customers to keep them from fighting each other. Both arguments were rejected by the all-white jury, which found for the African American plaintiff and awarded her two hundred dollars in damages.[25]

The verdict suggested that Chicago's white residents were not yet susceptible to racist fear mongering, and the conduct of the trial itself reinforced that impression; there is no indication of hostility to either the plaintiff or her African American attorney. Nor did the verdict for the plaintiff precipitate alarmed protests; on the contrary, several papers praised the outcome. Yet other events undermined the decision. Within days of the verdict, a second Chicago theater insisted that an African American patron sit in segregated seating. Before and after the trial, newspapers reported instances of blacks denied service in restaurants, ordered to use service entrances in hotels, or otherwise excluded from or segregated by businesses with a predominantly white clientele. Those who sought to segregate offered several rationales: Some echoed the theater owner's claim that mixing whites and blacks would lead to violence. Others argued the mere presence of African Americans drove whites away from the business, causing economic harm. Each business owner argued that some circumstance excused him from having to follow the law, an individualized theory of justice that threatened to undermine the law more generally.[26]

One popular excuse for segregation was that racial mixing was "incompatible with morality and health," as another prosecutor put it in a case brought in October 1888. Sam Wah, who was Chinese, was accused of hiring a fifteen-year-old German girl as a maid, raping her, and then forcing her to marry another man, Quong Kee. The prosecutor added that there was "a deep public sentiment against the union of different races. In my opinion," he went on, "it is inconsistent with morality and health, and it has to be stopped."[27]

Many of the discussions of vice in this period turned on racial mingling. When an unidentified white woman was found dead in a building on West Madison Street, the trail quickly led to a Chinese laundry that doubled, according to the police, as an opium den. The proprietor, Sam Lee, was particularly suspicious, since he had a white wife, and both were charged with the woman's death. At the same time, the victim's apparently white (though dark skinned) male companion was set free. The same point could be made more generally. The Levee's notorious Park Theater was not simply a dive, it was an interracial hell. Stories about the Levee made the connection concrete—racial mixing led to vice, and vice led to crime.[28]

There was another perspective on this issue of vice and race which is revealed by African American hostility to the Levee and gambling dens. In the late nineteenth century, African Americans who wished to integrate into middle-class Chicago deplored gambling and the saloons where lower-class whites and blacks consorted. This was partly an expression of their desire for respectability, much like that which drove Irish American attitudes toward working women. It also reflected an increasing (though in this period before the Great Migration, not overwhelming) African American concern with the effect of the Levee on the morals of other, particularly poorer, blacks. But it was fundamentally a defensive reaction, based on an all too well-grounded fear that whites would equate all African Americans with those they read about in tales of vice raids.[29]

The coroner's inquest was a moment where the jury spoke out about the Davis case, offering an interpretation that modified the one offered by Kent. It was a sign of the sort of jury independence that the *Daily News* had reservations about, and served as a modest sign of a civil society that defined itself in opposition to the State. But the jury's verdict and the reactions to it also provide an example of how different interpretations could arise, based on the different contexts that people brought to consideration of a problem. Just as the jury recast the coroner's comments, contemporaries had reason to read the verdict of the jury from a variety of perspectives. The result was a message that went to many people, in many different ways.[30]

In the days following the coroner's jury verdict, different groups in the city reacted to the events at Greene's. Not all of them did much. The grand jury met the afternoon following the inquest. Heeding the recommendation of the coroner's jury, it promptly indicted Zephyr Davis for the murder of Maggie Gaughan, but ignored the *Tribune*'s recommendation that it use the case as an opportunity to investigate violations of the child labor law. Other groups were far more active. A few days later, a labor-based political organization, the Trade and Labor Assembly, issued a statement attacking Greene's for hiring underage workers, in violation of a city ordinance prohibiting child labor, and demanded that the city prosecute the factory. When its demand appeared to be ignored, the Assembly threatened to file the complaint itself. Ultimately, its pressure paid off and the factory was brought to trial, where it was prosecuted by two city attorneys, including a very young Clarence Darrow.[31]

Evidence at the Greene hearing fit the murder into the story of unskilled labor in late nineteenth-century Chicago. Seven employees testified, six black and one white. One was as young as twelve, another as old as seventeen, the rest were fourteen. All agreed that their workday began at 7:00 A.M. and ended at 5:30 P.M., with a half-hour lunch break. They were paid by the piece; none made less than $1.50 or more than $2.50 a week, wages that were low even for women and children and far below the $4.00 a week that was deemed inadequate in *White Slave Girls*. The wage scale was clearly why Greene's employed this type of worker, and in that respect, the evidence at the hearing substantiated the *Labor Enquirer*'s concern about wage slaves.[32]

In his defense, Greene tried to argue that he was unaware of the law and that he permitted his employees to take a break whenever they wanted during the day, a claim they all conceded in their testimony. But the city's attorneys argued that neither Greene's ignorance of the law, nor the fact that other employers violated it, should prevent the court from punishing the factory, and Judge Lyons agreed. In his ruling, he laid special emphasis on the fact that the employees were so young—"mere infants," he called them, and "atoms of humanity." He ordered Greene's fined the maximum amount under the ordinance, two hundred dollars, and expressed the hope that the case would make the city and its businesses wake up to the problem of child labor.[33]

The *Times* reported on the hearing in a manner consistent with its anti-employer sentiments. It characterized John Greene as a whiny, pinched little man and made much of Judge Lyons's remarks at his sentencing. In particular, it highlighted the judge's declaration that it was time "that a stop was put to the pernicious habit of enslaving mere children at hard and confining labor for longer hours than their elders would work." The paper also captured the incompatible interests at stake when it repeated Lyons's assertion that the law was "necessary for the welfare of the children and for their elders."[34]

The problem of child labor was vexed on several fronts. It was on the decline in the 1880s, nationally as well as in Chicago, though it became more prevalent again during the depressions of the 1890s. Notwithstanding, many Chicago families, like their counterparts nationally, continued to depend on the labor of children to make ends meet. Even at that level of economic necessity, a variety of forces came into play. While the comments of Mary Gaughan implied that her daughter worked for pin money, not subsistence, that was atypical if true. The usual practice was that working girls gave their wages back to their parents, while boys who worked were allowed to keep some or all of their income. Similarly gendered assumptions drove wages, so that young white working women, like blacks of either sex, typically made less than young white male workers doing the same job.[35]

Those intrafamily economic issues competed with larger economic demands. The 1870s and 1880s were marked by efforts to encourage—or force, depending on one's perspective—children to go to school. Beginning in 1873, Illinois law required that children younger than fourteen go to school at least sixteen weeks in a year. A second law, passed in 1883, reduced the requirement, mandating that children between eight and fourteen attend school at least twelve weeks in a year. For many in the business classes, these reforms were intended to create an educated and disciplined workforce. In that vein, Victor Lawson, the reforming editor of the *Chicago Daily News*, continually pressed for improvement of the public schools. But pressure for public education came from other directions as well; some working-class families encouraged children to go to school, joining the demand for improved education, even as others insisted their children continue to work.[36]

As this suggests, not everyone opposed child labor. Employers favored it as a means of getting a very cheap workforce, and because it drove down adult wages. Working-class families insisted that their children work for a variety of reasons, sometimes out of economic necessity, sometimes because of cultural pressures, and sometimes as a way to control their children. There were reformers who favored child labor. The Citizens League of Chicago, a middle- and upper-class reform group, argued that child labor laws contributed to urban crime by denying young men the stabilizing influence of employment. The Trade and Labor Assembly had a different perspective, in part because the ordinance prohibiting child labor had been sponsored in the early 1880s by a socialist alderman associated with the Assembly's forerunner. The stronger reason was that workers like Maggie and Zephyr threatened the Trade and Labor Assembly's constituents, the adult male workers who were driven out of work by competition from child laborers.[37]

Activism on behalf of a community of interest, undertaken by organized groups acting at the margins of the formal political system, was at the core of Chicago's civil society. Much of that activism related to law; groups from across the political spectrum, including the Trade and Labor Assembly and the Citizens League, pushed to have laws enforced and protested when they were not. The Citizens League, which had a loose affiliation with the National Law and Order League of the United States, issued public reports cataloging violations of the laws, and the Trade and Labor Assembly initiated its own inspections of various public institutions. These groups, and others like them, monitored court enforcement and sometimes prosecuted violations of the law themselves.[38]

Smaller groups, organized at the neighborhood rather than the city level, engaged in similar conduct. The suburb of Hyde Park, for example, had an active Citizens League that fought to enforce liquor laws in that village. There, the League's use of the legal system was counteracted by the efforts of organized saloon owners who also resorted to the courts, on at least one occasion having an officer of the League arrested and detained overnight. Other groups periodically demanded legal reforms, as happened in the spring of 1886, when the

Bricklayer's Union protested the decision to use prison labor to provide the stone for the new county courthouse. In each case, these groups filled a double role. They opposed the State, demonstrating its failures to enforce its own laws and demanding reform. They also supplanted it when they had to, offering services or advocacy that it could not, or would not, provide.[39]

There was another organized reaction to the verdict which revealed a different aspect of Chicago's civil society, tying the case into a third legal and social context. Immediately after the coroner's jury's verdict was publicized, members of the African American community in Chicago met to protest the verdict for failing to respect the equality of blacks.[40]

John G. Jones, a lawyer and African American political activist, opened the session with the announcement that he hoped there would be an apology for the comments of the coroner's jury. He added that if none was forthcoming, Coroner Hertz and Deputy Coroner Kent should "be tarred and feathered." Some speakers echoed his violent sentiments, while others argued, and finally convinced the group, that violent mob action was not a suitable response to racial hostility. In the end, the meeting condemned the murder and extended its sympathy to the Gaughan family. It also passed a resolution demanding that Coroner Hertz fire Kent and then resign from office. The resolution closed by characterizing the verdict as a "vicious, slanderous, and wholly unwarranted attack on a law abiding class of citizens."[41]

An indignation meeting of this sort was not unique. African Americans held mass meetings with such regularity in late nineteenth-century Chicago that Jones, who called many of them, was known as "Indignation Jones." Sometimes, as was the situation with the Davis case, the meeting protested events or conditions in the city. In 1887, for example, a similar meeting denounced city and county government agencies for refusing to hire black employees. In other instances, protest meetings were intended to inform; for example, African Americans in Chicago sponsored public debates examining race relations in the South. Some meetings were called to confront disagreements within the African American community, and as the nineteenth century came to a close, such meetings increasingly involved debates that pitted advocates of self-help and self-segregation against those who favored integration into the city.[42]

Chicago's activist African American community was not unusual; around the country, African Americans held mass meetings, which were often led and organized by political leaders. But not all members of the community participated or participated equally. In Chicago, protest meetings were dominated by the black professional classes, made up of doctors, lawyers, and civil servants, with the support of the city's African American ministers, who usually loaned their churches as meeting places. In contrast, small business owners, even relatively prosperous ones, were not active in these protests, and the poorest African Americans rarely participated at all. Women had a significant but, at this point, chiefly passive role in these sessions. They attended, often in large numbers, and their presence helped establish that a session was both serious and respectable. Yet in the 1880s, they were not active participants, and reports of the meetings do not suggest that women spoke out at them. By the 1890s, things had changed, and Chicago's African American community developed a number of influential women activists, but in the days before Ida B. Wells arrived in the city, women were typically confined to a symbolic role.[43]

Protest meetings called by African Americans in Chicago built on a tradition of activism within the city dating to before the Civil War and reflected national patterns that continued well into the twentieth century. Before the war, protest meetings in Chicago centered on the issue of slavery; after the turn of the century, the meetings were often used to shore up the sense of community among African Americans in response to increasing segregation and racism. In between those periods, and particularly in the 1880s, the meetings protested affronts to African Americans and were chiefly designed to insist that African Americans be treated as a part of the larger community of Chicago.[44]

Underneath that demand for inclusion lay the fear that by designating themselves as a separate community, with distinctive aims or interests, African Americans would encourage those who sought to segregate them or limit their access to the public sphere. That fear shaped reactions at protest meetings, and the terms in which they were conducted. It also set the limits on what many African Americans were prepared to do, as the protests over the Davis case demonstrated. While the meeting that followed the coroner's inquest condemned the slight the jury's verdict offered to African Americans, it did not issue any statement on behalf of Zephyr Davis, and although some participants urged it, it did not even demand that he be given a fair trial.

The meetings called by African Americans resembled the ad hoc protest meetings called by radical groups, yet there were key differences. As in the African American community, radical protest meetings typically arose out of other, more formal organizations, like the political clubs that met in saloons and ethnic halls. Both sorts of protests were reactions to perceived threats to the interests of the group, for example, meetings to protest the Haymarket verdict or police treatment of strikers. As in the African American community, women attended these sessions in significant numbers, but in contrast to the practice among Chicago's African Americans, women spoke at the radical meetings (much to the amusement of the mainstream press, which liked to poke fun at the arguments of the "red women"). In further contrast to African American women, some radical women held leadership roles at their meetings.[45]

There was another, even more significant difference between these two types of protest meetings. Those called by Chicago's African American community in the late nineteenth century functioned to make African Americans part of Chicago and to protest efforts that excluded or marginalized them. In contrast, those called by radical groups were typically, though not always, intended to reinforce a sense of radical community that functioned in opposition to Chicago. As Bruce Nelson has demonstrated, this difference between radical groups depended on the tradition in which the particular group worked. Some, especially those coming out of German or Eastern European traditions, thought of themselves as part of an international radical movement and sought to separate themselves from, or place themselves in opposition to, Chicago and the larger Chicago community. Theirs was a challenge, not to the local State or specific aspects of the economic system, but to the idea of the State or the practice of capitalism. Other radical groups, especially those dominated by people of Anglo-American or Irish American origin, defined themselves within the working-class republican tradition of the United States. Many, but again not all, of those who fit into this second group considered themselves part of Chicago and sought, like African Americans, to influence the direction of life in that community.[46]

Ad hoc committees were not limited to radicals or African Americans. Neighborhood groups built on the tradition of civic republicanism in another way, protesting matters that had an impact on their surroundings. In contrast to those who used ad hoc protest meetings to maintain a sense of community separate from Chicago, or those who used them to integrate into the Chicago community, this third sort of group originated from a community. Their meetings built on the "powerful public policy" of the common law vision of a well-regulated society. In Chicago, more immediately, they were a reminder of the political culture that dominated city politics before the Chicago Fire.[47]

The community group banded together to protest harm done to its geographic interests. It might petition to demand that a nuisance be abated or that criminal activity in the area be brought to an end, as, for example, when the people living on Butterfield and Dearborn Streets organized to demand that the city raid houses of prostitution in their neighborhood. Sometimes, community sentiment manifested itself in more direct action. In 1875, a vigilante group burned down the Wahl Glue Works in Chicago to protest the smells coming from the factory and the lack of enforcement of health ordinances. In a letter to the editor of the *Chicago Tribune* written after the fact, the group explained that it had burned the factory down because "municipal officials were 'not disposed to do anything.'" As that suggests, a major difference between a mob and a protest meeting was that the mob acted to enforce its sense of what justice required, while meetings usually just called to have justice done. But the boundary between the two situations was not fixed; where nothing was done, a meeting could easily turn into a mob that took matters into its own hands.[48]

Protests might be called by elite, non-elite, and even marginalized people. Some groups had semiofficial status, others were suppressed. Yet despite their differences, all shared the sense they were entitled to articulate their views and be heard by the city at large. They were, regardless of their particular motivations for organizing or the ideological antecedents of their mobilization, intent on having their opinions influence the nature and enforcement of the laws. When the State failed to act, they were prepared to take the law into their own hands, sometimes by prosecuting cases themselves, other times by more violent means.[49]

Such protests were only one aspect of the interest Chicago's civil society took in things legal. There were public lectures on civil rights; ministers gave sermons on the meaning of law; bar associations held symposia on law. Individuals of all persuasions and conditions called for closer regard to law, stricter enforcement of laws on the books, creation of laws to provide greater protections, and an end to laws that seemed unfair. But while they were couched in terms of law, these discussions were concerned with *justice*, not legal rules. As the people of Bridgeport put it when they protested Chicago's failure to clean out a health hazard at Healy's Slough, their demand was for "a tardy act of justice," not the enforcement of a particular rule.[50]

Chicagoans had no love for particular rules of law. Instead, the operating principle seems to have been that only if a law was consistent with what a group (or an individual) thought was just, should it be strictly enforced; in contrast, a law that seemed inconsistent with one's sense of justice was a corruption to be opposed. Edgar Lee Masters, the poet and sometime lawyer who practiced with Clarence Darrow in Chicago in the late nineteenth century, noted, "As in many other particulars, the leading men disobeyed [one] law, while calling loudly upon the police to enforce [another] law." That attitude was hardly confined to the leading men. The Haymarket defendants and their allies frequently criticized the State for being selective in its respect for law and were in turn attacked for demanding the protections of some laws even as they denied the authority of others. Ironically, the judge who tried the Haymarket case was notorious for being selective about which laws he applied. According to one account, he was "fond of being a law unto himself in his own court; bristling with technicalities which tend conveniently to defeat justice; smart in his wit and indulgent in his conscience."[51]

While that attitude was pervasive, it was not universal. As the protest meeting over the coroner's jury's verdict indicated, for African Americans in Chicago the relationship between justice and law was complex. Many had great faith in the protections of formal law, but a close reading of comments published in the Western Appeal demonstrates the limits of that faith. The Appeal demanded equality under law, applauding instances when whites were subject to the same laws as blacks, as happened in Maryland, for example, with the decision to flog two white men convicted of wife beating. "Heretofore," the paper noted, "flogging in that state has been confined to colored men," so that the application of whips to white backs suggested that "a new era" of equal justice had dawned. The paper also denounced lawlessness, which it equated with mob violence, running any number of stories about lynchings that pointed out how the mere threat of lynch mobs kept blacks from voting or running for office. As a basic principle, the Western Appeal favored law and feared popular, extralegal conduct.[52]

Beneath that attitude lay the fear that racially motivated injustice was becoming as prevalent in the North as it was in the South. The Western Appeal reported, with growing distress, tales of lynchings in the Northeast and Midwest. It worried that a racial double standard was developing in the North and printed tales that supported that suspicion to point out how vital it was that African Americans call for justice through strict enforcement of the laws. That was the message the paper offered in July 1888 when it reported the story of Julia Payne, a recent arrival to Minneapolis who had sought housekeeping work by placing an advertisement in a local paper. She was contacted by a white man who invited her to meet with him, presumably for an interview. Instead of taking her to his home, he took her to an isolated spot and raped her. Although the black community in Minneapolis was up in arms over the incident and called for the lynching of the man involved, the Appeal urged caution, noting, we "do not advocate any such proceedings, as there is justice for all classes of citizens in the state."[53]

Justice, for the Appeal, always began with law. Each time it reported a lynching, its first reaction was that there should have been a trial. It highlighted cases like that of Albert Polk, "suspected, accused, and actually tried in court, in regular court, in Kansas City, Mo., on the charge of committing a rape on a white female, [and] was discharged." It reported, in order to denounce, instances where black men had been lynched only to have evidence turn up later that demonstrated they were innocent.[54]

But while the Appeal hoped that trials would provide protections for blacks, it admitted that law often failed, resulting in a trial that was no better than a lynching. The legal system failed in other ways as well, most typically by failing to act. In October 1887, the paper reported that the white sheriff of Minneapolis had shot and killed Tim Graham, a black man. The coroner's jury met and concluded that the shooting was justified. The *Appeal* interpreted this judgment to mean that "because a county officer, a white man, has killed only a Negro, nothing should be done about the matter." The paper called, rather helplessly, for a grand jury investigation into the incident, arguing that it would convince blacks that the prevailing theory was not "the principle that led Justice Taney to declare: A Negro has no rights which a white man is bound to respect." The conundrum for the *Appeal* was that law was only just when it was truly equal, but nothing internal to the legal system guaranteed equal treatment. The paper called on other African Americans to constantly monitor criminal law and demand that it act justly. While the *Appeal* opposed extralegal justice, it believed that law had to be subject to some sort of popular influence in order to make sure that it did conform to justice.[55]

At the same time, another factor influenced the *Appeal*'s attitude toward law and justice. In the 1880s, the paper, and many of its readers, believed that conditions in Chicago for African Americans were very good. For that reason, the paper frequently failed to report racial problems in the city, often taking a path of nonconfrontation in hopes that conditions would improve naturally. This reluctance meant it often shied away from controversy, as it did in the Davis case. The *Appeal* never protested the treatment Zephyr Davis received or reminded its readers that as a black man he needed the protections of the law. It barely mentioned the case at all and never wrote a line about his trial, other than to applaud the outcome. Faced with a case that might lead to racial backlash, the *Appeal* silenced itself, just as the *Irish World* had, for much the same reason.[56]

The arguments presented by the coroner's jury, by the Trade and Labor Assembly, and at the African American indignation meeting demonstrated that all those groups felt free to act within Chicago's civil society and to protest the failures of law. Their protests assumed that the people protesting had a right to be heard, and that there were problems with the law that needed to be addressed. But while all agreed that law had failings, they did not agree on what those failings were; nor were they equally free to voice their demands.

Several forces set limits on their ability to do so. One was the problem of equal access. Ideally, the papers provided the field in which views could be expressed to the widest audience and contest with one another. Press treatment of protests arising from the Davis case demonstrated that while in practice the field was accessible to many, it was hardly level. The success of the Trade and Labor Assembly

in gaining attention for its protest, and in using that publicity to make the city enforce its ordinance against Greene's, showed that private people could make law
work. The widespread reporting of the verdict of the coroner's jury demonstrated
that individuals could resist a message pressed on them by a government official
and use the formal setting of a hearing to articulate an alternative vision of what
was right or wrong. Coverage of the protest meeting by the African Americans established that even those at the margins of Chicago's civil society could voice their
concerns. At the same time, coverage of the jury's protests and the African Americans' meeting revealed how the impact of protests could be limited, and why.
When it reported the coroner's jury's verdict, the *Tribune* dismissed it and urged
its readers to do the same. In that particular instance, the paper's response had the
salutary effect of indicating that overtly racist appeals had no place in the public
debate, but the paper's condescending report of the African American meeting
demonstrated how much racism continued to influence its coverage of debates.[57]

The press also permitted others to undermine certain messages by treating
them with derision. On March 3, after the coroner's jury entered its verdict and
African Americans met to protest it, D. P. French wrote a letter to the editor of the
Chicago Inter-Ocean attacking the verdict as a "false, . . . malignant, and slanderous attack upon all intelligent and law abiding colored persons." The verdict, he
explained, implied that "all negro foremen murder white girls," an untruth that
ignored the fact that black boys and girls went to school with white boys and girls
without incident. He also pointed out that blacks and whites worked together in
many workplaces without "harm to public morals." He closed with a paragraph
condemning Davis's crime and asking everyone in the city to "judge men not by
the color of their skins, but by their deeds," so that "justice will be done to all."[58]

Deputy Coroner Kent responded to the letter in the same edition of the paper. Identifying himself as a Republican of Irish heritage, he declared, "There
[was] not a man in the world who would more cheerfully help a race or class of
men occupy their place among men than myself." He then attacked French as
"a crank" who wanted "to resurrect issues that were settled by blood and war
twenty years before." Kent declared that French had read racial issues into a
statement that had nothing to do with race, and had tried to "manufacture" the
idea that Kent was prejudiced. Having distorted French's argument, which attacked the language of the jury verdict, by demonstrating that it did not reflect
his statement to the jury, Kent dismissed not only French's specific protest but
also his general point that verdicts that reflected prejudice were inherently unjust. In Kent's hands, French's well-reasoned complaint became just another
case of race pleading by an African American who did not understand that racial
problems had been settled by the Civil War.

DAVIS' MOTHER.

Attitudes like Kent's explain the self-imposed silences of the African American community and also led to more subtle problems. To maximize their chances of integration into the larger Chicago community, many African Americans modified their behavior as well as their arguments in order to avoid problems with a society that, while not yet overtly racist, was unsympathetic to what it saw as claims of racial entitlement. The desire not to appear to engage in race pleading led some African Americans to frame calls for integration in such vague terms that they undermined their own appeals; other times it kept individual African Americans from going places where they might be attacked or challenged. In all too many cases, it led to arguments and choices based on assumptions about what white Chicago would prefer.[59]

One example of this last sort of self-censorship had an immediate impact on efforts to prepare a case on Davis's behalf. In the first few days after his arrest, Davis appeared before the coroner's jury, the grand jury, and an initial court hearing without counsel. In that same period, he repeatedly announced that he was ready to go to trial instantly. Those promises were used, by both judges and the prosecution, to defeat subsequent requests for continuances on his behalf. Shortly after he was indicted, two African American attorneys, Edward Morris and Fredrick McGhee, appeared on his behalf. As soon as they did so, they were removed from the case at the behest of Zephyr's mother, Sophia, who apparently did not want her son represented by two black men. Because of the earlier promises made by Zephyr and the initial delays caused by the confusion over who would represent him, the white attorneys she hired to replace Morris and McGhee, Jonathan Arney and Campbell Allison, were never able to get the time they needed to find witnesses. His mother's apparent fear that with two black attorneys her son's trial would turn into a race case meant that his defense was never prepared as well as it should have been.[60]

Popular reaction during the pretrial period concerned itself with the ways, and reasons why, law failed to conform to justice. In this stage of the case, protest groups acted in a variety of contexts, from the institutional setting of the coroner's jury to the ad hoc protest called by African Americans, demonstrating the range of Chicago's civil society in the process. In interest, if not in form, these groups were similar to the mobs that had dominated the first day and a half of the case, since they shared the mobs' concern with law's relationship to justice. Of course, the generally nonviolent approach of these civic associations lacked the mobs' violent aspect, although when groups acted to enforce their members' ideas of justice, they were extralegal forces in another sense of the term. Nor were groups unwilling to act as well as talk, as the threats of the African American meeting to tar and feather Hertz or the actions relating to the Wahl Glue Works demonstrated. In the end, the differences between a citizen's arrest by the Citizens League and the rough justice administered by a neighborhood mob were often nothing more than matters of degree and class.

The greatest difference was a less obvious one. Mobs formed and often were encouraged by the press, while the relation between protest groups and the press was more distant. The groups preserved an independence, but their messages were subject to considerable constraint, whether externally imposed by the papers or self-imposed by the groups themselves. The failure of Irish American papers to comment on Maggie's murder demonstrated that African Americans were not the only ones who stood silent for fear of backlash. But the fact that others did the same thing did not mitigate the damage created by censorship, self-imposed or externally compelled, or the extent to which that silence diminished all appeals to justice.[61]

3

Trial, March 28 to April 2, 1888

The battle between law and justice took on yet another aspect when the case moved to the courtroom as the trial began, rather slowly, shortly after 10 A.M. on Wednesday, March 28. That it began at all at the very end of the March term, ahead of the trials of others arrested long before Davis, demonstrated that public pressure had paid off. Newspapers expressed relief at the end of legalistic delays; Davis's attorneys denounced an urgency that seemed unjust.[1]

Under the circumstances, it was not surprising that the first matter Judge Kirk Hawes took up that morning was yet another defense motion for a continuance. In support of their motion, attorneys Jonathan Arney and Campbell Allison argued that they needed time to locate Kate Caldwell, the woman Davis had stayed with in Kansas City for four years before he moved to Chicago. In affidavits filed with the motion, Zephyr and his mother explained that in that period Caldwell had seen him have fits. Because her testimony about those fits was necessary to establish Davis's defense of insanity, the motion requested that the trial be postponed until Caldwell was located and brought to Chicago.[2]

Since it explained why her evidence was relevant to the case, and why no one else could provide it, the motion met all the conditions for granting a continuance, but procedural compliance never guarantees outcome. The state's attorney, Joel Longenecker (whose presence as the trial attorney indicated that he considered the case politically significant), opposed the motion because it failed to allege that Zephyr had had any spasms or fits during the year he lived in Chicago. Ignoring the defense response that it obviously intended to prove that as well, Hawes denied the motion and set the trial to begin that afternoon at 2 P.M. He then turned his attention to completing another case pending before him. Zephyr was returned to his cell, and the attorneys began preparing for trial.[3]

JUDGE HAWES.

It was not the crush that filled the courthouse during the Haymarket trial, but a good-sized crowd waited outside the courtroom that afternoon. Maggie's parents arrived and took seats in front, placed so they could see everything and easily be seen. Zephyr's mother was there as well, seated unobtrusively in a corner at the back. Some workers from Greene's came to watch, fresh from testifying at the hearing on the child labor ordinance the day before. The rest of the crowd consisted of "the usuals," although one paper noted there seemed to be more blacks than was typical. There were plenty of reporters as well.[4]

They all scrambled to find seats, only to have to leap to their feet when Hawes entered the courtroom. Once he had taken the bench and the clerk gaveled the court to order, the spectators settled back for the duration. As happened that morning, the hearing began with motions by the defense. One sought creation of a commission *de lunatico inquirendo,* a panel charged with examining Davis to determine whether he was insane. Any official finding of insanity would obviously help the defense, but the motion had a strategic as well as an evidentiary function. If the commission found Zephyr insane, the prosecution would have to prove that he had been sane when he committed the crime. Otherwise, the presumption was that he was sane at the time of the offense, and the burden was on the defense to create a reasonable doubt about his sanity. That motion also suggested, for the first time, that the defense intended to rely on several, mutually inconsistent, theories of Zephyr's insanity. One, indicated by the morning's motion for a continuance, was that he suffered from periodic fits of insanity. The other, implied by the afternoon motion, was that his insanity had a more persistent basis.[5]

Hawes swiftly denied the motion as well as a second one, which sought to quash the indictment on grounds that it didn't include a charge of manslaughter. Zephyr was called to the front of the courtroom and, having been read the indictment, pleaded not guilty. He then returned to his seat, and the trial got under way.[6]

More precisely, the complicated process of jury selection began. Consistent with the common though not universal practice in the Chicago courts, the clerk called twelve men from the pool of potential jurors and placed them under oath. These twelve were then divided into three panels of four, and attorneys for each side began *voir dire*. Longenecker went first, questioning the members of the first panel to decide which of its members to challenge and which to accept. Each side had twenty peremptory challenges (and could also ask to have an unlimited number of potential jurors excused for cause). Any panel member who was successfully challenged was removed and replaced by someone else. The prosecution continued its initial *voir dire* until it had accepted an entire panel of four. Then the first panel was turned over to the defense attorney, and the process of examination began again. It was not until all four members of one panel were accepted by both sides that the panel could be sworn in, and then the entire process begin again with a second panel of four. Needless to say, the procedure could be time-consuming, and it was especially protracted in the Davis case.[7]

The first panel, Thomas Sprague, J. E. McNichols, Charles A. Westberg, and M. H. Rhodes, were subjected to a perfunctory examination by Longenecker, who asked each the same five questions. Two explored their familiarity with the case, focusing on whether they had read about the murder and, if so, whether they had formed any opinions about it. If the answers to those two questions were yes, Longenecker asked each panel member if he "could lay this opinion aside and try the case simply on the law and the evidence." He also asked the prospective jurors whether they felt they would be prejudiced against Zephyr because of his race, and if they were opposed to capital punishment.[8]

The first four panelists answered the questions in a manner acceptable to Longenecker, so he sat down and the defense took its turn. While Longenecker's examination had been brief, defense attorney Jonathan Arney asked the prospective jurors an exhaustive and, in the eyes of the press, exhausting series of questions. Doubtless influenced by the tenor of the early coverage of the case, Arney asked each panel member if he had ever been to the South and how he felt about blacks. He also inquired about their views of the insanity defense. Those questions were mere preliminaries to Arney's major focus on the far more abstract issue of the burden of proof. He asked the prospective jurors whether they had already formed opinions about Zephyr's guilt and, when they said yes, whether they believed that the defense had the burden of changing their minds. Several of that first group of would-be jurors stumbled when answering his questions, and as they did so, it became apparent that Hawes had no intention of letting previously formed opinions keep anyone from serving on the jury.[9]

The first panelist, apparently Westberg, satisfied Arney; the second, Rhodes, struggled. When asked "if the opinions [you] hold would require evidence to remove," he repeated several times that "such evidence would have to be forthcoming," and was unwilling to commit to putting aside any opinions about the case that he had already formed. After several exchanges, Arney asked that Rhodes be removed for cause, arguing that his responses demonstrated he would put the burden of proving Davis not guilty on the defense. Hawes refused. "Suppose," he recommended, "you question again, and add 'if taken as a juror.'" Properly educated about what he needed to say, Rhodes affirmed that if called as a juror he would put aside his opinion, and Judge Hawes denied Arney's request to dismiss Rhodes for cause.[10]

Arney had better luck with the next panelist, McNichols. After admitting that he had formed an opinion about the case, McNichols likewise insisted that it would take evidence to change his mind. Fearful, perhaps, that this would not be enough to get him dismissed, he also, in the words of the *Inter-Ocean*, "manifested a disposition to display ignorance concerning very ordinary events and deductions." After listening a few minutes, Hawes interjected, demanding to know whether McNichols's answers were prompted by the desire to avoid jury duty. When McNichols admitted that he had no particular interest in serving, Hawes dismissed him, plainly more annoyed by his attitude than by his insistence that Davis prove his innocence. Interestingly, although sarcastic, the account in the *Inter-Ocean* interpreted this exchange sympathetically, reporting that as a "sewer architect" McNichols understandably did not "like to puddle around in a stench—moral or otherwise." In contrast to the suggestion that McNichols was legitimately disgusted by the case, and perhaps by the legal system itself, the *Chicago Tribune* recounted the incident with scorn. It approvingly quoted Hawes's pronouncement that "a man who will let his desire to escape jury service color his answers is not a fit man to serve." The difference reflected fundamentally opposed perspectives. For all the *Inter-Ocean* defended the legal system in theory, the actual workings of the law made it queasy. The *Tribune*'s response reflected its greater commitment to authority and a related hostility to those who shirked their civic duty.[11]

The rest of that first afternoon passed much the same way. The prosecution used two peremptory challenges to excuse panel members opposed to capital punishment; the defense successfully challenged two others. At the close of trial that first evening, not a single panel of four had been sworn in. When court resumed the next morning, Hawes's impatience, and his proclivity to help jurors avoid the pitfalls of the burden of proof, became more marked. Early in the day, he cut Arney off as he argued that a particular panelist should be dismissed for cause. Arney insisted that the potential juror's answers indicated that he would place the burden of proving his innocence on the defendant, but Hawes disagreed, noting, "He has to bring a verdict according to the law, and the law says he must give the prisoner the benefit of any doubt." When Arney pointed out that the juror had specifically said that he could not do so, Hawes responded, "I can't help that, he has also said that he would try the case according to the law, and I think he will."[12]

Hawes continued, "And while I'm talking I want to say you are consuming too much time. This case is no more important than many others and I shall limit you in your questions if you don't cut them off. I shall not permit you to take up a week getting a jury." Although Arney and Allison objected that they had to ask all the questions they felt needed to be asked, Hawes dismissed their claim. Told there was no precedent for cutting short *voir dire*, he replied that he would create one.[13]

The exchanges between Hawes and the defense attorneys during *voir dire* marked the first skirmish over how much influence popular ideas of justice could have at the trial, a question much confused by the state of the law. The general rule governing when jurors could be dismissed for previously formed opinions had been set down by the Illinois Supreme Court in 1841, in *Smith v. Eames*. There, the court held that "if a juror has made a decided opinion on the merits of the case, either from a personal knowledge of the facts, from the statements of the witnesses, from the relations [i.e., admissions] of the parties, or either of them, or from rumor, and that opinion is positive, and not hypothetical, and such as will probably prevent him from giving an impartial verdict, the challenge [for cause] should be allowed." The court continued by distinguishing opinions "merely of a light and transient character, such as is usually formed by persons in every community," concluding that such opinions as might "be changed by the relation of the next person met with" did not "show a conviction of the mind, and a fixed conclusion thereon." Challenges based on that sort of opinion would be denied, while those against prospective jurors whose opinions were more fixed would be allowed. Applying those principles to the case before it, the court in *Eames* concluded that a potential juror who had indicated that he had formed an opinion about the defendant based on rumors he had heard, but who had also indicated the opinion was not fixed, had properly not been dismissed for cause.[14]

According to *Eames*, the determination of whether a prospective juror should be dismissed for holding a previously formed opinion turned on fixity of opinion. A statute passed in 1874 appeared to modify that rule by shifting the inquiry to the basis of the opinion rather than its nature. That statute provided that where a "person called as a juror has formed an opinion or impression, based upon newspaper accounts (about the truth of which he has expressed no opinion)," that "should not disqualify him to serve as a juror in such a case, if he shall, under oath, state that he believes he can fairly and impartially render a verdict therein in accordance with the law and the evidence, and that the court shall be satisfied with the truth of such statement."[15]

A number of opinions followed, each trying to explain whether the statute modified *Eames*. In the first, *Plummer v. Illinois*, a prospective juror admitted to having heard rumors about the crime which had led him to form an opinion unfavorable to the defendant. He denied, however, that his opinion would keep him from rendering a fair and impartial verdict. On the basis of that second claim, a defense motion to dismiss him for cause was denied. A second prospective juror conceded that he had read news reports that tended to bias him against the defendant, and he also was permitted to serve. On appeal, the court distinguished between the two prospective jurors, holding that the second should have been dismissed for cause. Where "a juror has been exposed to influences, the probable effect of which is to create a prejudice in his mind against the defendant, which would require evidence to overcome, to render him incompetent, it should clearly appear that he can, when in the jury box, entirely disregard those influences and try the case without, in any degree, being affected by them." In essence, this was the rule from *Eames*, yet because *Plummer* implied that certain sources of information created a stronger, more permanent bias, it seemed to go beyond *Eames*, holding that news accounts were more dangerous than rumors. The rule after *Plummer* appeared to require both an investigation of how fixed an opinion was and consideration of its source.[16]

Six months before Davis came to trial, the Illinois Supreme Court revisited that statute in the appeal of the conviction of the Haymarket defendants. Although the court did not admit it was doing anything of the sort, its decision in *Spies v. Illinois* appeared to reverse *Plummer* and to reject the standard from *Eames* as well. In *Spies*, the state supreme court was faced with a trial that followed innumerable, and highly prejudicial, news accounts about the Haymarket bombing and the defendants. A large number of prospective jurors indicated that "it would take pretty strong evidence to remove the impression" they held about the defendants. As one potential juror, William Neil, put it, "I could not lay [my opinion] altogether aside during the trial. I believe my present opinion, based upon what I have heard and read, would accompany me through the trial, and would influence me in determining and getting at a verdict." Others made similar remarks; all were challenged for cause, and most of those motions, including the one involving Neil, were denied.[17]

The Illinois Supreme Court refused to reverse, specifically holding that none of the jurors who served were prejudiced by the news accounts they had read. The essence of the ruling was precisely the opposite of *Plummer*; any juror who formed an opinion based on news accounts could not be challenged for cause. As the court put it, admitting jurors who read the newspapers "tends to secure intelligence in the jury-box and to exclude from it that dense ignorance, which has often subjected the jury system to just criticism." So long as a juror paid lip service to the idea that he would rule based on the evidence, he could serve, regardless of how fixed the opinion he had formed based on his reading of the newspapers.[18]

Six years later, in *Coughlin v. Illinois*, the Illinois Supreme Court revisited the statute once again and reinstated the test from *Eames*. In *Coughlin*, coverage of the original murder and the ensuing investigation had been exhaustive, and during *voir dire* several prospective jurors admitted they had formed opinions about the case based on what they had read in the papers. When defense attorneys asked that these jurors be dismissed for cause, their requests were denied. On appeal, the Illinois Supreme Court reversed, concluding that a statement by a prospective juror that he has not been biased by news accounts "merely tends to show that the juror, while admitting he has prejudged the prisoner's case, believes in his ability to act as though he were impartial." The court went on, "[I]t is difficult to see how, after a juror has avowed a fixed and settled opinion as to the prisoner's guilt, a court can be legally satisfied of the truth of his answer that he can render a fair or impartial verdict." Once again, the emphasis was on how fixed the juror's opinion was, not on its source.[19]

Tempting as it is to ascribe the very different results in the last two cases to varying degrees of public pressure, circumstances do not warrant that interpretation. The *Coughlin* case, though at present all but forgotten, was at the time a major political and legal event. The allegations in the case, and in particular the fact that one of the defendants was a police officer, led many to fear a conspiracy among Irish Americans within the department and the city government, and those claims were widely reported before the trial. This situation, no less than Haymarket, seemed to involve a serious threat to the city.[20]

The different rulings in these cases reflected a larger debate over the influence of public opinion on law. That debate involved questions about the jury's role in the criminal process and the proper nature of the effect of news reports on matters before the courts. The connections between those issues, and the larger debate itself, were illuminated in a series of papers presented before the Illinois State Bar Association in the 1880s.

The authors of those papers were very confused about how much influence popular opinions should have on law. Several opposed popular influence, paying special attention to protests organized to oppose verdicts the protesters deemed unjust. To a man, they denounced such protests—even when they were entirely peaceful—for instilling "into the public mind the *poison* of disobedience to the law." But while David Davis, a former associate justice of the United States Supreme Court and president of the Illinois State Bar Association in 1885, joined with those who deplored protests, he argued that they had to be understood as a response to an actual problem. Jury verdicts, he pointed out, were rarely, if ever, the subject of popular protest. Instead, the protests were to decisions by judges and reflected popular dissatisfaction with the formal law. Others made the related point that the perception that judicial decisions that were too legalistic drove businesses and individuals to work outside the law.[21]

Judge Davis appeared to agree that much popular hostility to law arose from judicial devotion to rules of law, and as a judge he had not been above acting outside the law himself, as one famous (though perhaps apocryphal) incident demonstrated. One day, a railroad company appeared as a defendant in his courtroom, sued by a farmer who claimed that the railroad had defrauded him, buying his farm with worthless stock. After hearing the arguments, Judge Davis declared, "I am familiar with the laws governing this case and with all the statutes touching such cases, but I know of no law to prevent a railroad company from stealing a man's farm." Before the defendants could celebrate their victory, he added, "But so long as I sit on this bench I will not permit [a railroad] to keep" a farm it stole. Davis then entered judgment for the plaintiff, ordering the railroad to return the farm.[22]

Davis worried about judges who put law before outcomes that seemed just, and about the effect their decisions had on popular respect for the legal system. For Davis, it was the judge's obligation to decide when the demands of justice outweighed the rule of law. Other members of the Illinois State Bar Association agreed that legal results had to square with "popular conscience" but put the onus of making sure they did so somewhere other than on the judiciary. In a paper he presented in 1885, Van Buren Denslow argued that public opinion, rather than the rule of law, often determined the outcomes of cases, especially in criminal law. He did not rejoice in this wholeheartedly; as he put it, the "frequent looseness in the outcome of the administration of justice" was "conspicuous and revolting in the criminal law." But he conceded the result was an inevitable and legitimate aspect of a system based on local, popular control. Given the assumptions of the system, popular influence was not only inevitable but also worth preserving and defending, since "the forms of law" made tyranny possible. One protection against tyranny was to educate the people so that they had a firmer grounding in law. Another, more viable, course was to allow popular will to influence legal outcomes, on the theory that if law squared with community norms people would be more likely to obey it voluntarily. That, in turn, would prevent the twin dangers of revolt against the law and the imposition of law by force.[23]

By this argument, law was not a means of social control so much as it was the way society protected itself from oppression. Because they guaranteed the flexibility needed to provide that protection, juries served as the cornerstone of the legal system. Jurors gave law its looseness, since they let their personal sense of justice trump legal rules, but that was precisely how they helped guarantee that law squared with justice. Jury verdicts, in that sense, were a way to avoid protests and mob action, while at the same time permitting the popular influence on legal outcomes that was necessary to keep tyranny at bay. As Melville Fuller, another member of the Illinois State Bar Association who became Chief Justice of the United States Supreme Court in 1888, put it, in democracies law had to grow out of the will of the people. Fuller was no populist—he lamented "trial by newspaper" and clearly had reservations about how democratic law or society should be—but he conceded some popular influence on law was inevitable.[24]

By adding newspapers to the equation, Fuller tied the issue of popular influence on law back to the problem of juror bias. Newspapers were one way to inform and educate the public about the workings of law, which meant they were a way to maintain popular interest in law and to ensure some popular influence on it. At the same time, their coverage created the risk of too much popular pressure. A similar desire to strike a balance between too much and too little popular influence, and the related problem of how much newspaper attention was too much, created the circumstances that led the Illinois Supreme Court to render its inconsistent opinions on the question of juror bias.

The dispute between Hawes and Arney was a variation on these debates. Arney was not merely challenging the bias of particular members of the jury pool, he was arguing the general principle that jurors had to decide cases based on what they learned during the trial. A just verdict, in his view, was one derived from information provided in the courtroom by lawyers and their witnesses, filtered through legal rules. It had to be untainted by popular perceptions or by information about the case obtained from other sources. Hawes, in contrast, defended the right of prospective jurors to rule based on opinions they had formed outside the courtroom, or on information they had received from other sources, so long as they did not ignore the law they learned in court. Arney's vision of justice demanded a legal system quarantined from daily life; Hawes's favored legal decisions reflecting popular understandings of what justice, as mediated by judicial instruction, required.

While the papers defended their right to report on crimes and legal proceedings as part of their obligation to properly inform the public, that ideal did not influence the way they reported on jury selection. None of the Chicago dailies were enthusiastic, or particularly thoughtful, observers of the process in the Davis case. The *Daily News* described *voir dire* as dragging "wearily along"; the *Inter-Ocean* echoed that sentiment, referring to an "almost insufferable tedium." Both the *Herald* and the *Daily News* made it clear the fault lay with the defense's "tactics of delay." While the *Inter-Ocean* agreed, its irritation went further. After referring to the "wearisome policy of the defense," it characterized the proceedings as a farce on all fronts. "The challenges for cause were innumerable, the Court's interferences and adjustments were as plentiful, and then the ground of examination would be gone over again, until finally, despairing of entangling the candidate for jurorship, the right to peremptory challenge would be exercised, and fresh men would be sworn in." For the *Inter-Ocean*, the entire spectacle was yet more proof that there were serious problems with law in practice.[25]

Not everyone took it so hard; the *Tribune* found the process far more amusing than tedious. Reporting on the first day of the trial, it recounted with glee the way a "farmer" successfully countered every question he was asked by Arney. It was hard to say whether the paper had more contempt for the rustic or the lawyer, but their exchange enlivened what the *Tribune* considered an otherwise dismal day at the courthouse. In the same vein, its account of jury selection on Friday attempted to wring as much drama as possible from prospective juror John Barker's claim that he had known Zephyr Davis before the trial. Asked to elaborate, Barker explained that three years earlier Davis had sold papers at the corner of Wabash and Eighteenth Streets. Barker claimed he had bought newspapers there regularly, becoming acquainted with Davis in the process. The *Tribune* mockingly noted that Barker was advised that three years earlier Zephyr had been living in Kansas City, adding that Hawes denied a defense effort to challenge him for cause after Barker said he would give Zephyr a fair trial. While those moments may well have been amusing and bizarre, the frolicsome tone that the *Tribune* adopted in recounting them made it clear that it too believed that what was going on in Judge Hawes's courtroom was a monumental waste of time.[26]

ZEPH DAVIS IN COURT.

Whether from boredom or amusement, no paper paid much attention to defense claims that Hawes was preventing them from getting an impartial jury. The press was far more concerned with monitoring Zephyr's behavior. At one point or another, each paper commented, critically, on how he acted during jury selection. All agreed that he sat, slumped over, head in hand, at counsel table, seeming to ignore the *voir dire* going on around him. While all found his behavior significant, there was no consensus on how to read it. The *Daily News* described his position as one of bored, "stupid, stolid" indifference, and the *Tribune* seemed to agree. When it reported that he sat upright the second day of jury selection, it proposed that he did so only because his previous position hurt his back, not because he cared about what was going on. The *Herald* and *Times* were less inclined to attribute Davis's posture to stupid lack of interest. The *Times* suggested that it was part of the "nervous and erratic" conduct that made up his insanity act; the *Herald* agreed, noting his remarkable metamorphosis over the course of the case into "a driveling, gibbering idiot." The *Inter-Ocean* also dismissed his behavior in the courtroom as part of an act designed to support his defense.[27]

These reactions reflected a nearly universal skepticism about the insanity defense, in this period typically dismissed as "the insanity dodge." More concretely, they revealed the intensity with which defendants' actions were observed. Defendants, especially murderers, were supposed to look brutal or evil or both. Often the papers described defendants as monsters whose behavior at trial reflected the cruelty of their natures. Papers monitored whether they expressed remorse or dramatically paled when compelling evidence was presented against them. This interest in their reactions reflected a sense that trials were places where defendants revealed their guilt through their conduct, rather than a site in which guilt or innocence was determined. This was the problem the state supreme court would identify in *Coughlin*, and it was the danger lurking in Hawes's attitude during *voir dire*. The idea that jurors had a right to bring their previously formed opinions into the courtroom easily led to a trial that ratified a decision that had already been made.[28]

It took nearly a day and a half, but finally, at 4:30 Friday afternoon, the entire jury had been chosen. It apparently consisted of only twelve men (no alternates are listed in any records): William Davidson, John Inman, John Barker, H. Ramaker, Charles Gerold, Charles Westberg, M. H. Rhodes, Ferdinand Dugan, W. C. Searle, J. M. Eaton, Martin Stonebecker, and John Thompson. Of these, Rhodes and Westberg had been on the initial panel of four, when Rhodes had been unsuccessfully challenged for cause by the defense; Barker was the panelist who had so amusingly insisted he had known Davis previously. Once the jurors were put under oath, the prosecution started to present its case.[29]

Longenecker began with an opening statement that the *Herald* described as short. He "said that it would be shown by the evidence that Zeph Davis had attempted familiarities with the girl he afterward murdered, and that he had been repulsed by her." Longenecker reminded the jury that the defense did not deny that Davis killed Maggie Gaughan, and closed with a reference to the insanity defense. "If," he vowed, "the state cannot show [that Davis was sane when he committed the crime] to your satisfaction, we shall not ask for the defendant's conviction." With that, he called Mary Gaughan to the stand. She described her daughter to the jurors and told them that Maggie had worked at Greene's for about four weeks before the murder. Her testimony, clearly designed to start the state's case on a sympathetic note, was followed by evidence that the *Herald* described as shocking for the defense.[30]

That characterization was probably fair. The prosecution's second witness was a teamster, William E. Carpenter, who testified that on the morning of February 27, he was driving by Greene's factory on his way back from the Atlantic freight depot at Clark and Thirteenth Streets. He passed Greene's, he thought, around 7:30 or 7:45 A.M., keeping close to the buildings because of the wind. He drove by just in time to "distinctly [see] a young colored man"—whom he immediately identified in the courtroom as Davis—"opening the door of the factory with his right hand." "As the young white girl who was standing outside attempted to pass in," Carpenter said, he saw the young man "put his left arm around her neck and try to hug her."[31]

She "struggled and tore herself loose," Carpenter went on, "slapping the negro in the face." Then he "saw the negro try the same familiarity again as the girl passed in." Carpenter added that the girl he saw going into the factory was wearing a dark cloak with a hood over her head and a blue silk handkerchief around her neck, a description consistent with those offered in the earliest accounts of the incident. Prompted by Longenecker, Carpenter explained that he had not merely assumed he saw Zephyr and Maggie but had later confirmed he had done so. After reading about the murder in the papers, he went to the Gaughan house during her wake and peeked in her casket to see if it contained the girl he saw outside the factory. Once he had concluded that it did, he went to the jail to glimpse Davis and decided that he was the young man he saw with Maggie outside the factory that morning.[32]

With that, cross-examination began. Arney started by suggesting Carpenter's evidence rested on bias, drawing out that he had been born on a plantation in Virginia before the Civil War. But when Arney pressed the point, Carpenter flatly denied that his background influenced his testimony. Arney then tried to attack the evidence from another direction, suggesting that it was unlikely, given the cold sleet falling the morning of the murder, that Carpenter would have paid much attention to what was happening in a doorway. To the amusement of the reporters, Carpenter responded that he distinctly noticed the incident because, as he put it, when he saw Zephyr his first thought was, "That's a damned cheeky thing for a nigger to do." Having violated one of the first rules of cross-examination by asking a question that let the witness strengthen his story, Arney sat down.[33]

After the excitement generated by Carpenter's testimony, the courtroom quieted when John Greene took the stand to testify about the discovery of Maggie's body. In contrast to the gory reports following the murder, he insisted that the closet was the only place where there was any blood. Greene also described Zephyr's confession after his capture. When the direct examination of Greene ended, shortly after 6:30, the trial came to a halt for the night.[34]

Parts of a carefully crafted whole, the testimony of the first three witnesses built on the themes suggested in Longenecker's brief opening statement. Mary Gaughan began the prosecution's evidence with a portrait of the victim, establishing in the process that her daughter was as virtuous as she was attractive. That laid the groundwork for the prosecution's main claim, which Carpenter's testimony made concrete. His evidence demonstrated that Zephyr initiated physical contact with Maggie, which she repulsed. His evidence further suggested that the murder arose from Davis's frustrated sexual aggression, confirming Mary Gaughan's testimony about her daughter's virtue and offering a motive otherwise lacking, which made the murder seem more rational and less consistent with a claim of insanity.[35]

Carpenter's evidence was the centerpiece of the prosecution's theory of the case, but Greene's testimony, in particular his assertion that there was no sign of blood anywhere but inside the closet, was also vital. It undermined Zephyr's claim (in his confession) that his attack on Maggie began by the stove, as part of an argument. Having confined the attack to a private space, Greene strengthened the implication that the murder followed an attempt to rape Maggie, and weakened the insanity defense by demonstrating that Zephyr was lucid enough to choose an isolated setting. While that part of Greene's evidence wrapped up the statements of the previous witnesses, his testimony about Zephyr's confession reminded the jurors what the papers, and Longenecker, had already told them — Zephyr admitted he killed Maggie. Greene provided a powerful end to the first day's testimony, which left the jurors with a clear picture and a coherent explanation of the crime.

By offering a series of witnesses who provided a coherent narrative at the start of its case, the prosecution made it easier for the jury to render a verdict in its favor. A second factor helped make its story even more persuasive. The prosecution's basic narrative resembled the popular literary motif of the beautiful, virtuous female murder victim. That image, well established in literature to the point of being a cliché by the end of the nineteenth century, would have been familiar to the jurors, and its familiarity would have helped them fit the prosecution's case together and make it seem inevitable and obvious.[36]

But while the prosecution's case was similar enough to build on the jurors' familiarity with the image, the prosecution had to modify the traditional narrative in a fundamental way. As Daniel Cohen has demonstrated, in its classic form the motif required the murder of a beautiful, young, single woman by a young, single man. To this point, the image and the prosecution's story of the crime were identical. Yet the motif also required that the victim's virtue be overcome by her attacker, who then murdered her after seducing her. It was here that the prosecution's theory of the case diverged from the motif, since its theory was not that Maggie had died because she succumbed to Zephyr's advances, but rather because she resisted him.[37]

The prosecution had to present the case that way, since the evidence from the autopsy did not establish that there was even an attempted sexual assault. Just as important, by offering a narrative that strayed from the motif, the prosecution avoided the problems that a claim of interracial sex entailed. By the 1880s, those who wished to offer a justification for lynching in the South never had to worry about whether the audience might think the white woman had led the black man on, but the boundaries of racial sexuality were not so clear in Chicago. Stories that emphasized the promiscuity of working girls, or titillated with accounts of willing white women involved with black (or Chinese) men in the Levee, meant that Longenecker had to be very careful when he hinted that Davis's motive for killing Maggie was sexual. As a result, the prosecution's evidence on this particular issue never settled into a single, coherent piece.[38]

Seen as a response to a key witness whose evidence tied together the state's narrative of the case, Arney's cross-examination of Carpenter appears inadequate. He faced a difficult task: he had to neutralize Carpenter, yet had only a few ways of doing so. The most obvious approach would have been to use the cross-examination of Carpenter to raise the specter of working-girl sexuality Longenecker hoped to avoid, by suggesting Maggie provoked Zephyr's advances. Such an approach, while unappealing, was certainly a staple of criminal law. But tempting as it may have been to try to argue that Maggie had led Zephyr on, fear of the sentiment, already being expressed by some southerners (and doubtless known to Carpenter), that "rape is the most frightful crime which the Negroes commit against white people, and their disposition to perpetrate it has increased in spite of the quick and summary punishment that always follows" silenced Arney as much as fear of provoking references to the promiscuity of working girls silenced Longenecker.[39]

Deprived of that weapon, Arney could have tried to undermine Carpenter in a series of smaller attacks, pinning him down, for example, on his time frame, which was inconsistent with the published statements of almost every other witness. He might have gotten Carpenter to repeat that he was a teamster, setting up a later argument that Carpenter had concocted his testimony to help his fellow teamster Owen Gaughan. Or Arney might, having established that Carpenter was born in the South, have left well enough alone, to argue at the close of evidence that Carpenter's prejudice influenced his testimony. He could have done any of those things, but he did none of them.[40]

Ultimately, the course he chose, directly challenging Carpenter's vision and lack of bias, failed. Why, then, did Arney, described as an attorney specializing in criminal law, take the approach he did? The papers suggested that he was so flabbergasted by Carpenter's testimony that he simply grasped at anything he could, without thinking about where his questions might lead. Most trial

technique books argue that under those circumstances the best response is in-
action — simply letting the witness step down without being cross-examined. But
presented with a witness whose testimony seemed dramatic and harmful, Arney
probably felt he had to do something. The risk of doing nothing that first day of
trial, when the defense had no chance to put on evidence supporting its side of
the story before the jury retired for the night, was simply too great. Faced with
that, Arney probably felt compelled to cross-examine Carpenter.[41]

He did so in a manner that tried to raise doubts about the prosecution's
main witness without advancing an alternative narrative of the case. The approach
was consistent with his demand during *voir dire* that the jurors hew to the rule
that the state had to prove Zephyr guilty beyond a reasonable doubt. By cross-
examining Carpenter on several small points, Arney hoped that he could make
the jurors distrust all his evidence. His approach held the jurors to their statement that they believed that the state had to prove Davis guilty beyond a reasonable doubt, but it also depended on his success in revealing holes in Carpenter's
testimony. Unfortunately, his botched cross-examination did little to cause them
to question any part of the prosecution's case.[42]

Even so, at the end of the first day of trial, the jury had been offered two competing narratives, each assuming different theories of justice, one less obvious
than the other. The prosecution had laid out a narrative about the crime and provided a series of witnesses whose evidence fleshed out the basic account. Its story
gave the jury a reason to see that justice was done and Maggie avenged. Instead
of offering an alternative narrative of the crime, the defense used the first day to
begin to set out a narrative of the trial. Its story of the case was reflected in Arney's
dogged insistence throughout *voir dire* that justice required strict adherence to
the rule of law. By the end of the first day of testimony, it was clear how weak a
case could be when its only weapon was the rule of law.

When trial resumed Saturday morning, Greene returned to the stand for cross-
examination. This time, Arney did aggressively challenge the witness, but it is
not clear how much that helped. He forced Greene to admit that Zephyr had
been an excellent employee, and established that in the course of the five weeks
Davis had worked at the factory he had received one raise and was due to receive
another. But none of that evidence clearly helped strengthen the defense argument that Davis was insane; on the contrary, it might easily be read as evidence
he was not. According to the brief account in the evening edition of the *Daily
News*, Greene testified that Davis acted oddly the day of the murder, which
might have helped the claim of insanity, but no other paper mentioned that

testimony. Instead, both the *Chicago Times* and the *Daily News* reported that Greene stated that Davis had "always [been] bright, active and faithful up to this time." After Greene testified, he was followed by Ed McDonald, the driver on the State Street cable car the day of the murder. McDonald testified that when riding back from the Fair Zephyr got off the car in the middle of a block and went "the other way, seemingly afraid of the crowd seen in front of the factory."[43]

After McDonald, the state called Henry Meyers and Mary Johnson, who had been in the kitchen in the back of Conlon's shop when Zephyr came by to ask for hot water. Both recalled noticing blood on his hands and repeated their earlier statements that he told them he had cut himself chopping kindling. They were followed by two workers from Greene's factory. The first, Douglas Starks, a young African American, testified that when he came into work the morning of the murder Zephyr told him to help put sacks of leather into the closet in the back of the factory. He also recalled that Zephyr acted oddly that morning, keeping the workers waiting outside in the cold while he was at the back of the factory. Contrary to the testimony by Meyers and Johnson, which established that Zephyr had washed at the back of the store, Starks remembered that Zephyr had blood on his hands when he let them into the shop and that he said he had cut himself. Lizzie Lemke then took the stand to confirm Starks' account that they had waited outside for quite a while on the morning of the murder and could see Zephyr in the back of the factory as they waited. Her testimony contradicted Carpenter's time frame and called his entire story into question. More damaging to the defense, she also testified that when she went to the closet in the back of the factory to look for her work apron, Davis stopped her from going in and told her he had burned it that morning.[44]

The Greene's employees were followed by three law enforcement officials. The first, police officer James Swift, testified that he was called to the factory shortly after the discovery of Maggie's body. According to the *Chicago Times*, he described the way her cloak was partially unbuttoned, with her "clothes thrown over her head." At this point, another hole showed up in the state's strong narrative, suggesting once again that Arney's cross-examination bore fruit. Swift's evidence (which seemed to suggest that Zephyr had indeed tried to rape Maggie) was contradicted by the next witness, Cook County Physician Moyer. According to Moyer, who had performed the autopsy on the body, Maggie's wounds were made by the hatchet found under her body. Consistent with Carpenter's testimony, he also indicated that there was evidence that she had been grasped around the neck by someone's left hand. Contrary to Swift's testimony, however, Moyer said that he found no signs of attempted rape.[45]

Significantly, that bit of Moyer's testimony, although confirmed by the inquest report, was not widely reported. The *Chicago Times*, for example, neglected to include any mention of that detail in its lengthy account of the day's evidence. After Moyer's testimony concluded, Lieutenant Henshaw, chief of detectives on the Chicago police force, testified that Zephyr voluntarily confessed to him the morning he arrived at the police station in Chicago after being brought back from Forest. He recalled that Zephyr admitted to killing Maggie because she refused to follow his orders, but he denied raping her or otherwise touching her. On that rather muddled note, the prosecution closed its case in chief.[46]

After making yet another motion for a continuance that was, predictably, denied, Jonathan Arney gave the opening statement for the defense. As might be expected from the trial strategy revealed during *voir dire* and cross-examination, his statement emphasized the trial, not the crime. He focused on the insanity defense, although he admitted that the defense could not afford expensive expert witnesses, who cost "$100 a day." Instead, making one of his few appeals to popular opinion, he noted they would leave the decision about insanity to the "good sense of the jury." And with that, he called Zephyr's mother to the stand.[47]

Just as Mary Gaughan had testified first to create sympathy for her murdered daughter, Sophia Davis was the first defense witness because she could present her son's life in its most appealing light. She certainly told a tragic tale. She had been a slave in Missouri before the Civil War. Freed at war's end, she married another former slave and they had three sons. Zephyr was the eldest. Her husband had a violent temper, so frightening that she worried he would kill her or her children, and she finally left him as a result, taking their sons with her. Not only was her husband violent, he had fits as well, in which he foamed at the mouth and fell to the ground. She confirmed that others in her family had mental problems: one of her sisters had been diagnosed as mentally unsound, and two of her sons, including Zephyr, had fits like their father.[48]

Sophia Davis emphasized that even in these unhappy circumstances, Zephyr posed special problems. He had been sickly from birth, but his condition worsened after he fell off the roof of a shed when he was four, landing on his head on a stone stair. He was "laid up" for a month after the fall, and for a year after the incident he could not get around on his own. As he grew older, he started having fits that made him violent. During one, he threw a cup at her; another time he knocked down one of his brothers. Sometimes, his fits involved delusions; once he lashed around himself with a club because he thought there were burglars in the room. When these fits came upon him, he reacted violently to simple things; during a card game he tore up the playing cards and broke the table they were playing on. Typically, she said, he would start to foam at the mouth, then he would pull his hair and ears and roll on the ground. After that sort of a spell, he would be violent for a while and then would sit and stare. She admitted that people told her that he should be institutionalized, but she explained she had refused to do so because she did not want to send him away from home.[49].

She estimated that Zephyr had had five fits since arriving in Chicago the year before, the most recent occurring early Monday, the day of the murder. He had come home late, at nearly one in the morning, and gone to bed. Shortly thereafter, he got up and ran into the street without his clothes on. She went out with one of her other sons and brought him back into the house, but not long after they put him back to bed, Zephyr raced outside again. They found him once again and brought him inside. This time he stayed in bed, but when she woke him to go to work that morning, he was angry and excitable. She recalled that he dashed out from the house without eating breakfast or even fastening his shoes. She was cross-examined very briefly. In response to Longenecker's question about whether Zephyr had been drinking the night before the murder, she said she did not know if he drank and had no idea if he had been drinking that evening. She then sat down.[50]

Her testimony was followed by a string of corroborating witnesses. Mary Ann Lockery, a woman who lived with the Davises, described Zephyr's fits and testified that she had recommended that his mother have him institutionalized. One of his brothers and a friend, Alonzo Jones, told of seeing Zephyr act crazy and violent in the course of a fit. In contrast, Joseph Kemmerling, who kept the saloon near the Davis home, testified that he saw Zephyr at his saloon about five nights a week and that he usually was quiet and never drank much. Having countered Longenecker's effort to imply that Zephyr's fit early Monday resulted from intoxication, Kemmerling left the witness stand, and the trial ended for the night.[51]

The witnesses the defense called that first day were supposed to offer the sort of solid basis for the defense case that the prosecution's first witnesses had provided for the prosecution case. The testimony of Mary Ann Lockery, Zephyr's brother, and the friend Alonzo Jones was specifically designed to reinforce Sophia Davis's account of her son's episodic insanity, and in some respects it succeeded. It provided the bulk of the defense's evidence of insanity and described Davis's condition in simple, lay terms. That was no minor feat in light of the hostility that often accompanied expert evidence of insanity. Although expert witnesses were increasingly common in trial courts in this period, lay testimony about insanity continued to be acceptable so long as it focused on providing examples of insane behavior, and it was sometimes less frustrating for the jurors. Yet for all that it seemed based on common sense, the defense evidence about insanity was simultaneously too complex and inadequate. It was too complex because it offered several competing explanations of Zephyr's insanity; it was inadequate because it never managed to tie his condition to the crime.[52]

While the prosecution had limited itself to a single narrative, the defense failed to restrict itself to a single theory of insanity. Most of the witnesses' testimony focused on Zephyr's fits, consistent with the contemporary belief that epilepsy was a form of insanity. But Sophia Davis confused the issue by suggesting at various times that Zephyr had epilepsy, that he had inherited a more comprehensive form of mental illness, and that he had mental problems as a result of falling on his head. That sort of multifaceted explanation of insanity was common enough in the period, and to some extent scientific theory encouraged it by collapsing mental and physical debility together. In addition, such an agglomeration of evidence was necessary because, in contrast to their medical counterparts (and popular understanding), legal authorities were reluctant to equate epilepsy with insanity. They accepted its relation to criminality—epileptics often were institutionalized in both Europe and the United States on the theory they were insane, and Italian criminologist Cesare Lombroso argued that most criminals were epileptic—but precisely because criminals were presumptively epileptic, the leading treatise on criminal law in the late nineteenth century categorically denied that epilepsy provided grounds for an insanity defense. That meant that lawyers often tried to combine evidence of other forms of insanity with testimony about a defendant's epilepsy, in hopes they would appeal to both popular understanding and the requirements of law.[53]

As difficult as that made matters, the situation was further complicated by the state of the law. The basic test of insanity, set out by the Illinois Supreme Court in 1863 in *Hopps v. Illinois*, required evidence that "at the time of the act charged, the prisoner was not of sound mind, but affected with insanity, and such affection was the efficient cause of the act, [so that] he would not have done the act, but for that affection." This meant that a defendant's unsoundness of mind had to "create an uncontrollable impulse to do the act charged, by overriding the reason and judgment, and obliterating the sense of right and wrong as to the particular act done," such that the accused could not choose between right and wrong.[54]

In *Hopps*, the court specifically rejected as old and discredited the notion that a defendant could be found legally insane only if he "had so far lost the use of his understanding so as to [never] know right from wrong." With that, it raised the possibility that a person who usually appeared to know right from wrong could still be found criminally insane. This was not a temporal concept; there was no suggestion that a person could be legally insane at the very moment of the act but sane the moment before or after. Rather, as the court put it in *Hopps*, the distinction was physiological—total insanity was a constant state of affairs affecting all the mental organs of the accused, while partial insanity affected only one part of the defendant's life and mind.[55]

In *Hopps*, the defendant tried to prove he was insane by demonstrating that he believed, falsely but absolutely, that his wife was unfaithful, and had killed under the influence of his delusion. At trial, he was found guilty, but the Illinois Supreme Court reversed, remanding the decision and ordering a new trial on the grounds that the instructions given to the jury did not recognize the possibility of partial insanity. But while the idea that a person could claim insanity based on either total or partial insanity seemed straightforward, in application it became extremely murky. In trials after *Hopps*, defendants making very similar claims often lost. In 1888, Mathias Busch brought in expert witnesses to establish that he had killed his wife under the insane delusion that she was trying to have him fired from his job and wanted to divorce him. Even though the case was almost identical to *Hopps*, the jury refused to find Busch insane and sentenced him to life in prison. Six months later, he had to be removed from the prison and placed in an insane asylum.[56]

After *Hopps*, the greatest problem facing defendants trying to claim partial insanity was evidentiary. In a decision rendered in 1884, the Illinois Supreme Court complicated the problem when it held that a person could not be found legally insane if he could plan and carry out a murder with the appearance of rationality. The court concluded that when there was evidence the defendant planned the crime, threatened it beforehand, or concealed it afterward, the inference was that he or she knew the act was wrong, which justified the conclusion he or she was not insane. This ruling undermined the principle of *Hopps*, negating the idea that a person who appeared lucid might be insane. So long as a jury could find the defendant did anything that might be considered planning, or made any effort to conceal the crime, it could reject the defense.[57]

But while confusion over legal standards, and the differences between legal, medical, and popular understanding of insanity, complicated the insanity defense in the Davis case, another problem, a factual one, played at least as great a role. Even assuming that the jury accepted Sophia Davis's evidence about the fit her son suffered the morning of the murder, her story of the episode did not square with her accounts of his other fits. The time lag between his apparent fit at 1 A.M. and the murder six hours later was too long given her own description of his insanity's usual pattern.

The next day was Easter Sunday, and court was not in session. When trial recommenced at ten o'clock on Monday, the defense recalled Zephyr's mother to eliminate any confusion that juror John Barker might retain about whether he knew Zephyr. She testified that Zephyr had not been in Chicago three years earlier and had never sold newspapers on a street corner. Next the defense called William Parker, another friend of the Davis family, to offer more evidence about Zephyr's fits. When he was done, the defense called to the stand Assistant County Physician J. Lucius Gray, who had examined Zephyr while he was in jail. Gray, who worked part-time in the Detention Hospital for the Insane, was a terrible witness for the defense, since he denied there was any possibility that Zephyr was insane. County Physician Moyer followed, and he also testified that he had never seen Zephyr act insane. However, the *Inter-Ocean* reported that Moyer conceded that if Zephyr had fits of the sort described, he was probably epileptic. According to accounts in the *Daily News* and the *Tribune*, Moyer further admitted that epilepsy "predisposed one" to homicidal mania. The *Tribune* added that Moyer characterized Sophia Davis's testimony about her son's fits as "particularly strong in that respect."[58]

On that surprisingly helpful note, and without calling Zephyr to testify on his own behalf, the defense ended its case. The prosecution then put on a few rebuttal witnesses, calling some workers from Lee's Carpet Store, where Zephyr had been employed as an elevator operator before going to Greene's. They all agreed that he was "steady, capable and bright, and never showed any signs of insanity." Longenecker then called two guards from the jail, who also testified that in the entire time they had watched him, Davis had never acted insane. Other witnesses (unnamed in news accounts) denied that they ever saw Davis have fits. With that, both sides rested, and the morning session of court came to an end.[59]

That afternoon was set for final arguments. Before Longenecker gave his argument, Judge Hawes, at the jury's request, ordered him to refrain from waving Maggie's blood-soaked clothing during argument, lest some jurors faint at the sight. Longenecker's closing was as short as his opening statement and as rhetorically complex. He began by pointing out the weakness in the defense evidence, in particular its failure to tie the testimony of Davis's insanity to the murder. "If Davis did have fits," he argued, it did not matter, for he was evidently mentally in control at the time of the crime. In that respect, he noted, the "testimony of the teamster of the caresses Davis offered Maggie, and the disproval of his story of striking her by the stove, in that no blood was found outside the closet, was conclusive." Flirting briefly with the idea that the murder followed an attempted rape, Longenecker argued that Davis had apparently "tried to continue his liberties, followed her into the closet, and there being stoutly resisted had cruelly hacked her to death with the hatchet." Having rejected Zephyr's insanity defense, Longenecker turned the defense evidence against him as well. "Whether he had a dozen or one hundred fits did not matter," Longenecker argued. "The defense, by its own testimony, had shown him to be a boy of violent and uncontrollable temper, who attacked on slight provocation his mother, brothers, and playmates." After suggesting that Davis's problem was an ungovernable temper, not insanity, Longenecker offered a final, direct attack on the insanity defense. Relying on the Illinois Supreme Court standard, he reminded the jurors that Davis had concealed the murder and planned his escape after the event, acts that provided strong evidence he was sane when he carried out the murder.[60]

The defense attorneys both made closing arguments. In keeping with their approach to the case, Allison focused on the facts, attempting to point out the inconsistencies in the state's claims, while Arney set out the legal precedents that supported the defense of insanity. The papers ignored these arguments entirely, an indifference the *Inter-Ocean* justified by noting that the "jury listened listlessly" and "had evidently pretty nearly reached a decision, and their attention [to defense arguments] seemed only a matter of duty." In rebuttal, Longenecker dismissed the insanity defense and, according to one paper, "the sophistry of Mr. Arney." With that, arguments ended, and Hawes instructed the jury.[61]

Instructions, following local custom, had been prepared by both attorneys and offered to the judge for review. Depending on his view of the law that applied to the case, Judge Hawes accepted some, modified and accepted others, and rejected the remainder. He read the instructions he had accepted to the jurors, who then retired to deliberate.

The *Herald* protested that the instructions "muddled" the jury, but the paper gave no evidence that any juror felt confused. The *Inter-Ocean* reported that Hawes "liberally" gave instructions offered by the defense, but while several of them did seem to reflect the defense theory of the case, others undermined it considerably. During their motions at the start of the trial, the defense attorneys had been unable to convince Hawes to throw out the indictment for failing to include a charge of manslaughter. They did manage to convince him to instruct the jurors that they could find Davis guilty of manslaughter, as opposed to murder, if "they believe from all the evidence that the prisoner was actuated by an irresistible inclination to kill and was utterly unable to control his will or subjugate his intellect and was not actuated by anger, jealousy, revenge and kindred evil passions." But although that instruction was given at the defense's behest, it undermined its case. As it continued, the instruction advised the jurors that if they concluded Zephyr killed Maggie under some sort of irresistible passion, he could be convicted of manslaughter instead of murder. That meant that the jury was advised that if it found Davis suffered from partial insanity, it need not acquit—an instruction inconsistent with *Hopps*, which had indicated that a finding of partial insanity meant a defendant should be found not guilty. A second instruction advised the jury that if it found Davis insane it should acquit, so read in combination the two instructions suggested that total insanity would lead to an acquittal, while partial insanity should lead only to a reduction of the offense.[62]

Hawes properly instructed the jury that the defense did not have to prove that Zephyr was insane. Rather, he said, "If the defendant introduces evidence sufficient to raise in the minds of the jury a reasonable doubt as to his sanity at the time of the committing of the crime, it is the duty of the prosecution to then prove the sanity of the defendant at the time of committing the crime beyond a reasonable doubt before the jury can find the defendant guilty as charged in the indictment." But that instruction was mitigated by another that directed the jury that once the fact of killing had been established, "it devolves on the party who committed the act to excuse that killing unless the proof on the part of the prosecution shows beyond a reasonable doubt that the killing was justifiable or accidental." That second instruction seemed to place a much higher burden on the defense, and the potential for confusion between the two instructions was increased by Hawes's decision not to give another instruction offered by the defense which made the point that not all killings were crimes. That rejected instruction, clearly designed to prevent the jury from assuming that any killing had to be murder, might have kept the burden of proving all elements of the offense on the prosecution.

Or it might have done so if the jury been the least bit inclined to pay attention to the law. But it was not. After hearing the instructions, the jury went to deliberate at 6 P.M. Less than an hour later, it returned to the courtroom, and Davis was brought out from the jail. The verdict was passed to the clerk of the court, and Davis was taken to the railing of the courtroom to hear it. "We, the jury," the clerk read, "find the defendant guilty of murder, as charged in the indictment, and that he shall suffer the punishment of death." As Maggie's mother thanked the jurors for their verdict, Zephyr was led back to his cell.[63]

The length of the jury's deliberations suggests that the jurors could not have spent much time debating either the facts or the law, and comments jurors made after they returned the verdict made it clear they did neither. The foreman of the jury, John Barker, told a reporter from the *Inter-Ocean* that the jurors spent their time taking four votes. On the first ballot, they all agreed on guilt. On the second, the vote was 9 to 3 for hanging, on the third, it was 11 to 1 for hanging, and the last ballot was unanimous. The *Chicago Tribune* quoted an unnamed juror (probably Barker) to the effect that "the jury was unanimous in the opinion that it would have been a disgrace to Cook County to let so foul a deed go unpunished." That same juror added that "they could see nothing worthy in the insanity plea." Consistent with that statement, the *Chicago Herald* reported that the jury never considered Zephyr's age or his claim of insanity when deciding the case, an account that also accords with the speed of its deliberations.[64]

The unnamed juror's remarks suggest that confusion over the insanity defense, problems with the jury instructions, or weaknesses in the defense case did not matter much in the end. After all, the jury in the Davis case apparently rejected his defense without even taking the time to consider it. Writing about the insanity defense in Victorian England, Roger Smith argued that jurors often voted against it because they were offended by determinist arguments that the insanity defense so often entailed, and they rejected the idea that the defendant had to be sane to be held guilty of a crime. The juror's comments after the verdict in the Davis case rest on a simpler formulation. The jury seemed intent on punishing the harm to Maggie, so it ignored the question of Davis's mental state entirely and focused solely on his act.[65]

Arthur Train described a similar phenomenon in courts in turn-of-the-century New York. His experience as a prosecutor was that even in cases where the defendant's insanity was beyond question, jurors refused to acquit. In particularly gruesome cases, they convicted even insane defendants of first degree murder; in less grisly crimes, they reduced the sentence to manslaughter. Train speculated that this reflected their desire, particularly in the more extreme cases, to punish the act.[66]

If the jury did focus solely on Davis's act without giving any regard to his mental state at the time he committed it, it ignored one of the fundamental principles of criminal law—the doctrine "that criminal intent is an essential element in every crime." As a practical matter, the jurors had every right to do so. Since 1827, the criminal code in Illinois had provided that in all "trials for criminal offenses" juries "shall . . . be judges of the law and the fact." That grant of authority was confirmed by two decisions of the Illinois Supreme Court in 1859, each approving jury instructions setting out the scope of the rule. Jurors could ignore their instructions "if they can say upon their oaths, that they know the law better than the court does." According to the state supreme court, the jurors had a "duty to reflect whether, from their habits of thought, their study and experience, they are better qualified to judge the law than the court." Having done so, if they concluded "the court [was] wrong in its exposition of the law," the statute gave them the right to decide it for themselves.[67]

Instructions based on the statute were offered frequently in trials during the course of the nineteenth and early twentieth centuries. Even after 1895, when the United States Supreme Court rejected the concept of jury nullification in its decision in *Sparf and Hansen v. United States*, Illinois continued to recognize the jury's power to decide the law. It was not until 1931 that the Illinois Supreme Court finally put a stop to the practice.[68]

In the meantime, attorneys for both defense and prosecution regularly relied on the statute. An instruction based on it was read at the state's behest at the Haymarket trial in 1886, over the objection of the defendants, and the decision to give it was upheld on appeal by the Illinois Supreme Court in 1887. In the view of many contemporaries, as well as most historians, the outcome in the Haymarket trial was clearly, and disastrously, a reflection of popular will, not law. But given its instructions, the Haymarket jury had every right to impose its view of the law on its verdict. When the Illinois Supreme Court affirmed that instruction in *Spies v. Illinois*, it reiterated the legal authority for what the jury seems to have done in the Davis case. But while there was nothing remarkable about what the jury did as a matter of law, a technical problem remains—no instruction informing the jurors of that power was offered in the Davis case.[69]

Not only was no such instruction given, none was requested. That suggests that an account emphasizing the significance of a statutory grant of authority does not tell the whole story, and credit also has to be given to a general support for the idea that law in criminal cases had to reflect a popular sense of justice. Not everyone agreed. Davis's attorneys had tried to keep out any potential juror who demonstrated resistance to the rule of law. Nor were all juries equally quick to assert their right to nullify. Just weeks before the Davis case, a jury convicted August Heitzke of murder and sentenced him to death because it understood that that was the only penalty the law permitted. Rather than nullify the law with its verdict, the jury petitioned the trial judge to reduce the sentence, which he did.[70]

The papers read in the 1880s at the Illinois Bar Association demonstrate that views of the jury's power to impose popularly defined ideas of justice were not all of a piece. Nor were they particularly consistent. At several of the meetings in which those papers were read, the state bar association passed resolutions condemning the jury's power to decide the law. Even so, the outcomes of the Haymarket and Davis cases, as well as popular reaction to them, suggest there was a strong popular sentiment for the jury's power to decide the law.[71]

The Davis case came down to a battle between justice defined by the rule of law and justice determined by the jurors' sense of what was right. And in making their decision, those jurors were influenced not only by what they read in the papers about Maggie Gaughan's murder, and about law more generally, but also by conversations about this particular case and about the social conditions in which it arose. This information predisposed the jurors to believe certain things were right and other things were wrong. In turn, the standards they came up with constituted their sense of justice and, when they served on the jury, were brought to bear on formal law. In the Davis case, the system of criminal law worked just the way Van Buren Denslow said it did in his paper to the Illinois State Bar Association in 1885—popular standards of justice determined what murder was and how it should be punished.

Of course, the Davis trial was not just a grand struggle between formal law and popular justice. Arney's demand for strict adherence to the rule of law rested on something more concrete than mere formalism, and the jury's resort to its sense of what was right was a rejection of something larger than a legal rule. The *Western Appeal* argued that African Americans had to insist on law in order to achieve justice, and Arney fought to hold the line against popular influences on law precisely because popular justice made law subject to prejudice. His approach was not uncommon: Edward Morris, the African American who had briefly represented Davis before trial, was an impassioned advocate for the rule of law in civil rights cases. Yet Arney, in his devotion to the rule of law, failed to heed the lesson the *Western Appeal* taught its readers. Law alone, as the *Western Appeal* knew, could not guarantee justice. Nor, as Judge David Davis had pointed out to the railroad attorneys in his courtroom in the case recounted above, could law, divorced from the popular understanding of what justice required, easily persuade.[72]

4

Execution, May 12, 1888

On the morning of May 12, 1888, less than six weeks after his conviction and six months almost to the day after the execution of the Haymarket defendants, Zephyr Davis was hanged. Consistent with efforts to put a stop to the use of executions as public spectacles, a state statute required that the execution be conducted inside the walls of Cook County Jail. Davis was hanged within the jail walls, at the end of the north corridor, but it was hardly a private affair. Sheriff Canute Matson's proclamation that executions could only be viewed by officers of the court (including lawyers) did not guarantee lack of spectacle or prevent an audience. Politicians and reporters, to say nothing of people with political connections, could and did get tickets to the hanging.[1]

By early in the morning on Saturday, May 12, a crowd of several hundred ticket holders waited outside the prison, along with many more men and women who lacked tickets. When the gates opened, those fortunates who were entitled to a view crammed into the corridor, some finding positions in it, others on the gallery of cells that lined one side. At the front of the crowd, sitting in special seats placed at the foot of the scaffold, sat the sheriff's jury, a panel of twelve notable citizens whose job was to swear the condemned man had been executed. Among the doctors and lawyers on the panel, one in particular stood out: John G. Jones, the lawyer and activist, was the sole African American on the sheriff's jury.[2]

Executions were relatively infrequent in late nineteenth-century Chicago. In the 1880s there had been only six, though two—the "trunk murder," involving three Italian American defendants, and the Haymarket case—had multiple defendants. For that reason, among others, the Davis case remained news even after his sentencing. The papers reported his motion for a new trial, which Judge Hawes denied on April 7, the Saturday after the verdict. They also described efforts to have Governor Richard J. Oglesby commute the sentence or delay the execution, requests he denied twice, once in response to a series of letters and a personal request made four days before the hanging, and a second time in reply to a telegram sent to him the day before the execution by Sophia Davis. In that same period, the papers reported other, less significant events involving Davis.[3]

Those stories provide a further perspective on the case, although the wealth of coverage does not make this stage of the case particularly easy to understand. On the contrary, it was a most confusing month and a half, rendered the more so because the news accounts of the case were marked by a phenomenon that had not occurred previously—to a large extent several of them were nearly identical word for word. Beneath their similarities, subtle and not so subtle differences in the accounts guaranteed that the papers retained their distinctive voices, but the resemblances make isolating their voices more difficult.

In the immediate post-trial phase, discussion focused on efforts to explain and justify the verdict. Shortly after the verdict, the *Inter-Ocean* and the *Times* ran brief editorials on the trial. Both praised the verdict, and the *Inter-Ocean* used the occasion to dismiss any suggestion that Davis had been tried too fast because of his race. The *Times* ignored the race issue and simply applauded the case as an example of a good trial. Although courts had been criticized for being slow, here justice "marched with even step to duty." "So far as earthly tribunals can avenge little Maggie Gaughan," the paper went on, "she is avenged by the jury's verdict that condemns her murderer to death in a few weeks after his crime." The *Times*, as might be expected from its earlier attitudes, discerned justice in the manner in which the verdict had confirmed public opinion, giving formal confirmation to the anger and distress of the mob.[4]

There was, of course, at least one other point of view. From the moment his trial ended, several voices, Zephyr's the loudest among them, were raised on his behalf. According to the *Chicago Tribune*, seconds after the verdict was announced, he condemned it as reflecting prejudice. He repeated that claim at the hearing on the motion for a new trial the following Saturday. At that hearing, during a colloquy with Hawes, Davis complained that he was tried too fast by a jury whose foreman, John Barker, falsely claimed to have known him for three years. He also charged that Henshaw (the police lieutenant to whom he had allegedly confessed) had coerced his confession, and that Carpenter's story was a collection of lies. Having reported that protest, the *Tribune* expanded it. Its article ended with a summary of the interview its reporter held with Davis at the jail after the hearing. In the interview, Davis repeated his claims that he had been forced to confess and that his conviction rested on perjured testimony by Carpenter and unnamed others.[5]

In contrast to its elaborate treatment of Davis's claims, the *Tribune* gave short shrift to the formal presentation Arney offered on his behalf. As he had during the trial, Arney emphasized the insanity defense, arguing that because Zephyr was insane, as a matter of law he should not have been held responsible for his crime. Hawes dismissed that argument, and Arney's reference to Moyer's supporting testimony (to the effect that if Davis did have fits as described, he probably had epilepsy, which could predispose him to homicidal mania), commenting that after all his years on the bench he had ceased to believe experts. Nor did Arney's appeal to the rule of law noticeably inspire the newspapers, which reported this part of the hearing (to the extent that they mentioned it at all) with a collective shrug of indifference.[6]

Although the account in the *Daily News* also reported that at the hearing Davis protested that Barker should not have been on the jury and that Carpenter lied under oath, its report had a different tone. Offering a stronger version of his claim of racism than the *Tribune* had, it reported that Davis charged that if he "had been a white man" he would "never have been convicted." According to the *Daily News*, Davis was bitter, belligerent, sarcastic, and ultimately pathetic during the hearing, but he never displayed any sign of remorse. Although the paper reported that Hawes listened and responded patiently to Zephyr's outburst, it was also clear that he finally concluded that "further comments [were] useless" and called the session to an end.[7]

Like the *Tribune*, the *Daily News* amplified Davis's objections. One of its reporters also interviewed Davis in his cell after the hearing, and during their interview, Davis repeated his objection that the trial was too quick to be fair. In contrast to the interview reported in the *Tribune*, which emphasized his claims of unfairness, the account in the *Daily News* made much of Davis's admission that he had committed the murder. It also reported that he advised the reporter that because of his epilepsy, he did not always remember what he did.[8]

The other dailies ignored the hearing, reporting only the verdict itself. In its story on the end of the trial, the *Inter-Ocean* noted that Zephyr lost his air of despondency and stood alert and defiant when the verdict was read. As his sentence was announced, he chewed gum vigorously and then was "led silently away." The *Chicago Times* and *Chicago Herald* offered accounts of the verdict in language identical to the *Inter-Ocean*'s. Neither reported on the hearing on the motion for a new trial or presented Davis's objections in any other way.[9]

Editorials published the following week continued to endorse the verdict. Monday, April 9, two days after the hearing on the motion for a new trial, the *Daily News* ran an editorial dismissing Davis's basic claim of unfairness. Davis, it pronounced, "has received none too speedy treatment at the hands of the law."

Moreover, the "sentence of death which has been passed on him is none too severe." Even so, the paper conceded, when Zephyr claimed that if he were white, he "would not have had a hearing yet," he "gave expression to a stinging commentary—and one only too just, it must be confessed—upon the manner in which justice is executed in Cook County." With that, the *Daily News* reinterpreted Zephyr's remarks, twisting his charge of unequal treatment so that it became a rebuke to the criminal justice system. In the process, his case ceased to be evidence that the system had failed and became, instead, proof that it could, and occasionally did, work. While its recognition that the legal system had done the right thing because of racism was the recognition of a situation that would continue to influence the paper until the execution, the editorial offered no endorsement of Davis's claim of injustice.[10]

Three days later, the *Chicago Tribune* ran a longer, stronger editorial that also used Davis's claims as a platform for its own message. That editorial, a discussion of a meeting at the Chicago Union League Club on the state of criminal justice, offered the Davis trial as refutation of the optimistic claims of the meeting participants. According to the *Tribune*, the speakers at the session, including Kirk Hawes, had concluded that while there were some problems, the criminal law basically worked. The *Tribune* disagreed. It conceded that some much needed reforms in the system had occurred, but noted that they had followed, very slowly, on the heels of endless calls for change. The real problem was far more significant than anything those "minor reforms" corrected and could only be dealt with by major changes. Specifically, there could "be no radical change for the better until the criminal law [was] considerably modified" to get rid of "the various statutory amendments and additions made by the representatives of the lawyers' trade union" which permitted criminals to delay trials and escape judgment. The problem was that the rich could buy the very best lawyers, who would then delay matters until the system broke down, while poorer people, like Zephyr Davis, were tried promptly and dealt with efficiently by the system. Although it reads remarkably like a class-based attack, the editorial reflects the *Tribune*'s greater concern that lawyers manipulated law to keep justice from being done. Not until there were fewer laws preempting justice would the legal system truly work.[11]

The editorial in the *Daily News* twisted Davis's claim into the rueful admission that race explained the exemplary speed with which Zephyr was tried; the *Tribune* converted it into an attack on lawyers. That considerable difference aside, the two papers agreed that the speed of the trial was a salutary example of how the system could work rather than a failure or a reason to reconsider the verdict. Davis's protests provided them with a means to advance their aims, not his interests.

The papers' different attitudes toward the outcome of the trial shaped their reactions to Davis in the weeks before his execution. Significantly, the reactions of the *Daily News* were the most extreme, and its articles on Davis were uniformly hostile or dismissive. Stories emphasized that he was unrepentant, stupid, prone to violence even in the jail, and frequently "savage" in temperament. The paper detailed his angry reception of John Greene, who went to see him (out of kindness, the story claimed) after the trial. It recounted his "murderous assault" on a newspaper reporter, and the churlish manner in which he refused to see the grand jurors when, on a tour of the jail facilities, they asked to be taken by his cell. In the story it published the day of his execution, the *Daily News* reported that Davis had been so violent during his incarceration that he had to be shackled even while in his cell.[12]

While those articles characterized Davis as dangerous and uncontrollable, other stories from the *Daily News* offered an equally unattractive but different image. When not describing him as sullen and hostile, the paper usually depicted Davis as carefree and unconcerned. Several stories described the way he laughed and joked with jail personnel, another his mockery of the minister (and others) who came to see him. He sang, drew pictures, played games with childish abandon, and ate with the hearty appetite of the unconcerned. He was, in effect, "a negro of the chuckle headed type"—hardly the foul-tempered wretch the paper's other articles described, but not a remorseful or penitent convict either.[13]

Nor were those the only images that the *Daily News* offered of Davis. Notwithstanding its general claim that he was irreverent and unconcerned, it also reported that he asked to speak to a minister and that he listened with respect to the minister who came to see him. One story recorded the way tears came to his eyes the day before the execution as he thought about his fate. That same story, the one that also described him as "chuckle headed," added, a few paragraphs later, that "he was not at all the fool he is represented to be." As an example of his intelligence, it offered his "knack of stringing words together" and reported that he was writing the speech he would give on the scaffold.[14]

Largely because the two papers printed nearly identical stories about the various incidents involving Davis, articles in the *Tribune* also offered conflicting images of him. Yet in contrast to the accounts in the *Daily News*, the stories in the *Tribune* evolved over time, rather than continuing to circle around the same tired, hostile themes. Immediately after the trial, the *Tribune*, like the *Daily News*, tended to describe Zephyr as sullen, uncommunicative, and occasionally violent. It repeated the stories of the disagreement with Greene and accused him of trying to assault Assistant County Physician Gray. By early May, however, the tenor of its accounts changed. There were occasional lapses; on May 10, for example, the *Tribune* reported that Davis ignored several black women who came to pray for him. But generally in this period, its stories began to take on a forgiving though patronizing tone, summed up in the comment in one story that he appeared "more tractable and certainly acts in a more civilized manner."[15]

Right before his execution, the *Tribune*'s treatment of Davis became sentimental. While the *Daily News* harped on the way he spent his last day joking around, with his occasional moments of grief barely interfering with his horseplay, the *Tribune* offered a very different picture. Zephyr's last night, according to that paper, was marked by prayer and sad reflection on his life. As it passed, he reminisced about his sickly childhood, the problems he had getting work as a young black man in the South, the difficulties his family had after his parents' marriage ended. When he finally slept, he had nightmares about the murder and the trial — dreams that dragged him back into the fight with Maggie at Greene's, his frightened escape, and his anguish at the lies told during his trial. There is every reason to suspect that these nightmares reflected a reporter's imagination rather than Zephyr's own, but even so, the picture of a vulnerable and frightened young man was far from what the paper's earlier articles had presented. Its sentimentalism had much in common with the paper's earlier treatment of the Gaughan family's grief and probably served the same purpose. It kept the *Tribune*'s readership interested in the case and its protagonist.[16]

The *Herald* did not cover the case much after the trial was over, but when it did it offered a fairly sympathetic picture of Davis, marred only by its insistence that he was an idiot. Remarkably, the *Chicago Times*, which had done little to cover the case after the trial and when it did so had typically described Davis as vicious and unrepentant, also portrayed him sympathetically in his final days.[17]

In contrast, the *Inter-Ocean* presented him as defiant and hostile nearly to the end. In a story it published shortly before the execution, the *Inter-Ocean* reported that Davis, upon hearing a visitor to the jail announce that he would be "the first nigger to be executed" in Chicago, declared that he "didn't care if he was." Once again, the *Inter-Ocean* refused to consider the possibility that race influenced the outcome of the trial and offered the remarks as an example of Davis's loutishness. The paper did describe Davis's gradual shift from a sullen, morose prisoner who attacked John Greene and a reporter to a more docile person, but it was skeptical about the change, ascribing it to punishment inflicted by prison officials. On May 6, according to the *Inter-Ocean*, Davis refused to see the grand jury (the visitor's comment he overheard about being "the first nigger to be executed" was apparently made by a grand juror). Hearing of his reaction, the jailer ordered him cuffed in his cell as punishment. From that point on, the paper reported, Davis was brooding but generally civil. The *Inter-Ocean* had its doubts, suggesting that Davis probably was acting that way as "a ruse to get people near to attack."[18]

By the very end, even the *Inter-Ocean* unbent enough to offer a sympathetic description of Davis. The morning of the execution, it printed an exclusive interview with Zephyr in which he apologized for what he had done and declared he was ready to die to atone for Maggie's death. He also told the story—later confirmed, the paper claimed, by the Reverend Thomas W. Henderson, a well-known African American minister who had taken up Zephyr's cause—that he had been engaged to a young woman who told him, after the verdict was entered against him, that she would drown herself. And she apparently did so; her father later told Davis that she had disappeared. This was the only story in the *Inter-Ocean* that put a human face on Davis, but what sympathy it generated was mitigated by another article it printed the same day. There, in another interview, State's Attorney Joel Longenecker deplored the tendency "to let our sympathy for the living man about to be executed blind us to our sense of justice." Compassion for Zephyr Davis, he went on, should not lead people to forget what he had done to Maggie Gaughan. Longenecker and the *Inter-Ocean* apparently feared that too much maudlin sentimentality would detract from the message of the execution.[19]

Longenecker's remarks suggested a tension between humanizing the criminal enough to maintain public interest and making him so sympathetic that no one cared about the underlying crime. But few paid much attention to that worry, and sympathetic stories about the condemned were a general execution eve convention. Murderers from Frank Mulkowski to the defendants in the trunk murder case were cast in sentimental fashion in the stories that immediately preceded their executions, as were the Haymarket defendants. There was a basic pattern to the accounts, presenting personal details, family reminiscences, and the final religious observances of the accused. The only exception to that overall tendency in the Davis case was the intransigent hostility of the *Daily News*.[20]

Its descriptions of Davis were endless variations on the stereotypes of blacks that pervaded popular culture. When it portrayed him as happy-go-lucky, ignorant, and feckless, that fit one dominant stereotype; when it depicted him as cunning, malicious, or violent, that fit another. The *Daily News* was not unique in offering descriptions of Davis based on racist stereotypes; most of the papers, at one time or another, reduced him to the level of a minstrel clown, having him speak in "plantation darky" dialect. But if the use of stereotypes was endemic, no paper reached the depths of the *Daily News*. No other paper felt the same need to stoke the flames of popular hostility after the verdict, probably because no other paper was as convinced that the trial's outcome had turned on race. The *Inter-Ocean* flatly denied race played a role and that ended the issue so far as it was concerned. It was only anxious lest its readers forget why the execution was occurring. The *Tribune* and the *Times*, convinced as they were that the verdict was a just one untainted by any serious flaw, felt secure enough to give Zephyr a human face in the last days before his execution. The *Daily News*, most sensitive of the Chicago dailies to the dynamics racism played, reacted by continuing to portray Zephyr in the harshest possible light.

Otherwise, little shook the certainty that the verdict was just. Zephyr continued to protest that he had not received a fair trial, but no one publicly supported his claims that he had been convicted on perjured evidence or that his confession was coerced. Instead, his allies—his mother, Reverend Henderson, and a few others—couched the public statements they made on his behalf in terms of his insanity and began to shift the focus to the justice of his punishment. As part of that effort, they sought to have the governor delay Zephyr's execution rather than stop it, although Henderson admitted that they hoped an extension would give them an opportunity to re-plead Zephyr's case and lead to having his sentence commuted.[21]

The clemency file in the case consists of six letters and telegrams written on Davis's behalf. Of them, one, from Mrs. M. A. Miller, of Milwaukee, who described herself as "the prisoner's friend," was a general attack on the death penalty and a statement in support of the remaining Haymarket defendants. She mentioned Zephyr on the first page of her eight-page letter and never referred to him again. Of the others, one was written by Zephyr himself; two by men who had not previously been involved in the case; one by Arney, the trial attorney; and one by Kirk Hawes, which was endorsed by Joel Longenecker. There are no letters in the file from Henderson or Sophia Davis, apparently because they made their pleas for Zephyr in person.[22]

The authors of the letters asked that the sentence be commuted to life imprisonment, or delayed for a period of time, supporting their requests on a variety of grounds. Zephyr's letter alone questioned the justice of his punishment by emphasizing the injustice of his trial. He reiterated that he had not attempted to rape Maggie, or intended to do so, and explained that while he agreed he must have killed her, he could not remember doing so and would never have done it if he had been in his right mind. He expressed sorrow for what he did both at the start of the message and again at the end. In between, he assured Governor Oglesby that Carpenter had lied when he testified that he saw Davis put his arm around Maggie as she came into the factory.

Just as Zephyr's letter set out claims he had made previously, so did much of Arney's rehash the defense he had offered at trial. Arney never claimed the trial was unfair. Instead, he emphasized the evidence of epilepsy and argued that Davis's condition meant that he had killed Maggie "while impassioned and enraged, which unnatural and terrible condition of his mind was brought about in a dispute with his victim." Given the "great doubt" this raised about Davis's sanity, life in prison was, Arney argued, a more just verdict. In some respects, this was the argument equating the rule of law with justice that Arney had tried, and failed with, at the trial. But it was hardly a strong defense of Davis, and he never argued that Davis's insanity meant he should have been found not guilty by reason of insanity.[23]

Arney also offered a second argument, which was a departure from anything he had tried before. He claimed that Zephyr was "young, fatherless, homeless, moneyless, and friendless" and had "lived among strangers most of his life." Davis's environment created him, he argued, and led him to commit the crime. As a result, he should not be executed, since that was too extreme a punishment for a crime he had been prompted to commit by circumstances beyond his control. That argument was a variation of the environmental determinism that was just becoming popular as a means of explaining criminal behavior. It was also untrue. Zephyr may have been literally fatherless, but he was not homeless, and testimony at the trial had indicated that he had friends, family, and a steady if only marginally adequate income. It is impossible to say why Arney tried to redefine Zephyr in terms of social pathologies that did not accurately describe him or his family, or why he thought the reinterpretation would be persuasive. In the course of dealing with those petitioning him to reconsider Davis's fate, Oglesby had the chance to get a sense of Davis's friends and family, so it would have been easy for him to see how little the reality of the situation matched Arney's account.

Finally, Arney asked the governor to postpone Zephyr's execution if he would not commute it, in order to give Zephyr time "to accuse himself of his crime" and come to terms with his guilt. He added that a delay would let Davis "reconcile himself with man and his soul and his soul with God." Again, the argument seems strange: the idea that Zephyr needed to comprehend his crime and his role in it was hardly consistent with the claim that he was insane. But in this case, however, there is an obvious explanation. The plea put forward on Davis's behalf by Joel Longenecker asked that the execution be postponed "to see if the poor fellow can be induced to be spiritually influenced by the Rev. Mr. Henderson's efforts." Longenecker's note indicated that both Henderson and Sophia Davis had asked him to request a postponement for that reason, which suggests that Arney may also have been asked to add that point as well. Hawes, who wrote the letter to which Longenecker's comments were appended, indicated that he had no objection to the execution being postponed. Perhaps, he wrote, "it may be well under all the circumstances," but he did not explain what those circumstances were or indicate why, having set the date for the execution himself, he now thought postponing it made sense.

In his letter, Arney noted there "was an unaccountable prejudice" against Zephyr, which meant that the case had been brought to trial in great haste in response to public pressure. That circumlocution was odd, given his blundering attempts to confront racism during the trial. Two other letters, one by Henry McGill, who described himself as a seventy-six-year-old white man who did not know Zephyr, and the other by J. D. Tallmadge, who was apparently African American, addressed the issue of racial prejudice much more explicitly, though they used it to different effects.

Offering a variation on Arney's determinism, McGill argued that Zephyr's "ignorance and brutal tendencies [were] his, in a measure, as the inheritance of his down-trodden ancestry." Given the inherited condition of slavery and its effect on Davis and other African Americans, and considering Davis's youth, McGill argued that mercy was the more just course. He also argued that if Davis's sentence was commuted to life in prison, there was a better chance he would repent, and the punishment of his having to live with himself would be severe enough.

While McGill emphasized the social impact of slavery, arguing that a just punishment for Davis had to take it into account, Tallmadge took the position that the sentence itself was unjust for several reasons. Like Arney he emphasized Davis's insanity, though he did a much better job of tying it to the case. Turning Longenecker's argument at trial on its head, Tallmadge asserted that Davis's insanity was proved by the fact he committed the crime shortly before work was supposed to start, guaranteeing that he would be discovered. Tallmadge then connected Davis's insanity to the problem of racism, noting that had he "possessed a little more money, a little more commonsense, and a *white skin*, there never would have been a verdict more severe than manslaughter" (emphasis in the original). Building on that, he concluded that racism made both the trial and the punishment unfair. He blamed Davis's race for the speed with which he was tried and for the verdict as well. Where McGill had emphasized the social impact of the heritage of slavery, Tallmadge noted its legal significance. Echoing Justice Roger Taney's decision in the *Dred Scott* case, with an argument made familiar by the *Western Appeal*, he pointed out that in parts of the South "it is claimed that the colored man has no rights which the white man is bound to respect." The verdict in the Davis case indicated, he feared, that the same was true in Illinois.[24]

Having suggested that the legal problems Davis faced had their antecedents in slavery, Tallmadge offered an explanation that was only just becoming popular among Chicago's African American elites. He suggested that Davis's mental limitations were enhanced by "his course of living, his frequenting of saloons, which the law licenses and allows, and his associating with the rabble always to be found there," and that this combination of mental weakness and bad living had led to him to murder. The idea that the temptations of the city had proved too much for the poor, ignorant son of former slaves was another variation on the determinist arguments offered by Arney and McGill.[25]

After focusing most of his letter on factors that he felt should determine a just punishment for Davis, Tallmadge shifted his focus to the death penalty itself. It was, he asserted, objectionable to inflict "the extreme penalty on an individual entitled, both by law and humanity, to a verdict less severe." But the death penalty was not simply unjust in this particular case; it was unjust as a general principle because it was barbarous. It corrupted the community and degraded the law whenever it was allowed. Executions corrupted justice by brutalizing the societies in which they took place and therefore should not be carried out.

The papers' coverage of efforts to win a pardon was neither detailed nor particularly accurate. Several reported that the Reverend Henderson and Sophia Davis put together a petition for Governor Oglesby, asking him to delay the execution or commute the sentence to life in prison. But no petition was ever filed; the letters offered on Zephyr's behalf were all there was. None of the papers reported the various arguments made on Davis's behalf, although there was brief mention of the letter written by Arney, and considerable speculation about why Hawes and Longenecker supported the request for a delay. As a result, none of the elaborate explanations of why the execution was unjust reached the city at large.[26]

The letters did get to Governor Oglesby, and both the *Chicago Daily News* and the *Tribune* reported that he was impressed by the letter Davis wrote on his own behalf, declaring that Davis wrote better than he himself had at his age. But it did not matter. After a brief meeting with Sophia Davis and Thomas Henderson, Oglesby denied their requests. Davis's mother sent one final plea on her son's behalf the day before the execution, but Oglesby turned it down as well, in a telegram that arrived virtually the instant of the execution.[27]

Accounts of the hanging fit it into well-established literary and historical traditions, though once again the common narrative concealed a range of reactions.

DAVIS IN PRAYER.

The stories in the *Tribune*, which began the night before the execution and described Davis's mournful reflection on his childhood, fit most neatly into this genre. It reported that on the afternoon of the day before his hanging, Davis's mother and brothers were at the jail for a tearful farewell. That evening the Reverend Henderson stayed with him in the library of the jail until midnight, praying and reading the Bible with him. Once Henderson left, Davis remained alone in the library, struggling to sleep, until Dr. Gray gave him a sedative that sent him into his nightmare-filled sleep around 1 A.M. A couple of the papers reported that he spent part of the night autographing small pieces of paper, creating ghoulish souvenirs for his friends and the guards.[28]

The next morning, no reporter was allowed into the jail until 10 A.M. Outside, the building was ringed with police and deputy sheriffs, on duty to keep the crowd, which the *Herald* estimated at five hundred people, at bay. At about 10:30 ticket holders were allowed into the jail, and at roughly the same time, Sheriff Matson read the death warrant to Davis in the library. Then Davis, a deputy sheriff, and two ministers, Thomas Henderson and George Williams, proceeded out of the library and into the north corridor, where they climbed onto the scaffold. Davis and the ministers used his last minutes to address the audience inside the jail, and those who would read about the execution in the papers.[29]

Henderson began by reading a passage from the Book of Job, and then led the group on the scaffold in a hymn. After a prayer, Henderson read Zephyr's message to the crowd:[30]

> To my friends and fellow beings of this city, I wish to say that I am sincerely sorry for the act for which I am to suffer, and for all other wrongs I have ever done, for the girl whose life I took and for her parents. I am deeply and truly sorry and would give all I have in this world if it could be called back. But since it is done, and cannot be undone, I am ready to pay the penalty. I have nothing against anybody on earth, and I leave the world feeling full of love for all. I feel that by true, noble prayer and sincere repentance I have found forgiveness with God and I ask the forgiveness of all mankind.
>
> I ask all to be kind to my mother and my brothers, they are not to blame for any of my conduct. I never went to school a day in my life, and all I know about reading and writing I picked up by myself, and therefore never had much of education. I desire to say to all the boys with whom I have ever associated to take warning and always try to do right.
>
> I sincerely thank the officials of the law and all others for any kind acts they have done for me. I pray God bless them all. I feel at perfect peace with God, and do not fear to meet Him. Mr. Henderson has given me good instruction, and has prayed earnestly for my soul, and I feel that God has answered his prayers. Hoping to meet you all in heaven, I am ready to go.[31]

With that, Davis was prepared to be hanged. He was wrapped in a white sheet that covered his arms and legs, then bound with straps designed to hold his arms and legs close to his body. A noose was placed around his neck and his head covered by a hood that completely covered his face. Henderson asked Davis one more time if he believed in God, then, seconds after Davis responded that he did, the signal was given and the platform of the scaffold dropped; his body shot straight down until it was stopped by the length of the rope. According to one account, a loud snapping noise indicated that his neck had broken, but another paper reported that it was not until an assistant sheriff pulled down on Davis's legs that his neck snapped.[32]

For a few minutes, his body swung in the air as his legs jerked and twisted him around. When the swinging stopped, Moyer reached into the white wrap to take Davis's pulse. The first time he checked, he reported it was 112 beats per minute, then it raced up to 120. Nine minutes after the platform dropped, there was

RESIGNED TO HIS FATE.

no longer any pulse at all, and Moyer declared Zephyr Davis dead. As his body was unwrapped and placed in a coffin, the crowd that had watched him die dispersed.[33]

Davis's behavior in his final moments reinforced the sentiments in his statement. By confessing guilt, asserting a reborn religious faith, apologizing to the Gaughans, and asking that people forgive him and hold his family blameless for his deeds, Davis emphasized the repentance that custom, and community feeling, required. Significantly, he made no mention of the insanity defense or problems with the trial. His message was the right thing to say at the right time, and his calm demeanor on the scaffold convinced many of the newspapers (though not all) that he had come to terms with what he had done. Those papers, in turn, interpreted his dying words and conduct as signs that he was both brave and manly, a far better person than his crime had indicated. This was a desirable shift, and not one that everyone who was executed achieved. In this case, it represented a significant departure from the earlier images of Davis as hunted beast of prey, manipulator of the criminal justice system, and sullen lout.

That reinterpretation of his character was even more impressive given his race. Although a few African Americans, generally members of the professional class, were treated with respect in Chicago papers, most were described with amused contempt and rarely credited with either sense or courage. All too often, even respected leaders in Chicago's African American community were described in terms that suggested that they were silly, prone to excessive outbursts of temper or emotion, and generally unrestrained. As a group, African American men were emphatically not perceived to be respectable or manly in a time when respectability and manliness were virtues to be aspired to. In his last moments, Davis displayed self-restraint, bravery, and fortitude, all characteristics that won him admiration.[34]

While Davis's last words fit neatly into the genre of scaffold speeches and managed, at the same time, to alter his reputation, a mystery remains. Aside from repeating his statement of repentance, it resembled nothing that he had ever said about the case.[35]

One possibility is that it did not sound like anything he had ever said because Davis himself played no role in writing it. Most accounts claimed that he composed it in the afternoon or evening before his hanging, but the *Chicago Tribune* reported that Henderson wrote it for him. Given the resemblance between the apology for his life in the statement and the remarks made by Tallmadge in his letter to Governor Oglesby, it is also possible that some other member of the African American community drafted it for him.

Either possibility suggests that the decision to avoid Davis's earlier claims of injustice was made for the good of the larger African American community more than for his own. Certainly, many African Americans in Chicago found his case troubling for its potential effect on other African Americans; that was why the *Western Appeal* only mentioned the trial to applaud the verdict. Given the ongoing and quite reasonable anxiety African Americans had about how they were perceived by other Chicagoans, the temptation to use Davis's execution to try to improve his image, and the image of all African Americans, was probably strong.[36]

Yet there is no evidence that anyone from Chicago's black elite, other than Thomas Henderson, had access to Davis while he was in jail. It may be, of course, that Henderson wrote the statement and cast it in those terms, but since Davis's remarks were inconsistent with Henderson's own comments on the scaffold, that seems unlikely. Another, stronger possibility is that Davis wrote the comments himself, influenced either by the ideas of racial uplift preached by the *Western Appeal* or by his mother's strong concern about the way his case might be interpreted in racial terms. It was his mother, after all, who had determined that her son should not be represented by two African American lawyers, apparently because she was afraid of the image that would present. She might also have convinced Davis that he needed to present an argument that reflected sentiments that would appeal to both the African American and white communities of Chicago, to lessen the risk of racial backlash. Regardless of whose idea it was, it was a clever stroke to use the speech to emphasize personal responsibility and remorse. But it was one that squandered all the issues of justice that Davis had raised on his own behalf.

Arguments for justice were not, however, completely silenced during the execution, since Henderson offered a message designed to make the audience confront the problems of injustice that the trial and execution raised. He used Scripture to make his point, choosing material from the Book of Job, specifically Job's response to Eliphaz the Temanite. In the chapters preceding the verses Henderson read, Eliphaz assured Job that because the innocent were never punished, the punishment Job was suffering proved he must have been guilty of something.[37]

In response, Job emphasized his hopelessness and his confusion about what he had done to deserve punishment. The verses Henderson read came from this section, and while they were not among the most confrontational parts of Job's response (emphasizing human helplessness rather than the injustice of his punishment), they challenged the notion that punishment proved guilt. Considered in the light of the rest of the Book of Job, the passage Henderson chose raised the question whether Davis had done anything that justified the punishment he was receiving. The verses were an indirect condemnation of his conviction and punishment as unjust.[38]

Henderson's use of Job was the strongest statement anyone made on Davis's behalf, but it did not reach his intended audience. Presumably anyone at the execution with a passing familiarity with the Book of Job would have seen the significance of his choice, but the newspapers' coverage of the execution kept it from getting much further. Only one paper identified the passage as from Job, but it did not quote from the verses Henderson read, making it next to impossible for its readers to understand his message. Another two quoted the material accurately but confused the issue by attributing the verses to Psalms, so that their readers could not easily grasp the verses' context. A fourth concluded that Henderson read from the funeral service for the A.M.E. Church and also failed to quote the verses, so that its readers had no way of knowing what he had said. This rather suspicious lack of biblical literacy on the part of the local press kept Henderson's challenge from reaching the city at large.[39]

Instead of communicating Henderson's message, the papers offered their own interpretations of the execution. Several made much of the crowd that gathered outside the jail on the day of the execution hoping to get in to see the hanging. Although accounts varied, the consensus seemed to be that the crowd was a rough one, including people who drank, smoked foul cigars, and told vulgar jokes while waiting for the doors of the jail to open. In fact, it was a mixed crowd that included gamblers, aldermen, political hangers-on, and men about town, as well as the occasional youth of less than twenty who was unceremoniously barred from watching the seventeen-year-old Davis hanged. According to some accounts it was mixed in other ways as well, with men, women, blacks, and whites all standing together outside, anticipating the excitement.[40]

Those stories emphasized two distinct aspects of the crowd. In keeping with its racist brand of populism, the *Daily News* reported that one young man who had gone to see the execution left "after taking half a dozen steps" into the jail. "'I can't do it,'" the paper reported he said to a friend. "'I thought I'd see the _____ nigger hanged without a quiver, but when it gets so close as this I find I can't do it.'" Anyone, he apparently went on, "'who will voluntarily witness the mortal suffering of another is nothing more than a brute.'" The same paper recounted that others in the crowd had to fortify themselves with liquor and emphasized that several of those who watched the hanging were so moved that they made contributions to help pay for the funeral as they left.[41]

While the *Daily News* described the crowd at the execution as chastened by the event, and suggested that even the most callow and prejudiced were affected by the scene, other papers interpreted the situation very differently. The *Tribune*, first in a story and then in an editorial, denounced the people that went to the hanging as a mob. They "talked, and laughed, and joked, and some smoked" during the execution, revealing their lack of appreciation for the solemnity of the spectacle. The *Times* agreed, noting that the "rough crowd" that went to see the hanging "clattered and banged" as they streamed into the jail when the doors opened. Some climbed up into the galleries of the jail so that they could see better, laughing and joking and "uttering ribald remarks about the gallows and the hanging that was to amuse them." After the drop, when the hood was removed from Zephyr's face, "the most vulgar pushed forward to get a look at the swollen face" and were only restrained by the sheer size of the rest of the crowd. Even so, they continued to laugh and joke after the hanging was over.[42]

The *Herald*, like the *Tribune* and the *Times*, was contemptuous of the crowd. "Altogether," that paper put it, "it was about as disagreeable a lot of people as could have been selected to gaze upon a human being in the supreme moment of his last agony." As that implies, the *Herald*'s account focused on the execution itself. It provided the smallest details, noting Zephyr's pulse until he died and describing the process of preparing him for execution. But in contrast to the *Daily News*, which also gave a wealth of information, the *Herald* did so in order to condemn the proceeding. Its tone implied, far more than any other paper's did, that public hangings were barbaric, showing, much as Tallmadge had argued in his letter to Oglesby, that an execution brought out the worst of the crowd. Because it was an agonizing way to die, the entire event was "a terrible exercise." If, as the paper put it, "the epithet decency can be used in connection with the legal choking to death of a human being," the Davis execution was decent. Yet the actual scene, as the paper recounted it, made it clear that public hangings were inherently indecent. That sentiment permeated the paper's treatment of the case, to the point of influencing its descriptions of Zephyr, which emphasized his stupidity in order to make his hanging seem all the more inhumane.[43]

Both the *Times* and the *Herald* conceded that the crowd contributed to the burial expenses, but unlike the *Daily News*, they did not suggest that this reflected a general chastening of the spectators. On the contrary, the *Times* sarcastically reported that "the crowd that mocked the boy's death actually helped to bury him." So far as the *Times* was concerned, the indifference and insensitivity of the crowd were unchanged. The day after his execution, on a Sunday, Davis was buried in Oak Woods Cemetery, in a funeral service that was conducted in the presence of "a thousand men, women and children" who gathered there "out of morbid curiosity." The *Times* reported with outrage the way this crowd blocked the family from entering the cemetery and nearly disrupted the service itself in their "struggle" to see what happened. Quoting the director of the cemetery, the *Times* condemned the "disgraceful proceedings." The *Inter-Ocean*, although silent about the barbarity of the execution, also reported and condemned the spectacle at the funeral. Its outrage over crude thrill seeking was not, however, all that pure. The morning of the execution, it carried an advertisement from Epstein's New Dime Museum, which showed a sketch of Zephyr over an ad announcing it would soon feature his likeness in wax.[44]

There was a final word on the case and the hanging. Two days after the execution, the *Inter-Ocean* ran a letter to the editor from John G. Jones. In it, Jones complained about the *Tribune's* condemnation of the people at the execution and its description of their behavior as a "disgraceful exhibition." He wrote to differ. "I was at the execution," he wrote, and "in justice and fairness to all, so that the public may not be misled about the matter, I wish to state that the execution of Zeph Davis was in every way a solemn, orderly, and quiet affair." He went on, there "was no noise, laughing and smoking," and those who were present "were as highly cultivated and refined as any class of people you would find."[45]

Jones's letter shifted the focus away from the question of whether an injustice had been done to Davis, and away from the papers' intimation that executions encouraged barbarity. He did so in terms that echoed popular concerns about respectability, apparently under the impression that denunciation of the crowd at the execution reflected badly on all concerned, but especially, one suspects, given his general views, on Davis and on African Americans generally. His letter deploring the *Tribune's* reaction captures the ambiguities surrounding the entire case. In several respects, it was a sign of the strength of Chicago's civil society. It was a public statement by a man who felt his opinion should be heard and would be listened to. It was a challenge to a perceived racist slur by a man with a deserved reputation for racial advocacy, and it was intended to correct a slight that he felt had implications for race relations in the city. Yet his demand for justice on behalf of the crowd at the execution misinterpreted the papers' concerns. Even worse, it shifted attention away from Davis, and in particular away from Henderson's challenge on his behalf. It demonstrated how little the African American community had done to support Davis and also revealed the concerns that led them to remain silent.

Considered together, the comments of Henderson and Jones put popular justice in Chicago into perspective. One tried to use the scaffold as a stage from which to tell the city that it had judged a man unfairly and punished him unjustly. The other wrote to a major Chicago daily to explain that the execution demonstrated that the hanging of a black man could be a somber and decorous expression of society's judgment. That both were equally concerned with correcting perceived injustices cannot be denied; nor, given what we know about the temper of their times, can Henderson's concern about Davis, or Jones's concerns about African Americans more generally, be questioned. Both spoke publicly to offer their different messages, demonstrating their faith in Chicago's civil society and its capacity to listen and act justly. But it is most telling that Henderson's message was garbled by the press, while Jones's message did not need to be.

CONCLUSION

On January 1, 1887, the *Chicago Times* reported that a jury had made short work of the retrial of Eugene Dougherty, who had been charged with murdering Nicholas Johns. Dougherty, discovered a few feet from the corpse, a smoking gun literally burning a hole in his pocket, was arrested and promptly charged shortly after the murder. At his first trial in 1883, evidence established that Dougherty and Johns had quarreled shortly before the killing, and the jury entered a judgment against him.[1]

On appeal from the first trial, the verdict was reversed on the ground the prosecution had failed to establish the court's jurisdiction. A retrial followed at the end of 1886. This time the jury quickly entered a finding of not guilty, and the foreman of the jury was able to spare a moment before racing to a New Year's Eve party to explain that the jury ruled that way because it felt there was insufficient evidence tying the defendant to the crime. The report in the *Times* suggested that paper was more bemused by than aghast at that verdict. As well it might have been. But as Jeffrey Adler's statistics on the conviction rate for homicides in late nineteenth-century Chicago show, such a result was the norm, not the exception. Chicago juries acquitted any number of men, like Dougherty, who killed other men in the course of a fight or an argument.[2]

If the Dougherty verdict represented one type of case in which a Chicago jury followed its own sense of justice rather than the rule of law, the Davis case stood as another example of the phenomenon. Unlike Dougherty's case, Davis's crime did not arise in the context of the acceptable violence of plebeian male culture; it involved the murder of a young woman by an only slightly older man. Nor were the parties as forgettable as the young men and boys who fought and murdered each other in Chicago's saloons. Maggie Gaughan was not merely young and female, she was white; Zephyr Davis was not simply young and male, he was black. Yet it was because of those factors, not despite them, that the outcome in the Davis case, like the verdict in the Dougherty case, reflected the influence of popular justice far more than law. The rule of law played no role in determining what happened to Eugene Dougherty or Zephyr Davis. Although both were tried within the formal legal system, the factor that determined the respective outcomes of the two cases was what some Chicagoans felt was just. The modifier "some" is important. The two verdicts in the Dougherty case demonstrated that different juries disagreed about what he deserved.

The history of the Davis case in its entirety indicates, in far more detail, the power of popular justice in the late nineteenth century and the many means by which it influenced the law. But it also reveals how easy it was to limit the force of law to some views.

In the Davis case, each aspect of popular justice played a role. Popular justice worked through Chicago's civil society as individuals—acting through civic associations, mass meetings, protest sessions, and newspapers—reacted to the case and tried to influence the enforcement of laws. Sometimes those organizations failed; no public outcry followed the African American community's protest against the inquest verdict, nor did Republican voters heed its call to remove Coroner Hertz from office. Other times, a group's influence was indirect, and it often took several forces, working separately or together, to succeed in advancing a particular cause. The difference between success and failure depended on several things. Arguments and protests were sometimes subject to deliberate censorship by the newspapers, which reported what they did not approve of inaccurately or mockingly and ignored other matters entirely. Other times, groups silenced themselves, choosing not to present a particular view or otherwise to mute their protests, either from fear of offending or from fear of being ignored.

Popular justice also worked through civil society's turbulent alter ego—the mob—either indirectly, like the crowds that threatened to snatch Davis from police custody, or directly, like the mob at Forest that helped the police seize Davis. Both types of force were encouraged to varying degrees by the local papers, which often praised mob action in Chicago and frequently described the conduct of mobs in other places in glowing terms. The mob played another role as well, since the very idea that justice could be expressed through force excused the idea that the agents of the law could use force in the exercise of their official duties.

Finally, as happened in both the Dougherty and Davis cases, popular justice worked within the system. Just as some grand juries treated their position as a platform to express their own views of justice, the coroner's jury in the Davis case took the opportunity to publicize its views on the working conditions at Greene's Boot Heel Factory. Then, as had happened in the Dougherty case, the actual trial gave the jury the opportunity to decide what it thought justice required. The difference in outcome between the two cases, though stark, did not turn on a legal distinction. Rather, it was a reflection of the relative worth of the victims, and the relative danger the juries felt the defendants' acts posed to society.

Popular influence was able to be effective because people in Chicago believed that they could act against the State and ignore the law. They held that view because of the examples, printed frequently in the press, of mobs that acted out their will, or of groups that made demands about law, or of meetings that protested ways in which laws had failed. They also had the evidence of other trials in which juries had ignored their instructions, imposing their own sense of justice in their place. The notion that the popular sense of what justice required was a force to be reckoned with even shaped the thinking of those who officially opposed popular influence on law, as two statements from 1893 demonstrated. The authors of the two statements were Joseph Gary, the judge who presided over the trial of the Haymarket anarchists in Chicago in 1886, and John Peter Altgeld, then governor of Illinois, who freed the remaining Haymarket defendants in 1893.

In April 1893, Judge Gary wrote an article, published in *The Century Magazine*, which he intended as an apology. In it, he tried to answer both those who criticized his conduct of the Haymarket trial for playing to mass prejudice and those who praised him because the trial's outcome was consistent with public opinion. As Gary put it, "Mixed with all the approval of my own part in the conviction of the anarchists . . . there has been an undertone, like a minor strain in music, that the anarchists deserved their fate; that society has the right to enforce the first law of nature—self preservation; and therefore if I had a little strained the law, or administered it with too great rigor against them, I was to be commended for my courage in so doing." This conclusion, Gary went on, rested on a misunderstanding. Law existed to preserve order in the State, and those who enforced the law therefore had to follow its rules. If they went beyond the limits of law, overlooking its intent or misunderstanding the meaning of a particular doctrine, they erred, even if the result was the punishment the public demanded. "The end," Gary insisted, "however desirable its attainment, excuses no irregular means in the administration of justice." Gary claimed he had recognized and enforced the rule of law rather than popular justice in the Haymarket trial. The rest of his essay was intended to prove his claim but actually proved quite the opposite.[3]

Ultimately, try as he might, Gary could not completely separate formal law from popular ideas of justice. His chief problem was that he was unwilling to dispense with the idea that the people had a right to express their sense of justice outside the legal system. He began by admitting that there were types of wrong-doing that the law did not reach. Wife beating, for example, was offensive yet not illegal. Likewise, a salesman might bring contaminated goods into a community and sell them without violating any laws, yet because the act endangered society it was clearly wrong. Even though Gary claimed his position was that the "exist-ing order of society [could] be changed only by the will of the people," he did not follow this with the assertion that the representatives of the people should enact laws to deal with circumstances where the law did not forbid conduct that was clearly harmful.[4]

Rather, Gary suggested that in situations where law did not prohibit some-thing, popular justice was permissible. In the case of the beaten wife, for ex-ample, members of her family could retaliate by beating her husband. Similarly, in the case of the impure goods, the community could drive the salesman out of town and destroy his merchandise. In either instance, popular justice was the means by which social groups could protect themselves against harm and define correct behavior. The only limitation Gary recognized was that these acts had to be undertaken by those who were immediately harmed—family members in the first case and the members of the threatened community in the second.

These examples gave legitimacy to some acts of popular justice, but Gary at-tempted to separate formal law from popular justice by suggesting that extralegal behavior was legitimate only where formal law could not act. However, as he de-veloped his argument further, he was unable to sustain the distinction between extralegal acts and formal law. Even though he tried to show that the Haymarket defendants were legitimately convicted of conspiracy to commit murder, as defined by common law and the statutes of Illinois, at best he established no more than that the evidence put before the jury established that the defendants posed a threat to society. In the end, so far as he was concerned, that was proof enough. It justified a conviction because the purpose of the criminal law was the preservation of society. But that was also, of course, his justification of extralegal activity. This meant, as Gary ultimately conceded (without admitting the im-plications of the admission), that the legal system could do no more than ratify or formalize popular justice. Law codified commonsense understanding, which meant that the commands of statutes had to be judged against public expecta-tions, and verdicts had to reflect popular sentiment.[5]

In June 1893, Governor John Peter Altgeld pardoned the three remaining Haymarket defendants (four had been executed in 1887, one committed suicide in jail). The text of his executive pardon excoriated the conduct of the trial. Ju-rors, he noted, were selected because they were recommended as "safe" by busi-ness leaders. During jury selection, Judge Gary repeatedly refused to dismiss jurors who declared they had already made up their minds about the defendants' guilt. Instead, he examined those jurors himself and did so in such a way that he managed to get them to declare that if they were selected they would listen to the evidence. On the basis of that statement, he then declared that their bias was not so serious that they should be excluded, a conclusion Altgeld condemned as absurd.[6]

Altgeld added that witnesses called to the stand perjured themselves repeatedly, apparently because of police threats. At the same time, Gary prevented defense efforts to expose those lies by sharply limiting the defense attorneys' efforts to cross-examine witnesses for the state. In contrast, the state was given every opportunity to cross-examine defense witnesses, and when the prosecutor did not question extensively enough, Gary often stepped in and asked questions himself. Gary also commented on the nature of the evidence, usually in the presence of the jury and always in a manner hostile to the defense.[7]

For all these reasons, Altgeld concluded that the trial was so biased as to be unjust. In offering those criticisms, Altgeld emphasized the extent to which the trial failed to conform to law. He noted that Gary's efforts to rehabilitate jurors who admitted prejudice conflicted with the standards approved by the Illinois Supreme Court in the *Coughlin* decision. He offered several statements and affidavits in support of his conclusion that the police and prosecution had acted lawlessly in suborning witnesses and in the case of the police had actually provoked the events that gave rise to the trial. He denounced the very decision to prosecute the case against nine men none of whom had been clearly tied to the throwing of the bomb that night in Haymarket Square. None of the evidence presented at the trial, in his view, tied any of the nine defendants to the actual murder, and nothing established any conspiracy that led to the throwing of the bomb. Altgeld finished by quoting other judges who agreed that the decision to prosecute the defendants, in the absence of evidence tying them directly to the bombing, punished them for exercising rights to freedom of speech and assembly that were protected under the Illinois Constitution.[8]

This statement in support of clemency was fundamentally a defense of formal law, its rules and substance. Fundamentally but not exclusively, since at times Altgeld had to concede problems with the law. His entire statement was an admission that formal law depended on the integrity of judges, police officers, and lawyers, hardly a reassuring conclusion in light of his findings. Nor were Judge Gary and the state's attorney the only officers of the court who had cut corners or twisted rules in an effort to assure the convictions of the Haymarket defendants. Both the Illinois Supreme Court and the United States Supreme Court had upheld Gary's decision on appeal, ignoring the very problems that

Altgeld's statement claimed were clear violations of the law. Also problematic was the fact that *Coughlin*, the decision that Altgeld relied on, came down after the decision in the Haymarket case, and the Illinois Supreme Court claimed that the outcomes in the two cases were consistent. Clearly, there was less consensus than Altgeld claimed about what the rule of law had required, and more possibility that law would not bar unjust results than he was prepared to admit in his statement.

Altgeld's statement undermined his defense of the law in other ways as well. He supported his decision to pardon the remaining Haymarket defendants by repeated references to the many others, mostly members of Chicago's business and legal communities, who thought the trial's outcome was wrong. He reinforced that attempt to ground clemency on the popular will by noting that both Judge Gary and the prosecutor had, at various times, expressed doubts about the guilt of the remaining defendants, who had appeared to show appropriate respect for law and society. Because their guilt was unclear, and their attitudes and lives seemed acceptable, justice demanded that they be set free.

Ultimately, Altgeld's statement about the grant of clemency was an admission that law alone was not enough, that it somehow had to be tempered with a sense of justice that had popular roots. It was also a concession, similar to that offered by the *Western Appeal*, that the rule of law alone did not guarantee justice. But at the very moment that he indicated that law had to reflect justice, he demonstrated how perilous such an effort could be. For in the end, Altgeld did almost exactly what he charged Gary with doing. He used public opinion, actually a fragment of public opinion, to substantiate his argument about what justice required. And then he grounded his interpretation of law, and his decision to pardon, on that sense.

Late nineteenth-century Chicago was a place where popular forces influenced formal law, and where popularly defined justice often trumped the rule of law. In that, Chicago was not unique. The anxieties of Roscoe Pound, Arthur Train, and others writing at the time demonstrated that jurors in other cities were willing to let their views of what was right or wrong dictate verdicts. Train's remarks in particular made it clear that newspapers in New York encouraged jurors to act out their own sense of justice, and Lawrence Friedman and Robert Percival's study of criminal law in late nineteenth-century Alameda County, California, suggests that jurors on the other side of the country were doing much the same.[9]

And they were doing it because the idea that they should do so was still a powerful one. Peter Karsten has demonstrated that many judges in nineteenth-century civil cases ruled in accord with their senses of justice, entering rulings that reflected religious or ethical ideals rather than the pure rule of law. As Karsten notes, the fact that judges dispensed with law when they felt fairness required it argues for an alternative to the view that legal formalism dominated law or that the legal system was a tool of market capitalism. The idea connects law, or at least some law, with the community-oriented, populist, "heart-based" (to use Karsten's term) approach to society that influenced one branch of social science thought at the end of the century.

But while those judges and lawyers and social scientists who supported the principle of the heart over the law of the head gave credence to a vague sense that justice, not formal legal rules, should prevail, they did so in a context in which people were willing to act. Timothy Gilfoyle has demonstrated that civic associations and groups in New York made demands about crime and law up through the end of the nineteenth century, just as they were doing in Chicago during Zephyr Davis's trial. Law, whether in New York, California, or Chicago, was subject to justice.[10]

If the Davis case was a moment when formal law and popular justice came together, the question arises of how that process worked. In his study of nineteenth-century Chicago, Carl Smith described the Haymarket trial as a drama, "'written' and 'performed' to be viewed and reported in a way that would fulfill the authorities' and the public's aesthetic as well as legal standards for justice." According to Smith, the drama played out in the large courtroom in the Cook County Criminal Court in 1887 turned on the conflict between law and disorder, the struggle he felt characterized the era. And in the end, law prevailed because those who scripted the trial did so in a manner that appealed to the jurors.[11]

In her study of the murder trial of Harry K. Thaw in 1906, Martha Merrill Umphrey made a similar point, in a far more theoretically sophisticated manner. She concluded that the Thaw trial was a contest between different theories of criminal responsibility, one in which lawyers tried to win jurors over to their particular interpretation through carefully crafted arguments and testimony designed to appeal to the jurors' sensibilities. Umphrey's underlying point was that law evolves as a result of this sort of process, as lawyers have to reframe legal doctrines in ways that appeal to lay notions, and that the unpredictable nature of the jurors' input adds an element of randomness to law's growth. In that sense, she agrees with Smith, offering a view of the jury's role much like that held by Kirk Hawes, Joel Longenecker, and Joseph Gary. In this view, juries serve as a critical audience who bring their own perspectives to bear on the case before them, and who then filter the evidence and the law through that perspective as they determine the verdict.[12]

For both Smith and Umphrey, and some other historians of trials, those courtroom battles are instances where the ideas of formal law are introduced to the public and popular influences redirect law. With their emphasis on the active engagement of juries in the process of legal change, these works stand in contrast to most histories of criminal law. In these studies of trials, rather than sitting and absorbing whatever rules are put in front of them, jurors are consumers of ideas who make choices about what ideas to accept and which to reject.[13]

But while Smith, Umphrey, and others emphasize the active role of jurors, when they draw this picture of the juror as a consumer, they also set limits on the jurors' ability to act independently of lawyers and judges. Jurors may make choices, but they are influenced to do so by the persuasions of the attorneys' arguments and the seduction of their narratives. They are drawn into a particular interpretation and then rule accordingly.

The Davis case suggests a different process was at play. There, the public did not sit idly by, waiting to be persuaded by a particular perspective or engulfed by a certain narrative. Instead, even before the case went to trial, popular forces were at work, demanding to be heard on the subject of what justice required. People contested, actively, over the messages that they wanted attached to the crime and public response to it, and they did so from the assumption that the contest mattered. At the trial itself, jurors insisted on their right to ignore the law offered by the defendant, as well as the legal principles urged by the prosecution, and asserted their authority to decide the case in a way that they thought was good for Chicago. Even during the execution, while papers worried about popular reaction to the spectacle, Henderson used the scene to try to challenge both the crowds that watched the hanging and the process that had led to it. At each stage, people were not an audience, disengaged from the drama playing out in front of them; they were actors who helped decide what should be done. The unfortunate outcome in the case is, therefore, a result of the rule of justice, not law.[14]

NOTES

Introduction

1. *Chicago Tribune* 28 February 1888, 1; *Chicago Times* 28 February 1888, 3.

2. On the chase: *Chicago Tribune* 29 February 1888, 1; *Chicago Times* 28 February 1888, 3. On the trial and sentencing: *Chicago Daily News* 29 March 1888, 1; *Chicago Inter-Ocean* 30 March 1888, 7; *Chicago Times* 1 April 1888, 1; *Chicago Times* 3 April 1888, 8. Post-trial reactions: *Chicago Times* 4 April 1888, 4 (editorial); *Chicago Tribune* 12 April 1888, 4 (editorial).

3. See generally Friedman, *Crime and Punishment*; Hall, *Magic Mirror*, chap. 9. The major local studies of this shift are Steinberg, *Transformation of Criminal Justice* (a study of Philadelphia), and Friedman and Percival, *Roots of Justice* (a study of Alameda County). By now, the basic story of this change is so accepted it is assumed in social histories; see, e.g., Burrows and Wallace, *Gotham*, chaps. 46, 57, 65 (recounting the rise of the State and increased law enforcement in the period 1850–90). The story does not, of course, apply to the entire United States in the late nineteenth century. Historians generally agree that extralegal measures continued in the West and South. Hall, *Magic Mirror*, 187–88; and Friedman, *Crime and Punishment*, 186 (noting that a few northern vigilante groups, like the White Caps, continued to exist, but suggesting they were the exception to the rule).

4. On the shifts at the lowest level of the court system, see Steinberg, *Transformation of Criminal Justice*; Friedman and Percival, *Roots of Justice*, chap. 4; Friedman, *Crime and Punishment*, 239–41. On the reforms of law enforcement, see Lane, *Policing the City* (about reforms in Boston); Friedman, *Crime and Punishment*, chap. 7; Hall, *Magic Mirror*, 176–78. The decline in jury authority is discussed in Hall, *Magic Mirror*, 172–74; Friedman, *Crime and Punishment*, 251–52; Conrad, *Jury Nullification*. Changes in punishment are described in Masur, *Rites of Execution* (focusing specifically on execution practice), and Friedman, *Crime and Punishment*, chap. 7.

5. The quotation is from Wiecek, *Lost World of Classical Legal Thought*, 13. For the transformation of the civil, as opposed to criminal, aspects of common law, see Sellers, *Market Revolution*, 44–55, relying on Nelson, *Americanization of the Common Law*, and Horwitz, *Transformation of American Law, 1780–1860*. See also Hurst, "Release of Energy"; Wiecek, *Lost World of Classical Legal Thought*, Prologue, chaps. 1 and 2. For a study arguing that economic factors also determined the degree to which southern states accepted extralegal behavior, see Brundage, *Lynching in the New South*. The whole idea of the transformation of law in the nineteenth century has been called into question by Peter Karsten, who argues that it misreads legal opinions and overvalues the decisions of a few courts while ignoring the trends that influenced most of the courts in the country. Karsten, *Head versus Heart*. My study is in agreement

with Karsten's argument that appeals to justice played a larger role in the legal system, though it focuses less on legal sources and more on popular calls for justice.

6. Sellers, *Market Revolution*, 44–55. Others have argued that specific sorts of legal change in the nineteenth century were a product of ideological change, and specifically a triumph of particular ideologies over others. Tomlins, *Law, Labor, and Ideology* (labor law); Grossberg, *Judgment for Solomon* (domestic relations law, particularly laws relating to child custody).

7. The major study of the way popular culture advanced the interest of the State in criminal law reform is Papke, *Framing the Criminal*. See also Halttunen, *Murder Most Foul* (examining published accounts of popular trials). Aspects of the phenomenon are also discussed in Friedman, *Crime and Punishment*, 203–8. There are differences in those approaches—Papke's work is more clearly influenced by Gramsci, Halttunen's apparently by Foucault—but they share the view that people's thought was structured by popular works. Others who have studied the popular literature of the nineteenth century have argued, to the contrary, that people were able to read their own ideas and worldviews into those works and bring some agency into their own lives. See, e.g., Denning, *Mechanic Accents*. The issue of how historians should understand the messages people take from what they read is a complicated one, as many recent histories of the nineteenth century demonstrate. Compare, for example, Denning's argument that the fact that popular works are capable of being interpreted in many ways undermines the hegemonic power of an ideology, with Newman's argument, in *White Women's Rights*, 53, that the multiple meanings given to the phrase "woman as a civilizing force" demonstrate the "elasticity of this hegemonic discourse" and therefore its hegemonic power. See also Umphrey's discussion of multiple meanings of criminal responsibility, in "Dialogics of Legal Meaning."

In this work, I incline toward the approach taken by Denning and, to some extent, Umphrey. In late nineteenth-century Chicago, different people seem to have read the same works and events differently and acted accordingly, and that interpretive freedom sometimes increased public activity, sometimes decreased it. One problem, which Denning identifies in the afterword of *Mechanic Accents*, is how to determine what readers understood a work to mean. I try to use the arguments and actions of people as they are set out in other contexts as evidence of their interpretative assumptions. Like Umphrey's discussion, though in a slightly different way, this work (like other studies I have done) is influenced by the ideas of Bakhtin and Gramsci on interpretation. Dale, "Social Equality"; Bakhtin, "Discourse on the Novel," in *Dialogic Imagination*, esp. 292–94; Adamson, *Hegemony and Revolution*, chap. 6, esp. 174, 176, 179; and Holub, *Antonio Gramsci*, esp. 132–40.

8. Friedman and Percival, *Roots of Justice*, 260.

9. Friedman, *Crime and Punishment*, 254–55; Allen, *Habits of Legality*.

10. Friedman, *Crime and Punishment*, 252–55; Friedman and Percival, *Roots of Justice*, chap. 7. See also Papke, *Framing the Criminal*.

Interestingly, in the twelve years between *Roots of Justice*, a study of criminal law in Alameda County, Calif., which he coauthored with Robert Percival, and *Crime and Punishment in American History*, his synthesis of the field, Lawrence Friedman's interpretation of show trials underwent a change. In *Roots of Justice*, the authors argued that the extraordinary publicity given to show trials masked the real nature of the criminal justice system, which operated in the petty courts. Stories of such trials, with their emphasis on procedure and law, were part of a deliberate effort to lull people into the false belief that the rule of law they saw at work in those cases existed more generally. While hardly a ringing endorsement of criminal law in late nineteenth-century California, *Roots of Justice* at least suggested that the protections of the rule of law redeemed the show trials because people brought to trial on serious charges received protections of due process, recognition of their rights, and all the benefits of the rule of law. The rule of law in this account was a type of justice; the fraud lay in the fact that such protections did not exist at all levels of the criminal law system.

In contrast, *Crime and Punishment in American History* provided a much bleaker view. There, Friedman suggested that even in show trials, law and the protections promised by the rule of law were a sham. News accounts revealed law's bankruptcy, exposing "the tricks, the tomfoolery, the loopholes, the lawyer's machinations" that dominated even those trials. The different attitude of the two accounts may be explained by nothing more than Robert Percival's absence, or it may reflect a cynicism that says as much about law in the 1980s as it does about law in the 1880s.

11. Dale, "Social Equality"; Adler, "The Negro Would be More than an Angel," 297–98. See generally Spear, introduction to *Black Chicago*.

12. *Chicago Times* 4 April 1888, 4 (editorial). See also *Chicago Tribune* 12 April 1888, 4. For the civil rights case, see Dale, "Social Equality." See, e.g., *Frank Leslie's Illustrated Newspaper* 10 December 1887, 274 (outcome in a New York boodler case reflected "too much law and not enough justice"). That paper used the same language on other occasions, e.g., 10 September 1887, 50.

13. Train, "Sensationalism and Jury Trials" and "Tricks of the Trade." Compare the discussion of the first essay in Friedman and Percival, *Roots of Justice*, 237–38.

14. The address to the ABA is Pound, "Causes of Popular Dissatisfaction," 405–6. Friedman and Percival dispute Pound's interpretation in *Roots of Justice*, 256–58. Pound, "Need of a Sociological Jurisprudence," 610, 608.

15. Ireland, "The Libertine Must Die"; Hartog, "Lawyering, Husband's Rights"; Umphrey, "Dialogics of Legal Meaning." Stories from the *National Police Gazette* include 1 October 1887, 2 (wealthy residents of Staten Island propose a vigilante group to enforce laws); 8 October 1887, 1 (Mrs. Meadows of Harrisburg shot a man to save her honor); 22 October 1887, 3 (man who seduced his sister-in-law in Connecticut "skipped town some time ago to avoid a dose of tar and feathers"); 12 November 1887, 3 (two stories of women whipping men: one from Boston whipped an editor who insulted her husband, another from Cincinnati whipped a real estate agent who slandered her school); 18 February 1888, 3 (a mob in Indiana gave a man 50 lashes for deserting his wife and four children). See also the discussion of this sort of jury action in Dale, "Not Simply Black and White."

16. For discussions of the shifts in Chicago's political structure and system, see Einhorn, *Property Rules*; Schneirov, *Labor and Urban Politics*. For the structural changes that permitted the rise of a localized State in Illinois in this period, see Monkkonen, *The Local State*. The professionalization of the Chicago police force is described, with different degrees of applause, in Flinn, *History of the Chicago Police*, and Lindberg, *To Serve and Collect*, and its effect is outlined in Schneirov, *Labor and Urban Politics*. Lindberg notes that in Chicago this centralization was relative. The police department became more professional and more centralized, but its centralization lagged behind that of other cities. Lindberg, *To Serve and Collect*, chaps. 2, 3.

The economic shifts the city underwent in the nineteenth century are described in detail in the three volumes of Pierce, *History of Chicago*; Cronin, *Nature's Metropolis*; and more briefly in Miller, *City of the Century*.

17. Addams, *Twenty Years at Hull House*, chap. 9; Nelson, *Beyond the Martyrs*, chaps. 9–10 (discussing radical meetings, clubs, and newspapers in the 1880s and 1890s); Schneirov, *Labor and Urban Politics*. Here and elsewhere in this book, I am using the term *civil society* in a broad sense, to describe popular opposition to the State. My discussion resembles that in Ryan, introduction to *Civic Wars*, esp. 7–8, and elsewhere, and is also influenced by the discussion of civil society in Africa in the essays in Comaroff and Comaroff, *Civil Society and the Political Imagination*. See esp. Comaroff and Comaroff's introduction, 22–24 (noting the many meanings of the term).

Chicago's civil society was not strictly a public sphere in the sense associated with Habermas, with its emphasis on rational discourse, nor is the popular political debate of the sort described by Arendt. As with Ryan's popular democracy, it was a combination of debate, mob violence, and civic associations of various sorts. In its many facets, its emphasis on communication, and its potential for violence, it resembles San Francisco as described in Ethington, *Public City*, 14–24, although this type of civil society lasted longer in Chicago.

18. *Chicago Inter-Ocean* 29 February 1888, 7 (story on Bureau of Justice). For activities of various voluntary associations, see *Chicago Times* 9 January 1887, 6 (meeting of Citizens League with mayor); *Chicago Times* 18 February 1887, 1 (Citizens League prompts investigation into corrupt county officials); *Chicago Times* 19 January 1887, 8 (Woman's Suffrage Club meeting); *Chicago Inter-Ocean* 21 March 1888, 5 (Woman's Suffrage Club meets, outlines successes in getting aid for poor women); *Chicago Times* 7 February 1887, 7 (article on Trade and Labor Assembly's call for investigation into Cook County Hospital); *Chicago Times* 8 February 1887, 6 (mocking article on Trade and Labor Assembly's proposal for investigation into Cook County Hospital); *Chicago Times* 28 January 1887, 3 (meeting of Chicago Society for Political Education calls for police reform); *Chicago Times* 21 March 1887, 5 (Moral Education Society, a women's reform group, meets to discuss ways to combat vice and improve condition of the poor).

For discussions of group activity in Chicago during this period, see Pierce, *History of Chicago*, 3:398–400 (debating societies), 423–29, 445–55 (religious organizations), 483–92 (clubs), and chaps. 7–8 (labor organizations and newspapers). For evidence of the diversity of participation in popular discussion in Chicago, see ibid., 456–59 (women's organizations and the WCTU); for ethnic and labor organizations, 297–99; for African American organizations and papers, 48–50; for ethnic and labor papers, 255–61. See also Sawislak, *Smoldering City* (discussing group activities after the Fire); Schneirov, *Labor and Urban Politics* (discussing various radical groups in the last part of the nineteenth century); and Nelson, *Beyond the Martyrs* (discussing radical groups in the period after Haymarket). This discussion of civil society owes much to the essays in Comaroff and Comaroff, *Civil Society and the Political Imagination*.

19. It is difficult to draw a proper balance between the aspirations provoked by the abstract ideal of civil society and the very real problems some people have exercising any power within a civil society. This study tries to recognize the worth of the aspiration while describing the impediments that stood in the way of reaching the ideal. For other efforts to balance these two aspects of civil society, see Comaroff and Comaroff, introduction to *Civil Society and the Political Imagination*, 23–25, and the other essays in the book.

20. Chicago Police Department, *Homicides and Other Events*; I am indebted to Jeffrey Adler for the figures. For one instance of a trial where the jury acquitted a guilty defendant, see *Chicago Times* 1 January 1887, 6.

21. It is, as Linda Gordon put it in the context of her study of another case, the sort of strategic site for an investigation that can clarify larger questions. Gordon, *Great Arizona Orphan Abduction*, relying on the ideas of Robert K. Merton, "Notes on Problem-Finding in Sociology," in *Sociology Today*, xxvii–xxix.

22. For other accounts of late nineteenth-century lynch mobs in the North, see, e.g., Pederson, "Gender, Justice, and a Wisconsin Lynching" (late nineteenth-century lynching in rural Wisconsin); Cha-Jua, "'Join Hands and Hearts with Law and Order'" (a lynching in late nineteenth-century Decatur, Ill.); Friedman, *Crime and Punishment*, 184–86. See also Ethington, *Public City*, 405, quoting Isaac Milliken (from California) in 1898 to the effect that "there is no city in the union with a quarter of a million people . . . which would not be better for a little judicious hanging."

23. Consider the discussion in Wilder, "Practicing Citizenship," esp. 51.

24. Ryan, *Civic Wars*, 15 (describing civic ceremonies).

25. Compare the view set out in Steinberg, epilogue to *Transformation of Criminal Justice*, 224–32. For the argument that justice, no less than law, may be an instrument of power, see the essays collected in Garth and Sarat, *Justice and Power in Sociolegal Studies*.

26. The definition is from Silbey, "Ideology, Power and Justice," in Garth and Sarat, *Justice and Power*, 276.

27. Garth and Sarat, "Justice and Power in Law and Society Research," 13. Compare the arguments of Zinn, "Law, Justice, and Disobedience."

Chapter 1

1. *Chicago Tribune* 28 February 1888, 1; *Chicago Times* 28 February 1888, 3.

2. Maggie's family lived about a mile from Greene's, at 233 Twentieth Street. Zephyr's family lived about a mile and a half away, at Twenty-Second and Clark Streets. For the weather, see the various news accounts of the murder, and *Chicago Tribune* 28 February 1888, 5, 8 (reports for the previous day).

3. *Chicago Tribune* 28 February 1888, 1; *Chicago Inter-Ocean* 28 February 1888, 6.

4. The description in this paragraph and the ones that follow are based on accounts in *Chicago Tribune* 28 February 1888, 1; *Chicago Daily News*, 27 February 1888, 1; *Chicago Times* 28 February 1888, 3; *Chicago Inter-Ocean* 28 February 1888, 6; *Chicago Daily News* 28 February 1888, 1. See also the witness list, Inquest Verdict on the body of Maggie Gaughan, 28–29 February 1888, Verdict no. 4089.

5. On Greene's, see *Chicago Inter-Ocean* 28 February 1888, 6. The poolroom next door was described in another article. *Chicago Tribune* 2 May 1887, 9. Poolrooms, which were illicit offtrack betting rooms, are described in the *Tribune* story, and in Lindberg, *To Serve and Collect*, 99. For stories that give a sense of the Levee, see *Chicago Times* 1 January 1887, 1 (grand jury report on the Levee); *Chicago Daily News* 23 April 1885, 2 (story on sightseeing in the Levee); *Chicago Daily News* 15 March 1884, 8 (scenes from a dance hall in the Levee); *Chicago Daily News* 2 February 1884, 5 (article on Levee nightlife); *Chicago Inter-Ocean* 31 January 1887, 3 (lengthy story on a reporter's adventure in a gambling den in the Levee); *Chicago Inter-Ocean* 5 May 1887, 7 (article on efforts to close Levee dives). For a different perspective, see *Chicago Daily News* 2 February 1884, 5 (article on residential life in the Levee). See generally Miller, *City of the Century*, 253, 275, 508–13; Dedman, *Fabulous Chicago*, 135–47, 251–69. For

an example of contemporary views of Chicago's lawless image, see *Frank Leslie's Illustrated Newspaper* 27 March 1886, 83 (article on the evangelist Sam Jones noting that he was going to Chicago and declaring that he would find a visit there fruitful, given its dives, corrupt politicians, and contempt for the law). See also Smith, *Chicago and the Literary Imagination* (arguing that contemporary authors offered a range of interpretations of Chicago in this period, some negative, some positive).

6. For the ambiguity of race relations in this period in Chicago, see Dale, "Social Equality"; Spear, introduction to *Black Chicago*. For complaints about the rise in crime, see *Chicago Tribune* 4 September 1882, and *Chicago Tribune* 14 June 1896, quoted in Adler, "My Mother-in-Law is to Blame," 253. For the Chicago homicide records, see Chicago Police Department, *Homicides and Other Events*. Adler's study demonstrates that in the 1880s the homicide rate was actually dropping. 255 (table 1), 256–57. He also notes that the Homicide Report was a close but not completely accurate accounting (256), a point also made at the time. *Chicago Times* 4 April 1887, 4 (editorial notes that the police records for the year before seem incredible).

7. For details about the Snell murder, see generally Duis, *Challenging Chicago*, chap. 2. It was reported locally and nationally. For just some of the local coverage, see *Chicago Daily News* 9 February 1888, 1; *Chicago Daily News* 20 February 1888, 1; *Chicago Daily News* 21 February 1888, 1; *Chicago Daily News* 23 February 1888, 1. For examples of the national coverage of the crime, see *National Police Gazette* 25 February 1888, 6; *National Police Gazette* 3 March 1888, 6; *Irish World* 18 February 1888, 3; *Irish World* 25 February 1888, 3. The *Irish World* covered the case, briefly, in every weekly edition for over a month.

8. The Heitzke (or Heintke or Heintze, the papers and records offer several alternative spellings) and Busch cases are mentioned in *Homicides and Other Events* for 1888 (the Heitzke case is listed under the last name of his victim, Gillman). A hint of the coverage in February 1888 is offered in *Chicago Daily News* 7 February 1888, 1 (Busch); *Chicago Daily News* 17 February 1888, 1 (Heitzke). Both cases were also covered in March; see *Chicago Daily News* 6 March 1888, 1 (Heitzke); *Chicago Daily News* 30 March 1888, 1 (Heitzke); *Chicago Inter-Ocean* 31 March 1888, 6 (Heitzke); *Chicago Tribune* 31 March 1888, 6 (Heitzke); *Chicago Daily News* 6 March 1888, 1 (Busch); *Chicago Daily News* 7 March 1888, 1 (Busch). Adler discusses the shift toward murder as a domestic crime in "My Mother-in-Law is to Blame," esp. 261.

9. *Chicago Times* 28 February 1888, 3, but see *Chicago Inter-Ocean* 28 February 1888, 6 (reporting that Eddie had not had a chance to go home for lunch).

10. *Chicago Tribune* 28 February 1888, 1; *Chicago Inter-Ocean* 28 February 1888, 6. According to one account, Zephyr claimed he needed the hot water for "Mrs. Greene," which is unlikely, since the Greenes did not live above the factory. Inquest Verdict on the body of Maggie Gaughan, 28–29 February 1888, Verdict no. 4089.

11. *Chicago Inter-Ocean* 28 February 1888, 6.

12. *Chicago Tribune* 28 February 1888, 1; *Chicago Times* 29 February 1888, 3; *Chicago Inter-Ocean* 29 February 1888, 2. The *Times* report indicated that both his brothers were arrested that evening; the *Inter-Ocean* indicated that his brothers and his mother were put under arrest. The Chicago police department was, as this suggests, quite quick to arrest anyone it felt like during an investigation of a crime. Lindberg, *To Serve and Collect*, 32.

13. *Chicago Daily News* 27 February 1888, 1.

14. *Chicago Daily News* 28 February 1888, 1.

15. *Chicago Times* 28 February 1888, 3.

16. *Chicago Tribune* 28 February 1888, 1.

17. Maggie's father drove for Cook, Rathbone and Company, a local box company. *Chicago Times* 29 February 1888, 1; *Chicago Inter-Ocean* 29 February 1888, 2; *Chicago Tribune* 29 February 1888, 1. For a discussion of why different papers frame stories in different ways, see Tuchman, *Making News*.

18. *Chicago Times* 28 February 1888, 3. The series on working girls was published as a book later that year. Nelson, *White Slave Girls*. The series is discussed in Schneirov, *Labor and Urban Politics*, 271–72; Meyerowitz, *Women Adrift*, 33. For all the *Times* liked to think of itself as a supporter of the worker, it was hardly a radical working-class paper. Consider the arguments in "Remember the Haymarket," *Chicago Times* 5 April 1887, 4 (editorial, using Haymarket bomb as an argument for voting a particular way in the upcoming election). For a discussion of the *Times*'s politics, see Pierce, *History of Chicago*, 3:413; Schneirov, *Labor and Urban Politics*, 271–72; Mott, *American Journalism*, 466–67.

19. *Chicago Inter-Ocean* 29 February 1888, 2. The headline on the paper's story the day before referred to her as a wage earner. 28 February 1888, 6. Its series on working girls ran in the late summer and fall of 1887: 21 August 1887, 9; 28 August 1887, 9; 4 September 1887, 9; 11 September 1887, 9.

20. See the following stories from the *Chicago Inter-Ocean*: 5 December 1886, 6 (story of the abduction of two young women; both had always been obedient and stayed home at night until they met the suspect); 1 January 1887, 3 (story of an infanticide case, 19-year-old mother was seduced by her husband's employer); 17 April 1887, 2 (young woman of good reputation, now dead, came to Chicago from Wisconsin to find work; much speculation that her death was caused by a botched abortion); 7 June 1887, 7 (12-year-old girl came to Chicago looking for work, fell in with two men who took her to their room and tried to rape her); 4 July 1887, 8 (17-year-old girl killed herself; worked as a domestic and was impregnated by laborer who left her); 5 July 1887, 7 (a second story on the 17 year old; her case illustrates the problems of girls who have no one to support them and have to work); 7 July 1887, 3 (30-year-old woman who had been seduced and gotten pregnant threw herself into the lake); 1 August 1887, 3 (report of a sermon on "toiling girls" who seek love and find trouble).

The *Chicago Inter-Ocean* agonized about the problem of seduction and repeatedly called for laws that would punish men who seduced women: 5 August 1887, 4 (editorial); 3 January 1887, 8 (report on talk by Francis Willard on the subject of punishing men who seduce women); 21 October 1887, 4 (editorial calling for prompt prosecution of men in jail for assaults on women). But its readers were not certain whom to blame for the problem, and as a result, neither was the paper. It printed letters to the editor from some readers who felt that the fault lay with women for encouraging men by failing to shun those who were seducers — e.g., 19 January 1887, 8 (letter to the editor applauding calls for law making men criminally responsible for seduction but also noting that women are also to blame for not ostracizing seducers) — and from others who rejected that view, arguing that men and women should be taught from childhood that they should be sexually pure, and that if they were properly educated, there would be no seduction of young women by men: 2 January 1887, 3 (letter to the editor); 2 February 1887, 12 (letter to the editor); 25 September 1887, 13 (editorial calling on women in Chicago to deal with the working-girl problem).

21. *Chicago Tribune* 28 February 1888, 1; *Chicago Herald* 28 February 1888, 1. For discussion of the *Herald*'s and *Tribune*'s political attitudes, see Pierce, *History of Chicago* 3:411–14; Schneirov, *Labor and Urban Politics*, 272, 274–75; Mott, *American Journalism*, 466–68. Some specific examples of those papers' attitudes can be found at *Chicago Tribune* 1 July 1887, 5

(neighborhood protest meeting); *Chicago Tribune* 4 May 1887, 4 (police brutality in labor dispute acceptable); *Chicago Herald* 5 March 1888, 1 (sympathetic story on community of anarchists).

22. *Chicago Tribune* 28 February 1888, 1.

23. *Chicago Inter-Ocean* 29 February 1888, 2; *Chicago Tribune* 28 February 1888, 1; *Chicago Daily News* 29 February 1888, 1. Kathy Peiss and others have suggested that many parents found their working daughters hard to control. Peiss, *Cheap Amusements*; Odem, *Delinquent Daughters*. But Peiss also notes that most working women who lived at home with parents or family were expected to turn all or most of their wages over to their parents. *Cheap Amusements*, 68. The same practice obtained in Chicago; see Nelson, *White Slave Girls*, 87 (girls complain that they have to turn over nearly all of their salaries to their parents), and 122 (girl expresses wish that she were a boy, since they get to keep their wages). Theodore Dreiser's novel *Sister Carrie* describes a similar situation. If Maggie was indeed permitted to keep her salary for pocket money, she would have been exceptional.

For late nineteenth-century attitudes toward working women in Chicago, see Meyerowitz, *Women Adrift*. There were particular concerns about working women within the Irish American community; these are discussed in Diner, *Erin's Daughters in America*. For just one example of a contemporary argument that work made Irish women in particular immoral, see Brace, *Criminal Classes of New York*, 35–37.

24. On the treatment of female victims, see Halttunen, *Murder Most Foul*, chap. 5, esp. 136–51 (treatment of women, especially wives, murdered in domestic setting), and chap. 6 (women as victims of murderers outside the family circle). The first quotation in this paragraph is from MacAndrew, *Gothic Tradition in Fiction*, 179; the second from Halttunen, *Murder Most Foul*, 206–7.

Others have noticed that women murderers were often described in sexual ways. Knelman, *Twisting in the Wind*, 229–31. That was certainly the fate of the fifteen-year-old woman on trial in California in 1897 for murdering her lover whose story is set out in Friedman and Percival, *Roots of Justice*, 242–43. For stories that follow Halttunen's pattern, see, e.g., the following cases reported in the *National Police Gazette*: 13 October 1887, 6 (story of a woman murdered by her son treats her as a churchgoing woman trying to maintain her family); 8 October 1887, 6 (salacious account of the mysterious death of beautiful Lillie Hoyle, who died at the hands of an unknown man, apparently the result of an attempted abortion); 28 February 1888, 6 (death of a woman at the hands of an abortionist; story emphasizes how she went wrong even though she came from good, hardworking family). But see 22 October 1887, 6 (story of man, with grudge against a neighbor, who kills neighbor's elderly wife, presented as quiet, domestic type).

25. *Chicago Times* 28 February 1888, 3; *Chicago Tribune* 28 February 1888, 1; *Chicago Herald* 28 February 1888, 1. The comments of the women reflect the literary conventions of the day, which continued to associate beauty and purity. See MacAndrew, *Gothic Tradition in Fiction*, 52 (describing the phenomenon and noting that while it was on the wane in the late nineteenth century, it was still used in many books), 88–89 (offering examples); for an example written right around the time of the Davis case, see Donnelly, *Caesar's Column*, esp. 45, 47, 190, 201.

26. On Busch, see *Chicago Daily News* 7 February 1888, 1; *Chicago Daily News* 6 March 1888, 1; *Chicago Daily News* 7 March 1888, 1. On the Mulkowski case, see from the *Chicago Times*: 23 August 1885, 6; 24 August 1885, 2; 25 August 1885, 8; 26 August 1885, 8; 27 August 1885, 8; 28 August 1885, 8; 30 August 1885, 8; 5 November 1885, 8; 6 November 1885, 8; 7 November

1885, 11; 8 November 1885, 13; 10 November 1885, 7; 11 November 1885, 8; 12 November 1885, 3; 13 November 1885, 8; 14 November 1885, 6. On Heitzke, see *Chicago Daily News* 6 March 1888, 1; *Chicago Daily News* 31 March 1888, 1. For Snell, *Chicago Daily News* 20 February 1888, 1; *Chicago Daily News* 21 February 1888, 1; *Chicago Daily News* 23 February 1888, 1.

This was such a pattern that the *Inter-Ocean* occasionally wrote articles lamenting that loss of focus on the person who died. E.g., *Chicago Inter-Ocean* 12 May 1888, 6.

27. *Chicago Times* 28 February 1888, 3; *Chicago Tribune* 28 February 1888, 1.

28. *Chicago Daily News* 28 February 1888, 1.

29. *Chicago Tribune* 29 February 1888, 1.

30. Ibid. The details of the strike on the Q, as it was known, take up the entire front page of the *Tribune* on 27 February 1888.

31. This paragraph, and those following, are based on accounts in the *Chicago Tribune* 29 February 1888, 1; *Chicago Times* 29 February 1888, 1; *Chicago Inter-Ocean* 29 February 1888, 2.

32. Police brutality, especially during arrests, was a major problem in late nineteenth-century Chicago; see *Chicago Inter-Ocean* 18 March 1888, 6 (charge made that Chicago police officer was guilty of "brutal attack" on young, employed black man); *Chicago Inter-Ocean* 4 December 1887, 12 (editorial calling for investigation into police detective Murname, who has been accused of beating arrestees); *Chicago Daily News* 2 December 1886, 1 (another story on Murname's brutality, this time accused of beating two black men); *Chicago Daily News* 8 December 1886, 4 (article applauding conviction of two officers charged with assaulting citizen); *Chicago Times* 24 April 1887, 4 (editorial on police brutality). The Chicago Citizens Association complained about police brutality on at least one occasion in the 1880s. *Annual Report of the Citizens Association*, 1885, 20–22. See generally Lindberg, *To Serve and Collect*, 32–34. Chicago was not unique in this respect. Friedman, *Crime and Punishment*, 149–55.

33. Illinois law provided that a warrant was needed for an arrest except when the crime had been committed in the presence of an officer, which had not happened here, or when the arrest was of a person believed to be a fleeing felon. Illinois Revised Statutes, chap. 38, para. 352, p. 518; and para. 342, p. 516. Case law provided that an official could arrest without a warrant when circumstances made it probable that the person arrested had committed a crime. *Dodds v. Board*, 43 Ill. 95 (1867); *Marsh v. Smith*, 49 Ill. 396 (1868). Typically, this meant that the crime had to be committed in the officer's presence. *Cahill v. Illinois*, 106 Ill. 621 (1883). However, the Illinois Supreme Court had held that an officer could arrest someone without a warrant on the grounds that the person was "prowling the streets" in a suspicious manner. *Miles v. Westen*, 60 Ill. 361 (1871). It is a close question whether there was enough to seize Davis, though *Dodds* implies that there are grounds for an arrest without a warrant if it is done to prevent an escape.

For other contemporary accounts that equated force and law in much the same way as the *Tribune* did here, see *Frank Leslie's Illustrated Newspaper* 18 September 1886, 67 (story on the defeat of anarchists in Wisconsin noting that the governor simply ordered the police to fire on them), and 13 November 1886, 195 (story on same governor mentioning the same event).

34. The relevant statute concerning sentencing of criminals under eighteen appears to be chap. 38, para. 449, of the Illinois Revised Statutes, which provides that a person "under the age of 18 years shall not be punished by imprisonment in the penitentiary for any offense except murder, manslaughter, rape, robbery, burglary, or arson."

Compare the reactions of various papers to a lynching in Clinton, Ill., in 1882. Smith, "Devine is Doomed," 21, 32. Legal technicalities were often seen to thwart justice; see ibid., 30.

And compare the evolving reaction of *Frank Leslie's Illustrated Newspaper* to the decisions in the trial of the New York boodler Jacob Sharp: 10 September 1887, 50 (article accepting judicial opinion that reversed Sharp's conviction); 10 December 1887, 274 (further decision in the case reflected "too much law and not enough justice").

35. *Chicago Inter-Ocean* 29 February 1888, 2.

36. *Chicago Herald* 29 February 1888, 1.

37. *Chicago Herald* 5 March 1888, 1.

38. *Chicago Daily News* 29 February 1888, 1; *Chicago Daily News* 2 March 1888, 1.

39. *Chicago Daily News* 15 July 1886, 2 (denouncing lynching in Jacksonville); *Chicago Daily News* 28 April 1886, 4 (attack on lynching in Springfield, Mo.); *Chicago Daily News* 19 November 1886, 2 (article on "wholesale slaughter" of blacks in Mississippi). For articles denouncing attacks on Chinese workers, see *Chicago Daily News* 5 September 1885, 2; *Chicago Daily News* 10 September 1885, 2; *Chicago Daily News* 11 February 1886, 2. On lynch mobs during the Fire, see Smith, *Urban Disorder*, 51–57, 110 (discussing the stories and their reappearance in histories of the Fire).

40. The quotation about the strong rope is from *Chicago Daily News* 29 December 1886, 2. See generally *Chicago Daily News* 15 July 1885, 1 (14-year-old girl assaulted, lynching unsuccessful); *Chicago Daily News* 24 November 1886, 1 (attempted criminal assault on girl leads to the lynching of three); *Chicago Daily News* 14 May 1886, 2 (lynching of man who killed ex-girlfriend); *Chicago Daily News* 7 February 1884, 1 (father of girl who was assaulted shot the attacker); *Chicago Daily News* 21 October 1885, 2 (lynch mob removed man suspected of assaulting two elderly ladies from Winchester, Ill., jail and hanged him).

41. *Chicago Daily News* 10 January 1887, 2.

42. The quotation is from *Chicago Daily News* 15 August 1885, 1. For similar sentiments from the *Chicago Daily News*, see 7 November 1885, 2 (article on crowd that beat a man suspected of wife beating in Tennessee). See also 18 October 1886, 1 (Cady case); 5 November 1886, 1 (attack on five year old). For a contemporaneous discussion of the relationship between lynching and other types of mob action, see Cutler, *Lynch-Law*.

43. *Chicago Daily News* 10 June 1886, 1.

44. *Chicago Daily News* 11 September 1885, 1.

45. *Chicago Daily News* 16 January 1886, 1; *Chicago Daily News* 9 November 1885, 1. These were fairly typical arguments offered in justification of lynchings; see Cutler, *Lynch-Law*, chap. 7, esp. 193 (lynching justified by urgency), 195 (lynching justified in community "that had been injured and had no law to refer to"); *Detroit Free Press* 25 May 1893, reprinted in *The Lynching at Corunna*, Cumming, ed., 64–65 (arguing that suspect in murder was lynched because there was no capital punishment statute in Michigan); *Saginaw Courier-Herald* 26 May 1893, in ibid., 80–81 (the same argument).

46. *Chicago Times* 29 February 1888, 1.

47. *Chicago Times* 28 February 1888, 1; *Chicago Times* 29 February 1888, 1 (reporting the crowd that gathered at the Polk Street Station to get Davis). For examples of the *Chicago Times*'s reaction to lynchings from outside Chicago, see 10 January 1887, 5 (mob in Nebraska lynches but does not quite kill a man, since evidence of his guilt could not be completely established; no disapproval); 8 March 1887, 6 (African American man taken from jail and lynched in Mississippi; no protest); 4 April 1887, 2 (white man taken from jail and lynched in Iowa; no concern); 14 April 1887, 2 (African American lynched in Tennessee courthouse, after trial but before sentence was entered; no protest). But see *Chicago Times* 4 April 1887, 4 (brief

editorial referring to the Iowa lynching is sarcastic); 6 April 1887, 8 (four black men taken from jail and lynched in South Carolina; the paper reports the act was condemned by people in the state). For an example of the paper's acceptance of other sorts of extralegal violence, see 7 March 1887, 3 (story about women from Ellsworth, Ill., who raided local saloon). For examples of the paper's hostility to mob interference with elections and the hint of mob rule, see 3 February 1887, 6 (mob rule in Colorado condemned); 11 January 1887, 1 (hoodlums seem to have taken over Indiana politics); 5 April 1887, 4 (editorial warning voters of risk of radical, mob rule).

48. The quotation is from *Chicago Tribune* 1 July 1887, 1. Consider the paper's failure to condemn the lynching of three African Americans in West Virginia. *Chicago Tribune* 1 May 1887, 15. The paper's efforts to keep statistics on lynching is discussed in Williamson, *The Crucible of Race*, 529–30 n. 13; Cutler, *Lynch-Law*, 157–62.

49. *Chicago Tribune* 1 May 1887, 6 (editorial dismissing charges of police brutality admits that people were "more or less roughly handled by the police" but labels this insignificant); *Chicago Tribune* 4 May 1887, 4 (the same). Compare the attitude of the *Chicago Times* 11 January 1887, 8 (reporting claims that man arrested was beaten by police); *Chicago Times* 5 January 1887, 3 (article on Chicago police officer who was demoted, apparently for arresting someone; article suggests that most officers just beat people up); Citizens Association of Chicago, *Annual Report*, 1887, 11–12 (police brutality). On the *Tribune*'s attitude toward mob violence in the Davis case, see its report on the scene at Forest and its report on mob behavior in Chicago, both in *Chicago Tribune* 29 February 1888, 1.

50. *Chicago Inter-Ocean* 15 August 1887, 2 (white man lynches another white man in an Iowa town); 28 August 1887, 8 (story on near lynching in Centralia, Ill.); 10 September 1887, 4 (editorial on Bald Knobbers).

51. *Chicago Inter-Ocean* 16 December 1887, 6 (tarring and feathering incident); 20 October 1887, 6 (community group that put pressure on police); 31 March 1888, 1 (Minnesota case); 4 March 1888, 1 (Evansville case).

52. *Chicago Inter-Ocean* 24 August 1887, 4 (editorial relating to investigation of apparent murder; to keep people from leaping to wrong conclusions and demanding improper things, paper urges that all information on crime be made public); 13 September 1887, 4 (editorial deploring use of technicalities to keep from extraditing criminal wanted in Chicago; justice being destroyed by law); 15 September 1887, 4 (editorial praising verdict in Haymarket trial because it demonstrated that law could achieve justice).

53. *Chicago Tribune* 29 February 1888, 1; *Chicago Times* 29 February 1888, 2.

54. The quotation is from the *Chicago Times* 29 February 1888, 1. For just some examples of the shifting and conflicting descriptions of Davis, see *Chicago Daily News* 28 February 1888, 1 (bright and intelligent-looking); *Chicago Daily News* 29 February 1888, 1 (too dark to be mulatto but with "well-cut" features); *Chicago Times* 29 February 1888, 1 (a mulatto); *Chicago Inter-Ocean* 29 February 1888, 2 (a colored boy of no more than ordinary intelligence); *Chicago Inter-Ocean* 6 March 1888, 7 (no "Adonis even of the Ethiopian kind").

For treatments of "the three Italians," as the trunk murderers were known, and an equally dubious description of Mulkowski, see *Chicago Times* 13 November 1885, 8.

55. *Chicago Times* 29 February 1888, 1; *Chicago Tribune* 29 February 1888, 3.

56. *Chicago Inter-Ocean* 29 February 1888, 2.

57. Davis's claim that he never confessed is reported in *Chicago Tribune* 8 April 1888, 9. Interestingly, Henshaw left the force in April 1888, just a few days after Davis's conviction. His decision followed reorganization in the department that took away much of his power, so

although Henshaw claimed he quit, it seems possible that he was forced out. See discussion in *Chicago Inter-Ocean* 18 April 1888, 6. On the Chicago police department's reputation for abusive interrogation methods, see Lindberg, *To Serve and Collect,* 83 (recounting the beating of a suspect in an 1889 murder case).

58. E.g., *Chicago Daily News* 26 November 1886, 1; *Chicago Daily News* 21 December 1886, 1; *Chicago Tribune* 3 May 1887, 4. In contrast to the *Daily News,* which tended to condemn the entire criminal justice system from police officer to judge, the *Tribune* tended to conclude that the failings of the system did not lie in the hands of those who tried to execute or enforce the law. E.g., *Chicago Tribune* 2 May 1887, 10. At times, however, even the *Tribune* blamed parts of the system. *Chicago Tribune* 12 April 1884, 4. For examples of the *Chicago Daily News's* willingness to denounce the legal system, see 5 December 1885, 4 (editorial on closing laws); 10 December 1886, 1 (raid on Levee saloons); 23 January 1886, 1 (article on trial of saloonkeepers charged with violating Sunday closing laws); 5 October 1885, 2 (attack on selective prosecution in gambling house raids); 24 May 1886, 2 (article on racially selective enforcement of fines in gambling cases); 18 January 1884, 1 (article asserting that judge dismissed claim against black gambler in order to cater to the black vote); 18 January 1887, 1 (article on inspection of theaters in the city); 11 February 1886, 2 (article praising investigation of Sunday closing violations in Cincinnati); 4 January 1886, 2 (article on grand jury investigation of "dives").

On the reasons for this attitude toward the criminal justice system, consider the reactions when crimes went unsolved and uninvestigated. *Chicago Inter-Ocean* 14 August 1887, 9 (article on death of a woman as a result of a late-term abortion: "One thing is certain, the case is not being pushed. Some persons think there is a scheme to let these cases go by default."); *Chicago Times* 12 April 1887, 5 (doctor suspected in death of another woman, not yet arrested); *Chicago Times* 29 January 1887, 4 (editorial on proposed creation of police commission notes that there are serious problems with the department in terms of abuses and failures); *Chicago Times* 27 March 1887, 4 (editorial denounces decision by county commissioner not to fund medical examination of dead women to determine if they were poisoned); *Chicago Times* 5 January 1887, 3 (article on police officer who was disciplined argues that he was punished for doing his job, in this case arresting burglars). This lament was not confined to Chicago; see *Frank Leslie's Illustrated Newspaper* 16 April 1887, 130 (the chief obstacles to law enforcement in cities are political).

Chapter 2

1. Report of the Inquest on Maggie Gaughan, 28/29 February 1888, inquest no. 4089, p. 145. See also the discussions in *Chicago Inter-Ocean* 1 March 1888, 5; *Chicago Daily News* 29 February 1888, 1; *Chicago Times* 1 March 1888, 5.

2. *Chicago Daily News* 29 February 1888, 1; *Chicago Tribune* 1 March 1888, 7; *Chicago Inter-Ocean* 1 March 1888, 5; *Chicago Times* 1 March 1888, 5. The witness list is in the inquest report.

3. Report of the Inquest on Maggie Gaughan. *Chicago Daily News,* 29 February 1888, 1; *Chicago Tribune* 1 March 1888, 7; *Chicago Times* 1 March 1888, 5.

4. *Chicago Inter-Ocean* 1 March 1888, 5.

5. *United States Life Insurance Company v. William Vocke,* 129 Ill. 557, 563 (1889). See also *Chicago Daily News* 10 December 1888, 2.

6. *Chicago Daily News* 14 February 1888, 2.

7. Ibid.; see also *Chicago Daily News* 28 April 1886, 4 (article condemning coroner's jury in Missouri). See also *Chicago Times* 20 February 1887, 4 (editorial calling for abolishment of coroner's jury). For the *Daily News's* hostility to juries that decided the wrong way, see 15 November 1886, 1. The paper also objected to "professional juries." 7 January 1887, 1. But see *Chicago Daily News* 24 November 1886, 5; 4 January 1886, 2 (article and editorial on the same page).

8. For investigations and initiatives by grand juries, see *Chicago Daily News* 2 January 1886, 1; *Chicago Daily News* 15 November 1886, 1; *Chicago Daily News* 3 February 1888, 1; *Chicago Inter-Ocean* 2 April 1888, 7. The *Tribune* proposed a charge to the grand jury in the Davis case which was ignored; see *Chicago Tribune* 2 March 1888, 7.

9. This discussion is influenced by several different works on interpretation; see in particular Holub, *Antonio Gramsci*, esp. chap. 5; Bakhtin, *Dialogic Imagination*. Compare the use Martha Merrill Umphrey makes of Bakhtin's theory of the dialogic in "Dialogics of Legal Meaning." Although Umphrey and I both rely on Bakhtin, my interest is in how individuals bring personal context into their readings, while hers is on the way lawyers shape their arguments to contexts that are recognized by the community. As a result, my work has more in common with Denning, *Mechanic Accents* (considering the possibility that a working-class audience would read works with a particular "working-class accent"), and Holub, *Antonio Gramsci*, 132–40 (discussing a similar concern of Gramsci's and arguing that he was influenced by theories that Bakhtin was working with).

10. *Chicago Inter-Ocean* 1 March 1888, 5; *Chicago Times* 1 March 1888, 4 (W. F. Storey column). For the employment patterns of African Americans in Chicago in the late nineteenth century, see Dale, "Social Equality," 314–15; Spear, *Black Chicago*, 1–8. Compare the situation with respect to the role of race versus gender in the early twentieth-century South, in the context of a case in which the alleged defendant, Leo Frank, was Jewish and the victim was a young, Protestant (and white) girl. MacLean, "Leo Frank Case Reconsidered."

11. Nelson, *White Slave Girls*, 74, 86 (describing African American women and children working as maids, porters, or cooks). See also *Chicago Daily News* 9 July 1886, 1; *Chicago Daily News* 10 November 1886, 1 (African Americans as strikebreakers); *Western Appeal* 13 August 1887, 1 (article on African Americans applying for jobs). Compare the situation in Philadelphia, which Roger Lane describes as being similar. Lane, *Roots of Violence*, 29–30; but compare DuBois, *Philadelphia Negro*, chap. 16, esp. sec. 47. For the points made in this and the next few paragraphs, see Dale, "Social Equality"; Adler, "The Negro Would be More than an Angel." This picture of race relations in Chicago is not consistent with the situation discussed in Roediger, *Wages of Whiteness*, and Ignatiev, *How the Irish Became White*, since it sees ongoing evidence that black-white racism was not the only type of racism in Chicago.

12. For an example of attitudes toward Chinese men, see the story of Sam Wah, *Chicago Daily News* 1 October 1888, 1. He was eventually released but only after being held for two weeks. *Chicago Daily News* 15 October 1888, 1. For stories suggesting that black men were especially dissipated, see *Chicago Daily News* 23 April 1885, 2 (article on playing policy describes "coons," defined as "degraded colored men"); *Chicago Daily News* 15 March 1884, 8 (article on a "nigger dance"); *Chicago Daily News* 2 February 1884, 5 (article on blacks and whites drinking and dancing in a low-class resort). Compare Bruce, *Plantation Negro as a Freeman*, 83–85 (offering an early, c. 1880, Southern account of black men that suggests they want nothing more than to rape white women). For an extensive discussion of the evolution of the popular (white) image of black men as decadent, see Fredrickson, *Black Image in the*

White Mind, chap. 8. The evolution of Southern racist thought in the late nineteenth century is discussed in Hale, *Making Whiteness*.

13. The *Tribune* series is discussed in Meyerowitz, *Women Adrift*, 43–44, and chap. 3. For similar attitudes, see also Epstein, *Politics of Domesticity*, 138–41; and Denning, *Mechanic Accents*, chap. 9, esp. p. 180.

14. *Chicago Inter-Ocean* 21 August 1887, 9; *Chicago Inter-Ocean* 28 August 1887, 9.

15. *Chicago Times* 1 March 1888, 5 (the headline emphasizes racial mixing, while the story focuses on Greene's failure to protect Maggie). Nelson, *White Slave Girls*, 5–12 (economic exploitation at a lace company), 31–44 (problems with abusive female supervisors), 44–46 (middle-class man solicits sex from author simply because she appears to be a working girl). For her discussion of sexual exploitation in the workforce, see ibid., 50, 63, 65 (salacious remarks by male supervisors and coworkers), and 100–101 (woman working in book binding factory complains to health commission about supervisor who offered to ignore her bad work in return for sex). Nelson's book was first published as a series, "Life among the Slave Girls of Chicago," in the *Chicago Times* in July–August 1888. Consider also the assumptions of working women's sexuality offered in Dreiser's *Sister Carrie*.

16. For examples of assertiveness among the young women Nelson described, see Nelson, *White Slave Girls*, 73–74 (girls stick up for each other and provide assistance to each other), 104–5 (girls talk about picnic they plan to take and the boyfriends they have found since leaving school and going to work), 29–30 (mother accuses girl of lying to her), 38 (girl with headache decides to take afternoon off to go to the park), 49 (one girl at a shop complains about the way the others dance all night and never go home), 62 (girls at shop flirt with men during break). Nelson's conclusion that women needed help in protecting themselves was fairly common. See the articles on the Bureau of Justice, which emphasized that it was created to help working women who could not help themselves: *Chicago Daily News* 1 December 1888, 1; *Catholic Home* (Chicago) 28 April 1888, 2. See also Meyerowitz, *Women Adrift*, chap. 3 (discussing the treatment of working women's sexuality in reformers' writings); and MacLean, "Leo Frank Case Reconsidered" (describing similar reactions in the South).

Peiss, *Cheap Amusements*, makes a similar point, as does Odem, *Delinquent Girls*. Many of the arguments made about the sexuality of working women echoed statements made about regulation of prostitution. Best, *Controlling Vice*, chap. 3.

17. For the *Irish World*'s treatment of the Snell case, see 18 February 1888, 3; 25 February 1888, 3; 3 March 1888, 3; 24 March 1888, 3; 31 March 1888, 3; 7 April 1888, 3; 14 April 1888, 3; 21 April 1888, 3.

18. For the quotation about women, see *Irish World* 10 March 1888, 4. On the role of the *Irish World* in Chicago, and its ties to the Knights, see Schneirov, *Labor and Urban Politics*, 122, 123, 156. On Irish American attitudes toward working women, see Diner, *Erin's Daughters in America*; Hoover, "Supplemental Family Income"; McCaffrey, "The Irish American Dimension," in McCaffrey et al., *Irish in Chicago*, 3. For the argument that the Irish American community disapproved of working wives, see Roediger, *Wages of Whiteness*, 153–55; and McCaffrey, "Irish American Dimension," 3.

On working-class (and especially Knights of Labor) attitudes toward women, see Montgomery, *Fall of the House of Labor*, 140–48; Levine, "Labor's True Woman"; Denning, *Mechanic Accents*, chap. 3 (discussing working-class male attitudes). Denning particularly notes that dime novels for working-class women tended to describe them as able to stand up for themselves, in sharp contrast to the novels for middle-class women and dime novels for working-class men, which tended to assume that working women were victims who had to be saved by some-one else. For discussions of how Irish Americans positioned themselves against blacks, often quite hostilely, see Roediger, *Wages of Whiteness*; Ignatiev, *How the Irish Became White*.

19. Lindberg, *To Serve and Collect*, chap. 2 (on the ethnic breakdown of the Chicago po-lice department and the particular role of the Irish). For examples of the *Irish World*'s politics, see 12 November 1887, 1 (article on Haymarket defendants' execution); 21 January 1888, 4 (edi-torials on police and crime in Ireland); 23 June 1888, 3 (note about statute honoring police killed in Haymarket riot). The shifts in its politics, in particular those following Haymarket, are discussed in Rodechko, "An Irish-American Journalist," 533, and more generally in Schneirov, *Labor and Urban Politics*, 177.

20. For the argument that the *Alarm* became alienated from Chicago after Haymarket, see Nelson, *Beyond the Martyrs*, 214–15. He seems to have overstated the situation (see discus-sion in text). For the paper's attitude toward working women, see, in particular, the story of a young working-class woman who was raped by a police officer, *Alarm* 12 December 1884, 1, dis-cussed in Smith, *Urban Disorder*, 160–61; and *Alarm* 22 August 1885, 1 (article on sweatshops and working girls). The paper also suggested that business owners preyed sexually on young women. *Alarm* 3 April 1886, 2, discussed in Smith, *Urban Disorder*, 161–62. The paper did carry the occasional article on working women after it resumed printing, see 14 November 1887, 2 (editorial).

21. *Labor Enquirer* 2 March 1888, 2. See generally the discussion in Nelson, *Beyond the Martyrs*, 171. On debates over whether the *Labor Enquirer* was a true socialist paper, see Schneirov, *Labor and Urban Politics*, 173; Nelson, *Beyond the Martyrs*, 213–14. On the prob-lems female labor posed to male labor, see Meyerowitz, *Women Adrift*, esp. chap. 2.

22. *Western Appeal* 7 April 1888, 4.

23. *Chicago Tribune* 2 March 1888, 4. On workforces that included blacks and whites, see Nelson, *White Slave Girls*, 48 (cigar maker); Dale, "Social Equality."

24. Many of Nelson's examples of other sorts of racial mingling in the workplace involved Jewish employers; see *White Slave Girls*, 96–97 (bad bosses who spoke with accents, apparently Jewish), 63–65 (a bad, grasping Jewish manufacturer), 108–9 (grimy conditions in shop owned by Jewish man), 51–55 (sarcastic account of the boss who was a "good Jew"). For an example of the resentment inspired by Jewish workers, see *White Slave Girls*, 61–62. Another study of Chicago from this period, Pacyga, "To Live Amongst Others," indicates that workplace hostil-ity among the male workers went beyond black-white or religious divisions.

25. The history of the case is set out in Dale, "Social Equality."

26. Not all the stories on the trial were positive. See *Chicago Times* 17 March 1888, 3 (con-descending account of plaintiff). For other stories on segregation in public places and some lawsuits relating to the problem, see *Chicago Daily News* 10 October 1884, 1 (Palmer House dis-criminated); *Chicago Tribune* 13 September 1885, 16 (Polk Street restaurant charged with dis-crimination); *Chicago Daily News* 14 September 1885, 1 (article on the same case); *Chicago Daily News* 7 January 1886, 4 (same case); *Chicago Daily News* 15 March 1886, 1 (case brought against restaurant in Bloomington, Ill.). Compare the situation in Philadelphia. Lane, *Roots of Violence*, 17.

27. On Sam Wah, see *Chicago Daily News* 1 October 1888, 1.

28. *Chicago Daily News* 10 December 1888, 2; *Chicago Tribune* 1 October 1888, 1 (story about a murder in an interracial grog shop). As shocking to the *Tribune* was the fact that even after the grog shop's manager was murdered by a drinking companion during an evening of

drinking that extended well beyond closing time, the city reissued the saloon's license without a murmur. See also editorial, *Chicago Tribune* 2 October 1888, 4.

For examples of stories equating race and crime in the Levee and other dubious venues, see *Chicago Daily News* 2 February 1884, 5 (blacks and whites drinking and dancing together in dive); *Chicago Daily News* 15 March 1884, 8 (black men dancing with white women in dive); *Chicago Daily News* 23 April 1885, 2 (low-class blacks at gambling dens); *Chicago Daily News* 2 November 1885, 1 (arrest of women in disorderly house turns up women of "all descriptions, colors and ages"); *Chicago Daily News* 10 December 1888, 2 (a glimpse at conditions at the Park Theater).

Note that in each of these stories, the emphasis was on a mix of environmental forces (since immoral places bred criminal behavior) and heredity (since certain groups were prone to vice and crime). Some took a purely environmentalist attitude toward crime; see *Chicago Daily News* 15 October 1888, 2 (challenging the idea of "hereditary" criminals); Altgeld, *Our Penal Machinery*, 15–20, 23–24. At the same time, the notion that certain groups were particularly disposed to criminality made heredity a strong aspect of most debates. Even as staunch an environmentalist as Charles Loring Brace accepted that heredity played some role, assuming that members of certain ethnic groups, Germans for example, were prone to crime. Brace, *Criminal Classes of New York*. See the discussion in Hawes, *Children in Urban Society*, 110, 140–41 (noting these two aspects of Brace's approach).

29. Consider the class-based objections made during the discussion at a mass meeting of African Americans in Chicago in 1888. *Western Appeal* 11 February 1888, 1. For some indications of how the respectable, middle-class African American *Western Appeal* reacted to vice among lower class blacks, see 13 October 1888, 1 (article on "city wickedness"); 27 June 1885, 1 (story on licentiousness and race); 18 July 1885, 1 (article calling for the closing of all gambling hells frequented by African Americans); 9 July 1887, 1 (article on tendency of whites to lump all African Americans together at the lowest level). For discussions of this problem, see Dale, "Social Equality"; Gaines, *Uplifting the Race*; Drake, *Churches and Voluntary Associations*, chap. 1.

30. Compare the analysis of multiple interpretations offered by Umphrey and her suggestion that an effective narrative will transcend those different interpretive contexts, and Denning's assumption to the contrary that an audience has unlimited power to interpret. Umphrey, "Dialogics of Legal Meaning"; Denning, *Mechanics Accents*. In this instance, the situation seems to come closer to the condition described by Denning, since at least the jury resisted the narrative urged by Kent and offered its own alternative interpretation.

31. *Chicago Tribune* 2 March 1888, 4 (editorial); *Chicago Tribune* 5 March 1888, 3; *Chicago Inter-Ocean* 28 March 1888, 5; *Chicago Tribune* 2 April 1888, 3; *Chicago Tribune* 24 March 1888, 7. The *Chicago Times* also noted the Trade and Labor Assembly's role in having the case brought to trial; see *Chicago Times* 28 March 1888, 6. On the Assembly in general, see Nelson, *Beyond the Martyrs*, 40–44; Wade, *Chicago's Pride*, 234; Schneirov, *Labor and Urban Politics*.

The action against Greene's was brought under a city ordinance that provided "no person having the right and power to prevent the same, shall knowingly cause or permit any child under 15 years of age to be employed in any place where machinery is used, or more than eight hours in any day, at any grade of employment, and then only between the hours of 7 A.M. and 6 P.M." Municipal Ordinances of the City of Chicago, sec. 1357. See also "Opinion of the Corporation Counsel of the City of Chicago on the Sweat Shop Laws," in *Opinions of the Corporation Counsel*, 191–92.

32. On the salaries at Greene's, see *Chicago Tribune* 29 February 1888, 3 (workers at Greene's made $1.50 a week); *Chicago Tribune* 28 March 1888, 7 (Maggie made $2.00 a week). One study shows that by the time of the 1890 census, child laborers in Chicago earned on average $187.00 per year. Boys often worked in the stockyards, where their salaries were around $4.50 a week for a ten-month job. See Wade, *Chicago's Pride*, 227–29; *Chicago Inter-Ocean* 28 March 1888, 5. Women at the stockyards were paid higher salaries than other women: those who worked in stockyard offices made $11.00 a week; those who held blue-collar jobs made more than $6.50. Wade, *Chicago's Pride*, 229. Consider also the story in *Frank Leslie's Illustrated Newspaper*, 23 July 1887, 367 (on the poor girl from Chicago who earned $3.00 a week and could not afford to pay rent).

33. *Chicago Inter-Ocean* 28 March 1888, 5; *Chicago Times* 28 March 1888, 6. Other employers did violate the law with impunity. Stores in the Loop were allowed to avoid prosecution on the grounds that their young employees were able to take frequent breaks, which was one of Greene's claims. Pierce, *History of Chicago*, 3:294 (discussing selective prosecution of Loop stores).

34. *Chicago Times* 28 March 1888, 6.

35. Pierce, *History of Chicago*, 3:294; Peiss, *Cheap Amusements*, 68 (discussing the way girls had to turn their wages over to their parents); Nelson, *White Slave Girls*, 87, 122 (contrasting the way girls' wages were treated with those of their brothers).

36. Pierce, *History of Chicago*, 3:368–69 (Illinois statutes), 388–89 (Lawson and other business leaders), 367–68, 384–86 (working-class roles in education reform); Montgomery, *Fall of the House of Labor*, 132 and n. 34 (the same, noting the trend among the working class to encourage their children to go to school). But see Parsons and Goldin, "Parental Altruism."

37. Citizens Association of Chicago, *Annual Report*, 1883, 34; Parsons and Goldin, "Parental Altruism." Consider also the argument that there was good child labor and bad child labor, a distinction that turned on the attitudes of the child, not on the working conditions. *Frank Leslie's Illustrated Newspaper* 15 December 1888, 279. On the history of the ordinance, see Schneirov, *Labor and Urban Politics*, 91; "Alderman Meier's Amendment re Child Labor, 4 October 1880, Ordinances, Resolutions and Orders Introduced to the Chicago City Council by Socialist Aldermen During the Years 1878–1882," Carter Harrison II Papers.

38. For examples of the Citizens League's activities, see *Chicago Tribune* 6 March 1886, 8; *Chicago Tribune* 3 April 1886, 6; *Chicago Daily News* 10 December 1886, 1; *Chicago Daily News* 24 December 1886, 1; *Chicago Daily News* 18 January 1887, 1. Another, similar group calling itself the Reform Alliance also met during this period. *Chicago Tribune* 6 March 1886, 8. On the Trade and Labor Assembly's activism, see Schneirov, *Labor and Urban Politics*; *Chicago Times* 7 February 1887, 7 (article on its proposal to investigate Cook County Hospital); *Chicago Times* 8 February 1887, 6 (same).

The fondness of Americans in the early nineteenth century for civic associations of various sorts is well known. Tocqueville, *Democracy in America*, 2:114. They were no less popular among Chicagoans in the period after the Civil War. Einhorn, *Property Rules*, 66; Sawislak, *Smoldering City*; Schneirov, *Labor and Urban Politics*.

39. *Chicago Tribune* 7 October 1886, 3 (Hyde Park); *Chicago Daily News* 22 November 1888, 2 (Hyde Park); *Chicago Tribune* 2 April 1886, 1 (Bricklayer's protest). The use of prison labor was much debated in this period. See, e.g., "Opinion of the Corporation Counsel of the City of Chicago on the Employment of Prisoners at the Bridewell," in *Opinions of the Corporation Counsel*, 98–99.

40. *Western Appeal* 10 March 1888, 1. For a rather sarcastic account of this meeting, see *Chicago Tribune* 7 March 1888, 1.

41. *Western Appeal* 10 March 1888, 1. The African American press in Chicago mounted a campaign, which ultimately failed, to defeat Hertz's reelection bid. *Western Appeal* 22 September 1888, 1.

42. On Jones, see Spear, *Black Chicago*, 62–63. For examples of indignation meetings, see *Western Appeal* 20 October 1888, 1 (mass meeting to oppose Hertz's reelection); *Chicago Daily News* 1 February 1884, 1 (meeting of African Americans regarding civil rights failures in the South); *Chicago Daily News* 2 January 1884, 4 (mass meeting to celebrate emancipation proclamation); *Chicago Daily News* 10 March 1884, 4 (mass meeting to debate education's value to blacks); *Western Appeal* 11 February 1888, 1 (mass meeting to discuss comments made by Dr. Daniel Hale Williams, an African American civic leader, about blacks in Chicago); *Chicago Inter-Ocean* 1 August 1887, 8 (meeting to protest failure to hire blacks).

43. *Western Appeal* 10 March 1888, 1 (protest of coroner's verdict); *Western Appeal* 20 October 1888, 1. For examples of other civil rights activism from this period, see *Western Appeal* 2 July 1887, 1 (gathering in Oak Ridge, La.); *Western Appeal* 13 October 1888, 2 (mass meeting in Minneapolis). Chicago leaders in these mass meetings and protests were typically either politicians, like John G. Jones or Edward Morris, or ministers, like Thomas W. Henderson. The tradition of elite leadership among African Americans in the North in this period is described in Gatewood, *Aristocrats of Color*, and called into question in Gaines, *Uplifting the Race*. For discussions of the differences among African Americans within Chicago in the 1880s, and the suggestion that there were different degrees of activism between professionals and business owners, see Dale, "Social Equality"; Spear, *Black Chicago*, chap. 3. Ida B. Wells had not yet moved to Chicago in 1888, and at that time in Chicago no African American woman played a public role similar to the one she and other women did in the 1890s and early twentieth century. Spear, *Black Chicago*, 58–60. Bates, "New Crowd Challenges the Agenda," 340. For problems that African American women faced in taking an active role in church or public life, see Higginbotham, *Righteous Discontent*, esp. 120–21, 147.

44. Dale, "Social Equality." Indignation meetings were not unique to Chicago blacks. See Alfers, *Law and Order in the Capital City*, 47 (indignation meeting); *Frank Leslie's Illustrated Newspaper* 2 October 1886, 99 (report of such a meeting in New England). For a historical context for such protests, see Dittmer, *Local People*, chaps. 1, 2; Sugrue, *Origins of the Urban Crisis*; Gatewood, *Aristocrats of Color*; and Higginbotham, *Righteous Discontent*.

45. Nelson, *Beyond the Martyrs*, esp. chap. 6; e.g., *Alarm* 13 December 1884, 1 (article on meeting, women speakers).

46. The distinction between anarchists and the people he refers to as the English-speaking radicals is set out in Schneirov, *Labor and Urban Politics*, esp. 174–76; see also Nelson, *Beyond the Martyrs*. The distinction drawn between those who tried to maintain the public sphere and those who used it is based on Habermas, *Between Facts and Norms*, 369–70. The more radical, international groups could be described in two different ways. One might argue that they were participating in a larger, international public sphere, though whether they can accurately be described as acting against a State under those circumstances is another question. Alternatively, and perhaps more accurately, they were engaged in creating an oppositional social movement, while those like the African Americans were not. See Gamson, "Social Psychology of Collective Action," 53, and esp. 60–64.

47. The quotation is from Novak, *People's Welfare*, 235. For descriptions of Chicago's political culture before the Fire, see Einhorn, *Property Rules*; Sawislak, *Smoldering City.*

48. The localist, civic republican tradition and its connection to the mob is described in Novak, *People's Welfare*, and described in the Chicago context in Einhorn, *Property Rules*; Wade, *Chicago's Pride*, 135; and Sawislak, *Smoldering City.* See also *Frank Leslie's Illustrated Newspaper* 20 October 1888, 155 (brief account of Chicago neighborhood protest arising from streetcar strike).

49. Addams, *Twenty Years at Hull House*, chap. 9; she is also quoted in Smith, *Urban Disorder*, 171. Addams's conclusion, which is contrary to that offered by many historians of this period (who argue that after Haymarket there was a period of suppression), is substantiated by Schneirov, *Labor and Urban Politics*, chap. 8; and Nelson, *Beyond the Radicals.*

50. Einhorn, *Property Rules*, 4 (Healy's Slough). For other, informal group activities, see Nelson, *Beyond the Martyrs*, 40–44 (meetings of rival groups); Masters, *Tale of Chicago*, 212 (workers group's protest meetings); Sawislak, *Smoldering City*, 236–40 (rival meetings on saloon closing laws); Dale, "Social Equality," 315–16 (African American protest meetings).

For just a hint of the interest in law in this period, see *Western Appeal* 15 February 1890, 1 (public debate on civil rights law); *Chicago Daily News* 4 February 1886, 1 (sermon attacking law); *Chicago Tribune* 6 July 1885, 8 (sermon on the meaning of law); *Chicago Daily News* 5 February 1886, 2 (brief editorial on sermon the day before); *Chicago Tribune* 12 April 1888, 4 (bar association meeting in defense of law); *Chicago Daily News* 10 March 1884, 4 (lecture on the failures of civil rights); *Chicago Tribune* 2 March 1888, 4 (editorial refers to calls for child labor laws by Chicago's Ethical Culture Society); *Chicago Daily News* 1 February 1884, 1 (African American community holds protest meeting concerning nonenforcement of civil rights laws in the South); Sawislak, *Smoldering City*, 227–28 (ethnically diverse Committee of Twenty-five debates law enforcement), and 229–30 (formation of Committee of Seventy, which called for strict enforcement of "their moral and civic vision"); *Chicago Daily News* 25 December 1886, 3 (Citizens Association recommends reform of County Board); *Chicago Daily News* 18 January 1887, 1 (Citizens Association questions safety features of Chicago theaters, proposes to personally inspect them all); *Chicago Tribune* 1 July 1887, 5 (neighborhood gathering at Butterfield and Dearborn forces city to enforce laws against houses of prostitution in neighborhood).

The papers devoted much space to law as well. E.g., *Chicago Daily News* 3 July 1886, 4 (law being mocked in Chicago); *Chicago Daily News* 15 March 1886, 2 (failure to enforce liquor laws); *Chicago Daily News* 13 November 1886, 2 (attacking judge for creating a loophole). Sometimes this turned into an attack on lawyers. *Chicago Daily News* 1 March 1886, 2; *Chicago Tribune* 12 April 1888, 4 (editorial on legal system); *Chicago Herald* 13 May 1888, 4 (editorial on law's delay); and a letter to the editor on that same subject, *Chicago Herald* 2 March 1888, 4.

51. The quotation is from Masters, *Tale of Chicago*, 241, see also 279–80. Compare *Chicago Daily News* 23 December 1885, 2 (article condemning nonenforcement of criminal laws), with *Chicago Daily News* 13 November 1886, 2 (article condemning judge for a strict reading of a law in a criminal case).

For examples of the way appeals to law were made and rejected in the context of the Haymarket trial, see *Alarm* 28 November 1887, 3; *Alarm* 17 December 1887, 3; *Alarm* 14 January 1888, 2; *Chicago Inter-Ocean* 15 October 1887, 2; *Chicago Daily News* 4 August 1886, 2; *Chicago Tribune* 3 September 1886, 3; *Chicago Tribune* 4 September 1886, 4; *Chicago Tribune* 1

October 1886, 6; *Chicago Tribune* 1 October 1886, 4. This was not confined to Chicago. See, from *Frank Leslie's Illustrated Newspaper*, 30 October 1886, 163 (calling the Knights of Labor anarchists); 10 July 1886, 338–39 (anarchists like only one law, the one protecting their freedom of speech); 10 July 1886, 322–23 (quotation about Gary, judge in Haymarket trial); 24 November 1888, 231.

52. From the *Western Appeal*: 4 July 1888, 2 (Maryland story); 25 February 1888, 3 (recounting Klan activity in Mississippi); 22 December 1888, 2 (editorial discussing "Southern feelings towards the Negro" in light of "the lynchings, murders, and mobs that have followed the election"). On the treatment of black men accused of raping white women, see *Western Appeal* 2 July 1887, 1 (African Americans in Oak Ridge, La., protest against lynchings); 3 September 1887, 1 (young African American kills himself after being accused of rape); 24 December 1887, 1 (noting how odd it was that only after slavery ended did whites decide that blacks were rapists); 25 August 1888, 2 (black man shot for allegedly writing insulting letter to white woman).

53. *Western Appeal* 17 July 1888, 1.

54. *Western Appeal* 6 August 1887, 1 (Polk story); 13 October 1888, 2 (black accused of rape, tried, found not guilty); 9 June 1888, 2 (evidence discovered after victim lynched establishes his innocence).

55. *Western Appeal* 28 January 1888, 1 (trial leads to injustice); 1 October 1887, 1; 28 January 1888, 1.

56. See Dale, "Social Equality."

57. *Chicago Tribune* 2 March 1888, 4 (editorial).

58. *Chicago Inter-Ocean* 3 March 1888, 3. French apparently was the owner of one of Chicago's African American–owned catering services. See Spear, *Black Chicago*, 111.

59. For a more extended discussion of this dynamic, see Dale, "Social Equality"; Adler, "The Negro Would be More than an Angel."

60. On the motion for a continuance following a change of attorney, see *Chicago Tribune* 16 March 1888, 8. Affidavit of Zephyr Davis in Support of Motion for Continuance, dated 28 March 1888, and Affidavit of Sophia Davis in Support of Motion for Continuance, dated 28 March 1888, *People v. Zephyr Davis*; *Chicago Times*, 29 March 1888, 4; *Chicago Daily News* 28 March 1888, 1. See also Affidavit of Thomas Brown in Support of Motion for Change of Venue, dated 17 March 1888, and Affidavit of Charles J. Burks in Support of Motion for Change of Venue, dated 17 March 1888, *People v. Zephyr Davis*; *Chicago Daily News* 19 March 1888, 1.

61. Consider the discussion of similar problems of access in Ryan, *Civic Wars*.

Chapter 3

1. *Chicago Inter-Ocean* 29 March 1888, 6. To get a sense of the papers' reaction to the delays, see *Chicago Daily News* 20 March 1888, 8; *Chicago Daily News* 28 March 1888, 1; *Chicago Tribune* 20 March 1888, 6; *Chicago Times* 29 March 1888, 3. On law's delays more generally, see *Chicago Herald* 2 March 1888, 4 (letter to the editor from "Lex.") On the arrest dates of the various murder defendants, see *Chicago Inter-Ocean* 10 March 1888, 6.

2. Affidavit of Zephyr Davis in Support of Motion for Continance, dated 28 March 1888; Affidavit of Sophia Davis in Support of Motion for Continuance, dated 28 March 1888. *Chicago Daily News* 28 March 1888, 1; *Chicago Times* 29 March 1888, 4 (W. F. Storey column); *Chicago Daily News* 29 March 1888, 1; *Chicago Inter-Ocean* 29 March 1888, 6; *Chicago Her-*

ald 29 March 1888, 1 (paper claimed to have learned that Caldwell denied ever having seen Davis have fits); *Chicago Tribune* 29 March 1888, 3.

3. *Chicago Tribune* 29 March 1888, 3. The standards for a continuance were set out in *Dacey v. Illinois*, 116 Ill. 555 (1886). *Dacey* also discusses proof of insanity; see also the elaboration of the rule in *Langdon v. Illinois*, 133 Ill. 382, 404, 24 N.E. 874 (1890) ("As a general rule, where insanity is proven as existing at a particular period, it will be presumed to continue until disproved."); Wharton, *Treatise on Criminal Law*, 1:94, sec. 63. Although that rule might seem to have obliged Hawes to admit the evidence, it is not clear it applied in Zephyr's case, since his defense seemed to be a sort of temporary insanity based on his fits. The problem of proving insanity based on past evidence of insanity was an issue in the *Dacey* case. The issue of temporary versus permanent insanity, and the problems the legal system faced in trying to deal with claims of temporary insanity, are described in detail in Rosenberg, *Trial of the Assassin Guiteau*.

4. *Chicago Inter-Ocean* 29 March 1888, 5; *Chicago Times* 29 March 1888, 3; *Chicago Herald* 29 March 1888, 1. Trials, especially murder trials, were typically conducted before packed courtrooms. Compare the news accounts of the "trunk murder," *Chicago Times* 24 June 1885, 5; *Chicago Times* 26 June 1885, 6; and the Mulkowski murder case, *Chicago Times* 5 November 1885, 8. On the Haymarket trial, see Avrich, *Haymarket Tragedy*, chap. 7.

5. *Chicago Tribune* 29 March 1888, 3. Motion for the Creation of a Commission *de lunatico inquirendo*, 28 March 1888, *People v. Zephyr Davis*. Umphrey describes a similar commission in a New York case in "Dialogics of Legal Meaning." On the burdens of proof in insanity cases in Illinois, see *Dacey v. Illinois*, 116 Ill. 555 (1886); for a discussion of shifting the burden of proof, see Wharton, *Treatise on Criminal Law* 1:89, sec. 60.

6. The motion to quash is not in the court file, so it was probably an oral motion. According to one news account, the motion argued that the indictment was flawed because it charged murder but did not include the lesser charge of manslaughter. *Chicago Inter-Ocean* 29 March 1888, 3. The motion was also discussed in *Chicago Times* 29 March 1888, 3. The motion probably also reflected the defense desire to offer an insanity defense, since it seemed consistent with the principle that "when a defendant is charged with a deliberate homicide, and he offers evidence to show that the condition of his mind was such (by reason of insane predisposition) that he was incapable at the time of deliberation, then, if the jury has a reasonable doubt as to such capacity, he is to be acquitted of the higher grade and convicted of the lower grade of the offense." Wharton, *Criminal Law* 1:93, sec. 63. That was not, however, the standard in Illinois; see *Hopps v. Illinois*, 31 Ill. at 390–91.

7. The general procedure is described in Illinois Revised Statutes, chap. 28, secs. 21, 23. A different process was followed in the trunk murder case, where the lawyers passed on panels of twelve. *Chicago Times* 25 June 1885, 10 (discussing the change in procedure). There were different approaches used by different judges in the Cook County courts, though not all of them passed muster on appeal. *Donovan v. Illinois*, 139 Ill. 412 (1891) (judge did all the examining of prospective jurors; appellate court struck down practice and reversed verdict). The standard for a challenge for cause is set out in *Coughlin v. Illinois*, 144 Ill. 140, 163–66 (1893).

Jury selection could take a few hours or several days. Usually, in the case of a single defendant, the process took about a full court day. Consider the discussion of the Mulkowski jury selection in *Chicago Times* 5 November 1885, 8; *Chicago Times* 6 November 1885, 6. In cases with multiple defendants, like the trunk murder, it could take two or more. *Chicago Times* 24 June 1885, 5; *Chicago Times* 25 June 1885, 10; *Chicago Times* 26 June 1885, 6; *Chicago Times*

27 June 1885, 6. In the Haymarket trial in 1886, things took much longer; see Avrich, *Haymarket Tragedy*, 264–65. It took nearly a day and a half to pick a jury in the Davis case, a long time given that he was the lone defendant.

Compare the description of contemporary practice in New York in Winslow, *Recollections of Forty Years*, 304, and the discussion of jury selection in the early twentieth century in Goldstein, *Trial Technique*, sec. 221.

8. *Chicago Tribune* 29 March 1888, 3; *Chicago Inter-Ocean* 29 March 1888, 6.

9. *Chicago Herald* 29 March 1888, 1; *Chicago Tribune* 29 March 1888, 3.

10. *Chicago Inter-Ocean* 29 March 1888, 3. Compare Avrich, *Haymarket Tragedy*, 264–65. For a more contemporaneous, fictional account of jury selection in the Haymarket trial which makes it clear that the judge in that case also guided the jurors, see Herrick, *Memoirs of an American Citizen*, 89–90.

11. *Chicago Inter-Ocean* 29 March 1888, 6; *Chicago Tribune* 29 March 1888, 3.

12. *Chicago Inter-Ocean* 29 March 1888, 6; *Chicago Tribune* 29 March 1888, 3; *Chicago Daily News* 29 March 1888, 1 (Hawes's quotation). Scruples about the death penalty were typically considered grounds for granting a challenge for cause. See, e.g., *Chicago Times* 26 June 1885, 6 (trunk murder case).

13. *Chicago Daily News* 29 March 1888, 1; *Chicago Inter-Ocean* 30 March 1888, 7; *Chicago Tribune* 30 March 1888, 9.

14. *Smith v. Eames*, 4 Ill. 76 (1841).

15. *Smith v. Eames*, 4 Ill. at 80. Illinois Revised Statutes, chap. 78, sec. 14(3).

16. *Plummer v. Illinois*, 74 Ill. 361, 365–66 (1874).

17. Avrich, *Haymarket Tragedy*, 265, also 264–67.

18. *Spies v. Illinois*, 122 Ill. 1, 262–65 (1887).

19. *Coughlin v. Illinois*, 144 Ill. 140, 182–84 (1893). The decision was entered over the dissent of two justices. See 144 Ill. at 189–96.

20. Lindberg, *To Serve and Collect*, chap. 5; Luning, "Irish Blood," 31. See also Hunt, *Crime of the Century*; and "The Cronin Case," a pamphlet on the *Coughlin* trial (the victim's name was Cronin) published by the *Chicago Inter-Ocean*.

21. The quotation is from David Davis, "Annual Address of the President," 35, 42 (emphasis in original). Not every member of the Bar Association agreed that jurors had the power to disregard the law in criminal trials. See Green, "Arrest, Detention, Trial," 67, 71 (arguing that jurors had to follow the law they were given by the judge, and that the judge had the power to reverse any verdict that was not consistent with the law and order a new trial). See also Citizens Association of Chicago, *Annual Report, 1886*, 43–44 (proposing reforms of the jury selection process in the aftermath of the Haymarket trial), and *Annual Report, 1888*, 6–7 (discussing the failure of jury reform legislation and blaming press and political pressure).

Davis's argument that juries were a vital educational tool is set out in "Annual Address of the President," 38–41; for his argument about mob rule, see 42. See also Edwards, "Annual Address of the President," 35, 36. Consider also the arguments made by the various newspapers in this decade; e.g., *Chicago Inter-Ocean* 14 November 1886, 12 (editorial arguing that full disclosure of all information relating to a crime was a vital duty of the press); *Alarm* 17 December 1887, 2.

22. *Frank Leslie's Illustrated Newspaper* 17 July 1886, 347.

23. Denslow, "The Relation of the Organization of the Courts to Law Reform," 52, 54–55, quotation on 55. Although he went on to argue that law should be reformed, his concern was

punishment, not substance (62–64). See also Ewing, "Study of Law in Popular Education," 65, 70–71. For the argument that the passage of more laws would not correct social problems or protect the people, see Edwards, "Annual Report of the President," 44–45. There were judges who made the argument that tyranny acted through law; see, e.g., the discussion of law in the novel *A Century of Caste* by an Illinois judge, Abra Waterman (67–85), and discussion of the novel in Dale, "Social Equality," 332–33. For a contrary argument, see the discussion of the importance of judge-made law as compared to statutory law in Wiecek, *Lost World of Classical Legal Thought*, 98–100, esp. 99.

24. Fuller, "Annual Address of the President," 59, 60–61. Other members of the Bar Association argued that public attention to trials was a necessary part of a democratic, common law society. E.g., Greene, "Popular Opinions of Law," 88, 93. Others took no position pro or con, concluding merely that the legal system essentially worked. For an editorial attacking trial by newspaper as a form of intimidation, see *Frank Leslie's Illustrated Newspaper* 10 September 1887, 50.

25. *Chicago Inter-Ocean* 31 March 1888, 6; *Chicago Daily News* 30 March 1888, 1; *Chicago Herald* 30 March 1888, 2.

26. *Chicago Tribune* 30 March 1888, 9. The farmer was apparently named George Cole. For another account of his examination, see *Chicago Daily News* 29 March 1888, 6.

27. *Chicago Daily News* 29 March 1888, 1; *Chicago Daily News* 2 April 1888, 1 (quotation). *Chicago Tribune* 29 March 1888, 3; *Chicago Tribune* 30 March 1888, 9; *Chicago Times* 29 March 1888, 3; *Chicago Herald* 29 March 1888, 1; *Chicago Inter-Ocean* 31 March 1888, 6. On occasion, the *Chicago Daily News* also treated Zephyr's conduct as an act, e.g., 28 March 1888, 1.

28. Consider the descriptions of Heitzke, *Chicago Daily News* 15 February 1888, 1 ("sits stolidly, with a stupid, unmeaning stare on his face"); Mike Lynch, *Chicago Daily News* 18 January 1888, 1 ("has not a pleasant face. It is foxy, furtive, cunning, and about the mouth are lines denoting the man's cruel nature."). On Davis's behavior at the inquest, see *Chicago Times* 1 March 1888, 5 (defiant); *Chicago Daily News* 29 February 1888, 1 (unconcerned, jocular); and at a hearing, *Chicago Daily News* 28 March 1888, 1 (indifferent and stupid).

29. *Chicago Herald* 30 March 1888, 2; *Chicago Herald* 31 March 1888, 5. The spelling of the jurors' names changes depending on the paper. Rhodes was sometimes referred to as Rose, Gerold was sometimes Jerrold, and Ramaker was sometimes Reneaker. Compare *Chicago Herald* 31 March 1888, 5, and *Chicago Inter-Ocean* 30 March 1888, 7. The verdict form has their signatures on it, but they are not much help in determining the proper spellings of the names. Jury Verdict, *People v. Zephyr Davis*.

30. *Chicago Herald* 31 March 1888, 5. Compare the *Inter-Ocean*, which characterized Mrs. Gaughan's testimony as "of not much value," 31 March 1888, 6.

31. *Chicago Inter-Ocean* 31 March 1888, 6; *Chicago Herald* 31 March 1888, 5; *Chicago Tribune* 31 March 1888, 14. Interestingly, there is no subpoena for Carpenter in the court file, suggesting that he was a surprise witness.

32. *Chicago Herald* 31 March 1888, 5; *Chicago Tribune* 31 March 1888, 14.

33. *Chicago Herald* 31 March 1888, 5. The *Chicago Tribune* quotes Carpenter as saying it was a "damn pretty thing for a nigger to do," 31 March 1888, 14.

34. *Chicago Herald* 31 March 1888, 5; *Chicago Tribune* 31 March 1888, 14; *Chicago Inter-Ocean* 31 March 1888, 6.

35. See the discussion of the testimony in *Chicago Inter-Ocean* 31 March 1888, 6. On the need to provide convincing narratives of the crime for jurors, see Dee, "Constraints on

Persuasion," esp. 86, 89; Gobert, *Justice, Democracy, and the Jury*, 4; Umphrey, "Dialogics of Legal Meaning."

36. The motif is discussed in Cohen, "Beautiful Female Murder Victim." For histories that describe trials that successfully fit the facts of the case into a familiar or master narrative, see Carmichael, *Framing History* (a study of the Rosenberg case); Boyer and Nissenbaum, *Salem Possessed*. The necessity of developing a theory of the case, and explaining it clearly to the jury, is a standard of trial advocacy books; see, e.g., Goldstein, *Trial Technique*, secs. 649–50; McElhaney, *McElhaney's Trial Notebook*, chap. 5. The idea that a familiar narrative makes a case more persuasive and leads jurors to fill in gaps in the evidence is discussed in Brooks, "Law as Narrative and Rhetoric," esp. 17–18; and Umphrey, "Dialogics of Legal Meaning" (where the defense counsel creates a persuasive narrative by fitting it into contemporary theories of honor). See also the various essays in Brooks and Gewirtz, *Law's Stories*, especially Weisberg, "Proclaiming Trials as Narrative."

37. One way the image was familiar, of course, was through plays like *Othello*. On popular familiarity with Shakespeare, and *Othello* in particular, in this period, see Levine, *Highbrow/Lowbrow*, esp. 14–16. Levine notes that *Othello* was often turned into a racist farce or used as a basis of racist humor (16). And see the comments of John Quincy Adams, quoted in ibid., 39.

38. Chicago had a rather mixed-up understanding of interracial sex. There were interracial couples, and the discussions about Frederick Douglass's recent marriage to a white woman in the local papers were not particularly hostile. Dale, "Social Equality." At the same time, interracial sexuality was associated with the Levee and low-class decadence. *Chicago Daily News* 2 February 1884, 5 (story of dive full of interracial couples); *Chicago Daily News* 1 October 1888, 1 (prosecutor in Sam Wah case refers to "deep public sentiment against the union of different races").

39. The quotation is from Bruce, *Plantation Negro as a Freeman*, 83–85. Fredrickson, *Black Image in the White Mind*, chap. 9. Compare the discussion of defense strategies when faced with a coherent, and seemingly familiar, narrative, in Dershowitz, "Life Is Not a Dramatic Narrative," 99–100. Attacks by the defense on women victims worked sometimes and failed others; see Halttunen, *Murder Most Foul*, 148–49 (Earle case), 150 (Getter case), 184–86 (Cornell case). See also Cohen, *Murder of Helen Jewett*. Compare Wellman, *Art of Cross-Examination*, chap. 7.

40. In Chicago, the Knights of Labor had organized the teamsters across industries by 1886, so it is possible that Gaughan and Carpenter knew each other or felt some sort of guild tie. Commons, "Types of American Labor Organization," 401.

41. See Wellman, *Art of Cross-Examination*, chap. 7 (esp. the discussion of silent cross-examination).

42. The technique was not uncommon and could be quite successful. See Cohen, *Murder of Helen Jewett*, 306 and chap. 15 generally.

43. *Chicago Times* 1 April 1888, 1; *Chicago Daily News* 31 March 1888, 1.

44. *Chicago Times* 1 April 1888, 1; *Chicago Daily News* 31 March 1888, 1 (evening edition); *Chicago Tribune* 1 April 1888, 2.

45. Moyer's admission that there was no evidence of attempted rape was reported by the *Chicago Tribune* 1 April 1888, 2.

46. *Chicago Tribune* 1 April 1888, 2; *Chicago Times* 1 April 1888, 1.

47. *Chicago Times* 1 April 1888, 1; *Chicago Tribune* 1 April 1888, 2. Letting lay witnesses provide evidence of insanity was common enough in this period, though many defendants

used expert testimony. Rosenberg, *Trial of the Assassin Guiteau*; Ireland, "The Libertine Must Die," 160–61. While it helped to have money to pay for experts, there were working-class defendants who called expert witnesses to establish their insanity claims. Wharton, *Criminal Law* 1:87, sec. 56. See the reports of the experts called to testify in the Busch trial, *Chicago Daily News* 24 April 1888, 1; *Chicago Daily News* 25 April 1888, 1.

48. *Chicago Times* 1 April 1888, 1; *Chicago Tribune* 1 April 1888, 2.

49. *Chicago Tribune* 1 April 1888, 2.

50. *Chicago Times* 1 April 1888, 1.

51. Ibid.

52. For a case involving a combination of lay and expert testimony, see Pucci, *Trials of Maria Barbella*. Compare Rosenberg, *Trial of the Assassin Guiteau*, 66–68 (discussing expert testimony and the problems that could arise from its use). The rise of the use of experts in insanity cases corresponded, generally, to the increased reliance on experts in medical malpractice cases. De Ville, *Medical Malpractice in Nineteenth-Century America*; Cleman, "Irresistible Impulse," 625–26.

53. For the connection between the physical and the mental in contemporary theories of insanity, see in Skultans, *Madness and Morals*: Alexander Morison, "The Physiognomy of Insanity," 71–77 (describing the appearance of the insane); Henry Maudsley, "Illustrations of a Variety of Insanity," 86–94 (demonstrating how masturbation leads to insanity); and Furneaux Jordan, "Body and Character," 218–22 (body type as an indicator of temperament). In some of these arguments, heredity played a role; Jordan's analysis is a prime example. For examples of how the physical and the mental were confused in the criminal law setting, see the scholarly discussion of the explanations of insanity offered in the context of the Guiteau trial in Rosenberg, *Trial of the Assassin Guiteau*, 63–66 (discussing the intersection of the physical and the mental in general), 67 (discussing the effect of that intersection on trials), and chaps. 3 and 4 generally. A less scholarly but still careful example of similar legal confusion is set out in Pucci, *Trials of Maria Barbella*. See also Wharton, *Criminal Law* 1:94, secs. 63–64.

For examples of epileptics being institutionalized in criminal and noncriminal settings in Europe, see Hopf, "'Cretins' and 'Idiots,'" 19 (noting the practice in late nineteenth-century Austria); Harris, *Murder and Madness*, 41–42. For examples of epilepsy being relied on as proof of insanity in criminal cases, see Winslow, *Recollections of Forty Years*, 163–70, 170–74, 239–41. But see Wharton, *Treatise on Criminal Law* 1:62 n. 4, sec. 44, arguing that epilepsy was not insanity and could only mitigate punishment if proved. But compare ibid., 1:94, sec. 64 (insanity may be inferred from epilepsy). Several works suggest that the problem criminal law had with epilepsy was that the disease was closely associated with Lombroso's idea of a criminal mind, so it could not logically excuse criminal conduct. Harris, *Murder and Madness*, 69, 81; Rosenberg, *Trial of the Assassin Guiteau*, 69.

54. *Hopps v. Illinois*, 31 Ill. at 391–93 (1863), *Dunn v. Illinois*, 109 Ill. 635, 644–45 (1884).

55. *Hopps*, 31 Ill. at 390. See also Wharton, *Treatise on Criminal Law* 1:61–66, secs. 43–44 (discussing irresistible impulse theories of insanity).

56. *Hopps*, 31 Ill. at 389. With respect to the "right and wrong test," see Wharton, who defines it somewhat differently so as to require evidence that the defendant knew what was morally, not legally, right or wrong. *Treatise on Criminal Law* 1:55, sec. 37. Compare the test for temporary insanity set out in *Commonwealth v. Rogers*, 48 Mass. 500 (1844).

For Busch, see, from the *Chicago Daily News*, 7 February 1888, 1 (Busch presented as a remorseless monster but sane); 9 March 1888, 1 (jail officials dismiss Busch's claim of insanity as faked); 13 March 1888, 1 (Busch "playing crazy"); 24 April 1888, 1 (article questioning witnesses who try to establish Busch was insane); 25 April 1888, 1 (expert testimony on Busch); 28 April 1888, 1 (instructions in Busch case). On Busch's transfer to the insane asylum, see *Chicago Daily News* 19 October 1888, 1.

57. *Dacey v. Illinois*, 116 Ill. 555 (1886). This was not the general rule, which provided "a man may act without the concurrence of a responsible will, though he is not raving, though he knows what he is about, and lays and executes his plans with great sagacity." Wharton, *Treatise on Criminal Law* 1:74–75, sec. 47, quoting Sir James Stephens. Compare *Rogers*, 48 Mass. at 503. On juror hostility to insanity defenses, see Train, "Insanity and the Law," 246–47.

58. *The Medical and Surgical Directory of Cook County, Illinois, 1888–1889; Chicago Inter-Ocean* 3 April 1888, 5; *Chicago Daily News* 2 April 1888, 1 (evening edition); *Chicago Tribune* 3 April 1888, 2. In contrast, the *Chicago Herald* reported that Moyer denied that Davis was insane, 3 April 1888, 1.

59. *Chicago Inter-Ocean* 3 April 1888, 5; *Chicago Herald* 3 April 1888, 1. Jail officials were notoriously unwilling to admit prisoners were insane. See *Chicago Daily News* 9 March 1888, 1 (officials explain Busch's suicide attempt as part of his insanity act).

60. *Chicago Inter-Ocean* 3 April 1888, 5; *Chicago Herald* 3 April 1888, 1.

61. *Chicago Herald* 3 April 1888, 1; *Chicago Inter-Ocean* 3 April 1888, 5. Multiple arguments were not unusual; see Cohen, *Murder of Helen Jewett*, 314–16. The jury instructions are in the court file.

62. The actual instruction that the court gave was:

> the court instructs the jury that unless you [unintelligible word] from the evidence beyond a reasonable doubt that the homicide was committed with aforethought either expressed or implied, then you cannot find the defendant guilty of murder. The court instructs the jury that if after hearing all the evidence there exists in your mind a reasonable doubt as to whether the homicide was committed with malice or whether the same was the result of an irresistible passion, then you should not find the defendant guilty of murder.

Writing about his experiences as a prosecutor in the New York court, Arthur Train noted that jurors tended to reduce the punishment rather than acquit when there was evidence of insanity. "Insanity and the Law," 248–49. See also the discussion in Wharton, *Criminal Law* 1:93. The rule from *Hopps* that a finding of partial insanity should lead to an acquittal had been affirmed in *Dacey*, 116 Ill. at 571.

63. *Chicago Inter-Ocean* 3 April 1888, 5.

64. *Chicago Inter-Ocean* 3 April 1888, 5; *Chicago Herald* 3 April 1888, 1; *Chicago Tribune* 3 April 1888, 2; *Chicago Times* 3 April 1888, 8.

65. Roger Smith, "Boundary Between Insanity and Criminal Responsibility in Nineteenth-Century England," in Scull, *Madhouses*, esp. 373. Compare the discussion of strict liability and cases involving psychiatric defenses in Hart, "Principles of Punishment," in his *Punishment and Responsibility*, 19–20.

66. Train, "Insanity and the Law," 250–51. This may explain another phenomenon that historians have identified. Studies have shown that when a husband killed his wife's paramour, or a woman killed a man who had seduced and betrayed her, juries were willing to acquit based on insanity. When a jury found the underlying act incomprehensible or distasteful, however,

it punished it regardless of any evidence concerning the defendant's mental state. This seems like another example of a jury punishing (or not punishing) an act, and using the insanity defense as a means of doing so. Ireland, "The Libertine Must Die," 168–70; Hartog, "Lawyering, Husband's Rights" (explicitly makes the argument that verdicts in those cases reflected social assumptions about marital relations, not law); Umphrey, "Dialogics of Legal Meaning."

67. The quotation about criminal intent is from Bishop, *Commentaries on Criminal Law* 1:235, sec. 375. The statutory grant of the power of nullification was first set out in the Laws of Illinois (1827), sec. 176, p. 163. It was definitively interpreted in *Schnier v. Illinois*, 23 Ill. 17, 30 (1859), and *Fisher v. Illinois*, 23 Ill. 283, 294 (1859). See the discussion of this issue in Dale, "Not Simply Black and White."

68. *Sparf and Hansen v. United States*, 156 U.S. 51 (1895). The Illinois Supreme Court upheld an instruction to the jury about its power to judge the law in 1908. *Illinois v. Campbell*, 234 Ill. 391, 394–95 (1908). It was not until *Illinois v. Bruner*, 343 Ill. 146, 148–56 (1931) that the court held that *Sparf* meant that juries in Illinois could no longer be judges of the law. Even then, one justice dissented. 343 Ill. at 163, 168–71.

69. On the use of this statute in the Haymarket case, see *Spies v. Illinois*, 122 Ill. 1, 252 (1887). For the account of one contemporary who deplored the Haymarket verdict, see McConnell, "Chicago Bomb Case," 730.

70. *Chicago Daily News* 17 February 1888, 1.

71. For other calls to reform the criminal jury, see Capen, "Jury System in Illinois," 54, 63; Gregory, "Trial and Procedure," 51, 59; and the resolutions the Illinois State Bar Association offered in 1883 and 1885, see *Proceedings*, 1883, 38, 40; *Proceedings*, 1885, 22.

72. On Morris, see Dale, "Social Equality."

Chapter 4

1. The Haymarket defendants were executed on November 11, 1887. Avrich, *Haymarket Tragedy*, chap. 23. On reform of executions, see Masur, *Rites of Execution*. For a discussion of Sheriff Matson's effort to close off executions, see *Chicago Tribune* 14 May 1888, 4 (editorial); *Chicago Herald* 13 May 1888, 17 (suggesting that the law barred the public from executions). The execution is described in *Chicago Daily News* 12 May 1888, 1; *Chicago Times* 13 May 1888, 17; *Chicago Herald* 13 May 1888, 17.

The relevant statute provided that executions would be by hanging, and that they should be conducted within the walls of the prison or in a "yard or enclosure adjoining such prison." It also provided that the sheriff "shall invite" the judge, prosecuting attorney, clerk of the court, together with two physicians, and twelve respectable citizens to the execution. The defendant could invite three ministers and members of his immediate family. Prison officials could also be present. *Illinois Laws*, 1885, 533–34, para. 441.

2. On Jones, see the listing in *The Colored Men's Professional and Business Directory of Chicago*, 22–23, 25; and Spear, *Black Chicago*, 62–63. The other members of the jury, in addition to Jones, were Moyer, Dr. A. Doe, Captain Jack Stephens, Thomas Currier, F. F. Caundy, C. I. Danielson, George H. Williams, Dr. A. L. Curry (or Corry), A. B. Hart, Dr. Malcolm Guan (or Gunn), C. J. Adams, H. J. Mitchel, and John Enders. *Chicago Daily News* 12 May 1888, 1. But see *Chicago Herald* 13 May 1888, 17 (which has a shorter list). The George Williams on this jury might also be African American — there was a George Williams who was pastor at the Allen Chapel, a local African American church — but that seems unlikely, since at least one

paper reported that that George Williams was on the scaffold with the Reverend Henderson and Davis. *Chicago Tribune* 13 May 1888, 1. For the creation of that jury, see *Illinois Laws, 1885,* 533–34, para. 441.

3. On the executions in the previous six years, see *Chicago Herald* 13 May 1888, 17. See also *Chicago Daily News* 7 April 1888, 1 (on hearing denying motion for a new trial); *Chicago Times* 5 May 1888, 3 (on preparation of the petition); *Chicago Times* 10 May 1888, 3 (indicating two days before the execution that the governor had decided against the petition); *Chicago Daily News* 12 May 1888, 1 (on telegram the day of the execution denying petition).

Executions were popular subjects not just for the press in Chicago; they were generally popular aspects of Victorian literature, and they were covered in all sorts of accounts. See discussion in Knelman, *Twisting in the Wind,* esp. chap. 2.

4. *Chicago Times* 4 April 1888, 4 (editorial); *Chicago Inter-Ocean* 4 April 1888, 4 (editorial).

5. *Chicago Tribune* 8 April 1888, 9.

6. Ibid.

7. *Chicago Daily News* 7 April 1888, 1.

8. Ibid.

9. *Chicago Inter-Ocean* 3 April 1888, 5; *Chicago Inter-Ocean* 4 April 1888, 4 (editorial); *Chicago Times* 3 April 1888, 8; *Chicago Herald* 3 April 1888, 1. The beginnings of these articles are quite different; it is only about halfway through that they become identical. That is the general pattern: stories that are the same at the beginning often had different endings, those that began differently sometimes ended the same way.

10. *Chicago Daily News* 9 April 1888, 2.

11. *Chicago Tribune* 12 April 1888, 4.

12. *Chicago Daily News* 10 April 1888, 1 (fight with Greene); *Chicago Daily News* 20 April 1888, 1 (reference to assault on reporter, which took place the previous week); *Chicago Daily News* 5 May 1888, 1 (grand jury visit); *Chicago Daily News* 12 May 1888, 1 (shackled because of violent outbursts).

13. *Chicago Daily News* 7 April 1888, 1 (drawing pictures and acting childishly sullen); *Chicago Daily News* 13 April 1888, 1 (shows unconcern about fate); *Chicago Daily News* 8 May 1888, 1 (good spirits, singing, laughing); *Chicago Daily News* 11 May 1888, 1 (chuckleheaded, mocks minister).

14. *Chicago Daily News* 13 April 1888, 1 (sees minister); *Chicago Daily News* 7 May 1888, 1 (asks to see minister); *Chicago Daily News* 11 May 1888, 1 (writing scaffold speech).

15. *Chicago Tribune* 4 April 1888, 8 (says nothing, acts sullen); *Chicago Tribune* 11 April 1888, 7 (scene with Greene); *Chicago Tribune* 14 April 1888, 8 (morose and sulky); *Chicago Tribune* 24 April 1888, 8 (assaults Dr. Gray); *Chicago Tribune* 9 May 1888, 8 (good-natured); *Chicago Tribune* 10 May 1888, 8 (ignores black women).

16. *Chicago Tribune* 13 May 1888, 10.

17. *Chicago Herald* 12 May 1888, 2 (sad scenes with family, but paper continues to describe Davis as stolid, not very bright, and incapable of understanding what is going on). *Chicago Times* 10 May 1888, 3; *Chicago Times* 13 May 1888, 17 (first page of the third sec.). Compare the *Times*'s description in an editorial of Davis immediately after the trial, 4 April 1888, 4 ("a savage as destitute of feeling as a mad dog").

18. From the *Chicago Inter-Ocean:* 11 April 1888, 7 (attack on Greene); 14 April 1888, 7 (sullen attitude); 15 April 1888, 6 (attacks reporter, demands to be "sent to the dungeon"); 6 May

1888, 6 (scene with grand jury); 7 May 1888, 8 (no longer brutish but may be a ruse); 8 May 1888, 6 (subdued and polite seeming); 10 May 1888, 5 (stolid reaction to churchwomen).

19. *Chicago Inter-Ocean* 12 May 1888, 6 (interview with Davis, includes story of girl-friend); *Chicago Inter-Ocean* 12 May 1888, 7 (interview with Longenecker).

20. *Chicago Times* 12 November 1885, 3 (last days of the three Italians in the trunk case); *Chicago Times* 26 March 1886, 6 (Mulkowski). On the accounts of the Haymarket defendants, see Avrich, *Haymarket Tragedy*, chap. 23 (relying chiefly on labor papers). Michael Schaack, whose study is an apology for the outcome of the trial, also suggests that the defendants were described more sympathetically in their last days. Schaack, *Anarchy and Anarchists*, 640–41. Also on the Haymarket defendants, see, from the *National Police Gazette*, 19 November 1887, 8–9 (discussion of defendants' deathwatch); 26 November 1887, 1 (full-page sketch of the execution), 8–9 (a page of scenes of the defendants from the evening before the execution); 3 December 1887, 1 (picture of Lucy Parsons, wife of one of the defendants, sobbing at her husband's coffin).

21. *Chicago Times* 11 May 1888, 8. Henderson was the minister at Quinn Chapel, an African American church originally founded in 1847. On Henderson, see Harris, *Colored Men's Professional and Business Directory*, 11; Drake, *Churches and Voluntary Associations*, 72 (discussion of Quinn Chapel); the listing for Quinn Chapel, A.M.E. Church, in *Chicago Lakeside Directory*, 1888; and the discussion in Spear, *Black Chicago*, chap. 5.

22. Application for the Pardon of Zephyr Davis, No. 953, May 9, 1888.

23. In this respect, Arney's letter repeated the weak claim of insanity that was set out in the jury instruction and ignored the actual rule of *Hopps*.

24. E.g., *Western Appeal* 1 October 1887, 1; *Western Appeal* 28 January 1888, 1.

25. Gaines, *Uplifting the Race*, esp. chap. 6.

26. *Chicago Times* 10 May 1888, 17; *Chicago Times* 13 May 1888, 17; *Chicago Tribune* 9 May 1888, 8 (discussing Hawes's motivations in petitioning the governor).

27. *Chicago Daily News* 11 May 1888, 1; *Chicago Tribune* 12 May 1888, 2 (this is one instance where the language in the two accounts is identical). See also the mention of the petition in *Chicago Times* 10 May 1888, 17; *Chicago Times* 12 May 1888, 4 (James J. West column). There is no record of her telegram or Oglesby's response in the clemency file.

28. *Chicago Tribune* 13 May 1888, 10 (the only account that describes the nightmares); *Chicago Times* 11 May 1888, 8; *Chicago Times* 12 May 1888, 2 (last day described; the first part of this article is almost identical to the account in *Chicago Tribune* 12 May 1888, 20; *Chicago Herald* 13 May 1888, 17). For the literary tradition, see Papke, *Framing the Criminal*, 62; compare Avrich, *Haymarket Tragedy*, chap. 23.

29. *Chicago Times* 13 May 1888, 17; *Chicago Herald* 13 May 1888, 17.

30. The passage was Job 7:1–9.

31. The different papers punctuate the speech differently, but all have essentially the same account. *Chicago Times* 13 May 1888, 17; *Chicago Daily News* 12 May 1888, 1; *Chicago Tribune* 13 May 1888, 10; *Chicago Herald* 13 May 1888, 17. See also the different ways that the *Chicago Daily News* treated this in different editions dated 12 May 1888, 1 (earliest story does not describe the prayers, hymn, or speech; later edition mentions all).

32. *Chicago Times* 13 May 1888, 17; *Chicago Times* 13 May 1888, 4 (James J. West column). Compare the descriptions of earlier executions in Masur, *Rites of Execution*; Gatrell, *The Hanging Tree*.

33. *Chicago Daily News* 12 May 1888, 1; *Chicago Herald* 13 May 1888, 17.

34. The exception to the consensus that Davis had behaved bravely was the *Chicago Herald*, which concluded that his conduct was evidence that he was too stupid to know what was happening. *Chicago Herald* 13 May 1888, 17.

Henderson was described in a respectful fashion in the accounts about the Davis case, as were other African American ministers in other stories. E.g., *Chicago Daily News* 12 July 1886, 4 (describing a black Catholic priest from Quincy, Ill.). So, too, African American lawyers were typically described in complimentary terms. *Chicago Inter-Ocean* 6 March 1888, 4 (briefly describes Frederick McGhee, black lawyer who represented Davis, in terms that made it clear he was much more impressive than Davis). But status did not guarantee polite treatment in the press. *Chicago Daily News* 9 November 1888, 1 (article mocks African American court clerk who went into a panic and foolishly predicted a race war). For a more extended discussion of descriptions of African Americans in this period, see Dale, "Social Equality." On notions of manliness, and the significance of race in defining it, see generally Bederman, *Manliness and Civilization*; and Gaines, *Uplifting the Race*, esp. 52, 199.

35. Papke, *Framing the Criminal*, 61–62.

36. For a discussion of how those concerns played out in other situations, see Dale, "Social Equality."

37. In chapter 3 of the Book of Job, Job cursed his fate. In the next several chapters, Eliphaz responded and reprimanded Job.

38. The comments of Eliphaz are at Job 4:1–5.27. Job's response is at Job 6:1–7.21.

39. *Chicago Daily News* 12 May 1888, 1, and *Chicago Tribune* 13 May 1888, 10 (both claiming verse was from a psalm); *Chicago Times* 13 May 1888, 17 (correct identification but not quoted); *Chicago Herald* 13 May 1888, 17 (from A.M.E. funeral service).

40. *Chicago Tribune* 13 April 1888, 10; *Chicago Times* 13 April 1888, 17; *Chicago Daily News* 12 May 1888, 1 (noting that the crowd within the jail was composed of blacks and whites, and that those who were not 21 or older were excluded).

41. *Chicago Daily News* 12 May 1888, 1 (the "_____" is in the original quotation).

42. *Chicago Tribune* 14 May 1888, 4 (editorial). These descriptions of the crowd also fit within a general pattern, albeit one that most scholars claim was manifested in the antebellum period. Masur, *Rites of Execution*, 19–24.

43. *Chicago Herald* 13 May 1888, 17.

44. Ibid.; *Chicago Times* 14 May 1888, 5; *Chicago Inter-Ocean* 14 May 1888, 8; *Chicago Inter-Ocean* 12 May 1888, 15.

45. *Chicago Inter-Ocean* 15 May 1888, 6.

Conclusion

1. *Chicago Times* 1 January 1887, 6; *Chicago Inter-Ocean* 1 January 1887, 7. The case is reported at *Dougherty v. Illinois*, 118 Ill. 160 (1886).

2. *Chicago Times* 1 January 1887, 6; *Dougherty*, 118 Ill. at 162; Chicago Homicide Records, under Nicholas Johns. Once again, I am indebted to Jeffrey Adler for the statistics. See also his discussion of male-on-male homicide in Chicago, in "My Mother-in-Law is to Blame," 255–57.

3. Gary, "Chicago Anarchists," 803, 809, 809.

4. Ibid., 836. While spousal abuse might be grounds for a divorce in some states, it was not subject to criminal prosecution. See discussions in Edwards, *Gendered Strife*; Siegel, "Rule of Love," 2117.

5. "The law," as he put it, "is common sense." Gary, "Chicago Anarchists," 802, 836, quoting his speech at the sentencing of the Haymarket defendants.

6. Altgeld, "Executive Pardon Issued at Springfield, June 26, 1893," in *Mind and Spirit of John Peter Altgeld*, 63, 66–81.

7. Ibid., 94–95, 103.

8. Ibid., 86–88, citing Illinois Constitution, sec. 17, art. 2.

9. Friedman and Percival, *Roots of Justice*, 237–38.

10. Gilfoyle, *City of Eros*, esp. chap. 14.

11. Smith, *Urban Disorder*, chap. 8. On trials as narratives, see Batt, "American Legal Populism," 651 (esp. his discussion of Gerry Spence's trial technique); McElhaney, *McElhaney's Trial Notebook*, chap. 5. See generally Brooks and Gewirtz, *Law's Stories*. On trials as struggles between law and justice, with the judge representing law and the jury justice, see Gobert, *Justice, Democracy and the Jury*.

12. Umphrey, "Dialogics of Legal Meaning."

13. See generally the essays in Brooks and Gewirth, *Law's Stories*.

14. This discussion is influenced by Holub, *Antonio Gramsci*, esp. chap. 5.

BIBLIOGRAPHY

Manuscript Collections and Court Records

Application for the Pardon of Zephyr Davis, no. 953, May 9, 1888. Executive Clemency Files, Illinois State Archives. Springfield, Illinois.

Carter Harrison II Papers. Newberry Library, Chicago.

Case file, *People v. Zephyr Davis*, indictment number 21222a, term number 1158, Circuit Court of Cook County, Illinois. Box 3a-32-b-48, Cook County Court Records, Cook County Archives. Chicago, Illinois.

Chicago Foreign Language Press Survey. Special Collections, University of Chicago. Boxes 10, 15, 22.

Chicago Police Department, *Homicides and Other Events, 1870–1910*. Roll no. 30-2293, Illinois State Archives. Springfield, Illinois.

Cases and Other Published Legal Materials

Commonwealth v. Rogers, 48 Mass. 500 (1844)
Coughlin v. Illinois, 144 Ill. 140 (1893)
Dacey v. Illinois, 116 Ill. 555 (1886)
Donovan v. Illinois, 139 Ill. 412 (1891)
Dougherty v. Illinois, 118 Ill. 160 (1886)
Dunn v. Illinois, 109 Ill. 635 (1884)
Fisher v. Illinois, 23 Ill. 283 (1859)
Hopps v. Illinois, 31 Ill. 385 (1863)
Lyons v. Illinois, 137 Ill. 602, 27 N.E. 677 (1891)
Plummer v. Illinois, 74 Ill. 361 (1874)
Schneir v. Illinois, 23 Ill. 17 (1859)
Smith v. Eames, 4 Ill. 76 (1841)
Spies v. Illinois, 122 Ill. 1 (1887), 122 U.S. 131 (1887)

Newspapers

The Alarm (Chicago)
Catholic Home (Chicago)
Chicago Daily News
Chicago Herald

Chicago Inter-Ocean
Chicago Times
Chicago Tribune
Frank Leslie's Illustrated Newspaper
Irish World and American Industrial Liberator (New York)
The Nation
National Police Gazette
Western Appeal (Chicago and Minneapolis)
Western Catholic

Articles

Adler, Jeffrey S. "'My Mother-in-Law is to Blame, But I'll Walk on her Neck Yet': Homicide in Late Nineteenth-Century Chicago." *Journal of Social History* 31 (Winter 1997): 253–77.
———. "'The Negro Would be More than an Angel to Withstand Such Treatment': African American Homicide in Chicago, 1875–1910." In *Lethal Imagination: Violence and Brutality in American History*, edited by Michael A. Bellesiles, 295–314. New York: New York University Press, 1999.
Bates, Beth Tompkins. "A New Crowd Challenges the Agenda of the Old Guard in the NAACP, 1933–1941." *Journal of American History* 102 (April 1997): 340–77.
Batt, John. "American Legal Populism: A Jurisprudential and Historical Narrative, Including Reflections on Critical Legal Studies." *Northern Kentucky University Law Review* 22 (Summer 1995): 651–761.
Brooks, Peter. "The Law as Narrative and Rhetoric." In *Law's Stories: Narrative and Rhetoric in the Law*, edited by Peter Brooks and Paul Gewirtz, 14–23. New Haven: Yale University Press, 1996.
Capen, Charles L. "The Jury System in Illinois." *Proceedings of the Illinois State Bar Association*, 1883, 54–63. Springfield, 1883.
Cha-Jua, Sundiata Keita. "'Join Hearts and Hands with Law and Order': The 1893 Lynching of Samuel J. Bush and the Response of Decatur's African American Community." *Illinois Historical Journal* 83 (1990): 187–200.
Cleman, John. "Irresistible Impulse: Edgar Allan Poe and the Insanity Defense." *American Literature* 63 (1991): 623–40.
Cohen, Daniel A. "The Beautiful Female Murder Victim: Literary Genres and Courtship Practice in the Origins of a Cultural Motif." *Journal of Social History* 31 (Winter 1997): 277–306.
Commons, John R. "Types of American Labor Organization—The Teamsters of Chicago." *Quarterly Journal of Economics* 19 (1905): 400–433.
Dale, Elizabeth. "Not Simply Black and White: Jury Power and Law in Late Nineteenth-Century Chicago." *Social Science History* 25 (Spring 2001): 7–27.
———. "People versus Zephyr Davis: Law and Popular Justice in Late Nineteenth-Century Chicago." *Law and History Review* 17 (1999): 27–56.
———. "'Social Equality does not Exist among Themselves, Nor among Us': *Baylies vs Curry* and Civil Rights in Chicago, 1888." *American Historical Review* 107 (April 1997): 311–39.
Davis, David. "Annual Address of the President, 1885." *Proceedings of the Illinois State Bar Association*, 1885, 35–44. Springfield, 1885.

Dee, Juliet. "Constraints on Persuasion in the Chicago Seven Trial." In *Popular Trials: Rhetoric, Mass Media, and the Law*, edited by Robert Hariman, 86–113. Tuscaloosa: University of Alabama Press, 1990.

Denslow, Van Buren. "The Relations of the Organization of the Courts to Law Reform." *Proceedings of the Illinois State Bar Association*, 1885, 52–64. Springfield, 1885.

Dershowitz, Alan M. "Life Is Not a Dramatic Narrative." In *Justice and Power in Sociolegal Studies*, edited by Bryant G. Garth and Austin Sarat, 99–105. Evanston: Northwestern University Press, 1998.

Dunbar, William H. "The Anarchists' Case Before the Supreme Court of the United States." *Harvard University Law Review* 1 (February 1888): 307–26.

Edwards, B. S. "Annual Address of the President, 1886." *Proceedings of the Illinois State Bar Association*, 1886, 35–46. Springfield, 1886.

Ewing, James S. "The Study of Law in Popular Education." *Proceedings of the Illinois State Bar Association*, 1885, 65–72. Springfield, 1885.

Fisher, William W., III. "Texts and Contexts: The Application to Legal History of the Methodologies of Intellectual History." *Stanford University Law Review* 49 (May 1997): 1065–110.

Fuller, Melville. "Annual Address of the President, 1887." *Proceedings of the Illinois State Bar Association*, 1887, 59–68. Springfield, 1887.

Galliher, John F., Gregory Ray, and Brent Cook. "Abolition and Reinstatement of Capital Punishment during the Progressive Era and Early 20th Century." *Journal of Law and Criminology* 83 (Fall 1992): 538–76.

Gamson, William A. "The Social Psychology of Collective Action." In *Frontiers in Social Movement Theory*, edited by Aldon D. Morris and Carol McClurg Mueller, 53–76. New Haven: Yale University Press, 1992.

Garth, Bryant G., and Austin Sarat. "Justice and Power in Law and Society Research: On the Contested Careers of Core Concepts." In *Justice and Power in Sociolegal Studies*, edited by Garth and Sarat, 1–18. Evanston: Northwestern University Press, 1998.

Gary, Joseph E. "The Chicago Anarchists of 1886: The Crime, the Trial, and the Punishment." *The Century Magazine* 45 (April 1893): 803–37.

Gordon, Robert W. "Introduction: J. Willard Hurst and the Common Law Tradition in American Legal History." *Law and Society Review* 10 (1975): 9–55.

Green, E. B. "The Arrest, Detention, Trial, Conviction and Punishment of Criminals." *Proceedings of the Illinois State Bar Association*, 1884, 67–75. Springfield, 1884.

Greene, H. S. "Popular Opinions of Law and Those Who Administer It." *Proceedings of the Illinois State Bar Association*, 1887, 67–75. Springfield, 1887.

Gregory, S. S. "Trial and Procedure." *Proceedings of the Illinois State Bar Association*, 1888, 51–61. Springfield, 1888.

Haller, Mark H. "Urban Crime and Criminal Justice: The Chicago Case." *Journal of American History* 57 (December 1970): 619–35.

Haney, Lynn A. "Engendering the Welfare State: A Review Article." *Comparative Studies in Society and History* 50 (October 1998): 748–67.

Harcourt, Bernard E. "Imagery and Adjudication in the Criminal Law: The Relationship Between Images of Criminal Defendants and Ideologies of Criminal Law in Southern Antebellum and Modern Appellate Decisions." *Brooklyn Law Review* 61 (Winter 1995): 1165–246.

Harriman, Robert. "Performing the Laws: Popular Trials and Social Knowledge." In *Popular Trials: Rhetoric, Mass Media and the Law,* edited by Harriman, 17–30. Tuscaloosa: University of Alabama Press, 1993.

Hartog, Hendrik. "Lawyering, Husband's Rights, and the 'Unwritten Law' in Nineteenth-Century America." *Journal of American History* 84 (June 1997): 67–96.

Hoover, Greg A. "Supplemental Family Income Sources: Ethnic Differences in Nineteenth-Century Industrial America." *Social Science History* 9 (Summer 1985): 293–306.

Hopf, Gundrun. "'Cretins' and 'Idiots' in an Austrian Alpine Valley in the Late Nineteenth and Early Twentieth Centuries: Social Norms and Institutions Involved in the Attribution of 'Imbecility.'" *Crime, History, and Societies* 3 (1999): 5–27.

Hughes, John S. "Labelling and Treating Black Mental Illness in Alabama, 1861–1910." *Journal of Southern History* 63 (August 1993): 435–60.

Hunt, Alan. "Anxiety and Social Explanation: Some Anxieties about Anxiety." *Journal of Social History* 32 (Spring 1999): 509–28.

Hurst, James Willard. "The Release of Energy." In *Law and the Conditions of Freedom in the Nineteenth-Century United States.* Madison: University of Wisconsin Press, 1956.

Ireland, Robert M. "Insanity and the Unwritten Law." *American Journal of Legal History* 32 (April 1988): 157–72.

———. "The Libertine Must Die: Sexual Dishonor and the Unwritten Law in the Nineteenth-Century United States." *Journal of Social History* (Spring 1989): 27–44.

"Journal of the American Medical Association 100 Years Ago: The Insanity Dodge." *Journal of American Medicine* 279 (April 15, 1998): 1232A(1).

Kettler, David, and Volker Meja. "Legal Formalism and Disillusioned Realism in Max Weber." *Polity* 18 (Spring 1996): 307–31.

King, Nancy J. "Juror Delinquency in Criminal Trials in America, 1796–1996." *Michigan Law Review* 94 (August 1996): 2673–751.

Levine, Susan. "Labor's True Woman: Domesticity and Equal Rights in the Knights of Labor." *Journal of American History* 70 (September 1983): 323–39.

Lipin, Lawrence M. "Burying the 'Destroyer of one Happy Home': Manhood, Industrial Authority, and Political Alliance Building in the Murder Trial of Ira Strunk." *Journal of Social History* 28 (Summer 1995): 782–800.

Luning, Paul. "Irish Blood." *Chicago History* 22 (1993): 20–37.

Lupton, John A. "'In View of the Uncertainty of Life': A Coles County Lynching." *Illinois Historical Journal* 89 (1996): 134–46.

MacLean, Nancy. "The Leo Frank Case Reconsidered: Gender and Sexual Politics in the Making of Reactionary Populism." *Journal of American History* 78 (December 1991): 917–948.

McConnell, Samuel P. "The Chicago Bomb Case: Personal Recollections of an American Tragedy." *Harper's Monthly Magazine* 166 (May 1934): 730–39.

Pacyga, Dominic. "To Live Amongst Others: Poles and Their Neighbors in Industrial Chicago." *Journal of American Ethnic History* 16 (Fall 1996): 55–73.

Parsons, Donald O., and Claudia Goldin. "Parental Altruism and Self-Interest: Child Labor among Late Nineteenth-Century Americans." *Economic Inquiry* 27 (1989): 637–59.

Pederson, Jane M. "Gender, Justice, and a Wisconsin Lynching, 1889–1890." *Agricultural History* 67 (1993): 65–82.

Posner, Richard. "The Problematics of Moral and Legal Theory." *Harvard Law Review* 111 (May 1998): 1637–709.

Pound, Roscoe. "The Causes of Popular Dissatisfaction with the Administration of Justice." Reprinted in *Roscoe Pound on Criminal Justice*, edited by Sheldon Glueck, 57–73. Dobbs Ferry, N.Y.: Oceana Publications, 1965.

———. "The Need of a Sociological Jurisprudence." *The Green Bag* 19 (1907): 607–15.

Rodechko, James P. "An Irish-American Journalist and Catholicism: Patrick Ford of the Irish World." *Church History* 39 (1970): 524–40.

Scalia, Antonin. "The Rule of Law as a Law of Rules." *University of Chicago Law Review* 56 (Fall 1989): 1175–88.

Schauer, Frederick. "Rules and the Rule of Law." *Harvard Journal of Law and Public Policy* 14 (Summer 1991): 645–95.

Scheflin, Alan, and Jon Van Dyke. "Jury Nullification: The Contours of a Controversy." *Law and Contemporary Problems* 43 (Autumn 1980): 51–115.

Siegel, Reva B. "'The Rule of Love': Wife Beating as Prerogative and Privacy." *Yale Law Journal* 105 (June 1996): 2117–207.

Silbey, Susan S. "Ideology, Power, and Justice." In *Justice and Power in Sociolegal Studies*, edited by Bryant G. Garth and Austin Sarat, 272–308. Evanston: Northwestern University Press, 1998.

Smith, Beverly A. "'Devine is Doomed, And So are High Prices': The Hanging of Patsey Devine in Clinton, 1882." *Illinois Historical Journal* 91 (Spring 1999): 21–40.

———. "The Murder of Zura Burns: A Case Study of Homicide in Lincoln." *Illinois Historical Journal* 84 (1991): 218–34.

———. "*People v. Weyrich* (1877): A Nineteenth-Century Murder Case." *The Old Northwest* 14 (1988): 107–29.

Snow, David A., and Robert D. Benford. "Master Frames and Cycles of Protest." In *Frontiers in Social Movement Theory*, edited by Aldon D. Morris and Carol McClurg Mueller, 133–55. New Haven: Yale University Press, 1992.

Streib, Victor L. "Death Penalty for Children: The American Experience with Capital Punishment for Crimes Committed While Under Age Eighteen." *Oklahoma Law Review* 36 (1983): 613–41.

Train, Arthur. "Insanity and the Law." In *Courts and Criminals*, 234–65. Reprint, New York: Arno Press, 1974.

———. "Sensationalism and Jury Trials." In *Courts and Criminals*, 57–69. Reprint, New York: Arno Press, 1974.

Umphrey, Martha Merrill. "Dialogics of Legal Meaning: Spectacular Trials, the Unwritten Law, and Narratives of Criminal Responsibility." *Law and Society Review* 33, no. 2 (1999): 393–423.

Warner, Charles Dudley. "Studies of the Great West: Chicago." *Harper's New Monthly Magazine* 76 (May 1888): 869–79.

Weisberg, Robert. "Proclaiming Trials as Narratives: Premises and Pretenses." In *Law's Stories: Narrative and Rhetoric in the Law*, edited by Peter Brooks and Paul Gewirtz, 61–83. New Haven: Yale University Press, 1996.

Wilder, Gary. "Practicing Citizenship in Imperial Paris." In *Civil Society and the Political Imagination in Africa: Critical Perspectives*, edited by John L. Comaroff and Jean Comaroff, 44–71. Chicago: University of Chicago Press, 1999.

Zinn, Howard. "Law, Justice and Disobedience." *Notre Dame Journal of Law, Ethics and Public Policy* 5 (1991): 899–920.

Books

Adamson, Walter L. *Hegemony and Revolution: A Study of Antonio Gramsci's Political and Cultural Theory.* Berkeley: University of California Press, 1980.

Addams, Jane. *Twenty Years at Hull House.* New York: Macmillan, 1924.

Alfers, Kenneth G. *Law and Order in the Capital City: A History of the Washington Police, 1800–1886.* Washington, D.C.: George Washington University, 1976.

Allen, Francis A. *The Habits of Legality: Criminal Justice and the Rule of Law.* New York: Oxford University Press, 1996.

Altgeld, John Peter. *The Mind and Spirit of John Peter Altgeld: Selected Writings and Addresses.* Edited by Henry M. Christman. Urbana: University of Illinois Press, 1960.

———. *Our Penal Machinery and Its Victims.* Chicago: Jansen, McClurg & Co., 1884.

Avrich, Paul. *The Haymarket Tragedy.* Princeton: Princeton University Press, 1984.

Bakhtin, M. M. *The Dialogic Imagination: Four Essays by M. M. Bakhtin.* Edited by Michael Holquist. Translated by Caryl Emerson and Michael Holquist. Austin: University of Texas Press, 1981.

Bederman, Gail. *Manliness and Civilization: A Cultural History of Gender and Race in the United States, 1880–1917.* Chicago: University of Chicago Press, 1995.

Best, Joel. *Controlling Vice: Regulating Brothel Prostitution in St. Paul, 1865–1883.* Columbus: Ohio State University Press, 1998.

Bishop, Joel. *Commentaries on Criminal Law.* 7th ed. 2 vols. Boston: Little, Brown and Co., 1882.

Boyer, Paul. *Urban Masses and Moral Order in America, 1820–1920.* Cambridge, Mass.: Harvard University Press, 1978.

Boyer, Paul, and Stephen Nissenbaum. *Salem Possessed: The Social Origins of Witchcraft.* Cambridge, Mass: Harvard University Press, 1974.

Brace, Charles Loring. *The Criminal Classes of New York and Twenty Years Work among Them.* 1880.

Brooks, Peter, and Paul Gewirtz, eds. *Law's Stories: Narrative and Rhetoric in the Law.* New Haven: Yale University Press, 1996.

Bruce, Phillip Alexander. *The Plantation Negro as a Freeman: Observations on His Character, Condition, and Prospects in Virginia.* New York: G. P. Putnam's Sons, 1889.

Bruce, Robert V. *1877: Year of Violence.* Chicago: Ivan R. Dees, 1989.

Brundage, W. Fitzhugh. *Lynching in the New South: Georgia and Virginia, 1880–1930.* Urbana: University of Illinois Press, 1993.

Burrows, Edwin G., and Mike Wallace. *Gotham: A History of New York City to 1898.* New York: Oxford University Press, 1999.

Calhoun, Craig, ed. *Habermas and the Public Sphere.* Cambridge, Mass.: MIT Press, 1996.

Carmichael, Virginia. *Framing History: The Rosenberg Story and the Cold War.* Minneapolis: University of Minnesota Press, 1993.

Citizens Association of Chicago. *Annual Reports, 1874–1896.* Chicago, 1874–96.

Cohen, Patricia Cline. *The Murder of Helen Jewett: The Life and Times of a Prostitute in Nineteenth-Century New York.* New York: Alfred A. Knopf, 1998.

Colored Men's Professional and Business Directory of Chicago, The. Chicago: I. C. Harris, 1886.

Comaroff, John L., and Jean Comaroff, eds. *Civil Society and the Political Imagination in Africa: Critical Perspectives.* Chicago: University of Chicago Press, 1999.

Conley, Carolyn A. *The Unwritten Law: Criminal Justice in Victorian Kent.* New York: Oxford University Press, 1991.

Conrad, Clay S. *Jury Nullification: The Evolution of a Doctrine.* Durham, N.C.: Carolina Academic Press, 1998.

Cronin, William. *Nature's Metropolis: Chicago and the Great West.* New York: W. W. Norton, 1991.

Cronin Trial: Extracts from the Evidence at the Inquest. London, 1890.

Cumming, John, ed. *The Lynching at Corunna.* Mount Pleasant, Mich.: The Private Press of John Cumming, 1980.

Davis, David Brion. *Homicide in American Fiction, 1798–1860: A Study in Social Values.* Ithaca, N.Y.: Cornell University Press, 1957.

Dedman, Emmett. *Fabulous Chicago.* New York: Random House, 1953.

Denning, Michael. *Mechanic Accents: Dime Novels and Working-Class Culture in America.* 2d ed. New York: Verso, 1998.

De Ville, Kenneth Allen. *Medical Malpractice in Nineteenth-Century America: Origins and Legacy.* New York: New York University Press, 1990.

Diner, Hasia R. *Erin's Daughters in America: Irish Immigrant Women in the Nineteenth Century.* Baltimore: Johns Hopkins University Press, 1983.

Dittmer, John. *Local People: The Struggle for Civil Rights in Mississippi.* Urbana: University of Illinois Press, 1995.

Donnelly, Ignatius. *Caesar's Column: A Story of the Twentieth Century.* Chicago: A. M. Donohue and Co., 1918.

Drake, St. Clair. *Churches and Voluntary Associations in the Chicago Negro Community.* Works Projects Association. Report of Official Project 465–54–3–386. Chicago, December 1940.

Drake, St. Clair, and Horace R. Clayton. *Black Metropolis: A Study of Negro Life in a Northern City.* New York: Harcourt, Brace, 1945.

DuBois, W. E. B. *The Philadelphia Negro: A Social Study.* Philadelphia: University of Pennsylvania, 1899.

Dugdale, R. L. *The Jukes: A Study in Crime, Pauperism, Disease and Heredity.* 4th ed. New York: G. P. Putnam's Sons, 1888.

Duis, Perry R. *Challenging Chicago: Coping with Everyday Life, 1837–1920.* Urbana: University of Illinois Press, 1998.

———. *The Saloon: Public Drinking in Chicago and Boston, 1880–1920.* Urbana: University of Illinois Press, 1983.

Edwards, Laura F. *Gendered Strife and Confusion: The Political Culture of Reconstruction.* Urbana: University of Illinois Press, 1997.

Eigen, John Peter. *Witnessing Insanity: Madness and Mad-Doctors in the English Court.* New Haven: Yale University Press, 1995.

Einhorn, Robin L. *Property Rules: Political Economy in Chicago, 1833–1872.* Chicago: University of Chicago Press, 1991.

Elias, Norbert. *The Civilizing Process.* Translated by Edmund Jephcott. Oxford: Blackwell, 1994.

Ellis, Havelock. *The Criminal.* London: Walter Scott, 1890.

Epstein, Barbara Leslie. *The Politics of Domesticity: Women, Evangelism and Temperance in Nineteenth-Century America.* Middletown, Conn.: Wesleyan University Press, 1981.

Ethington, Philip J. *The Public City: The Political Construction of Urban Life in San Francisco, 1850–1900.* New York: Cambridge University Press, 1994.

Flinn, John J. *History of the Chicago Police.* Chicago, 1887. Reprint, New York: AMS Press, 1973.

Fredrickson, George M. *The Black Image in the White Mind: The Debate on Afro-American Character and Destiny, 1817–1914.* New York: Harper and Row, 1971.

Friedman, Lawrence M. *Crime and Punishment in American History.* New York: Basic Books, 1993.

Friedman, Lawrence M., and Robert V. Percival. *The Roots of Justice: Crime and Punishment in Alameda County, California, 1870–1910.* Chapel Hill: University of North Carolina Press, 1981.

Gaines, Kevin K. *Uplifting the Race: Black Leadership, Politics, and Culture in the Twentieth Century.* Chapel Hill: University of North Carolina Press, 1996.

Garth, Bryant G., and Austin Sarat, eds. *Justice and Power in Sociolegal Studies.* Evanston: Northwestern University Press, 1998.

Gatewood, Willard B. *Aristocrats of Color: The Black Elite, 1880–1920.* Bloomington: Indiana University Press, 1990.

Gatrell, V. A. C. *The Hanging Tree: Execution and the English People, 1770–1868.* New York: Oxford University Press, 1994.

Gilfoyle, Timothy J. *City of Eros: New York City, Prostitution, and the Commercialization of Sex, 1790–1920.* New York: W. W. Norton, 1992.

Gleason, Timothy W. *The Watchdog Concept: The Press and the Courts in Nineteenth-Century America.* Ames: Iowa State University Press, 1990.

Gobert, James. *Justice, Democracy and the Jury.* Aldershot; Brookfield, Vt.: Ashgate/Dartmouth, 1997.

Goldstein, Irving. *Trial Technique.* Chicago: Callahan and Co., 1935.

Gordon, Linda. *The Great Arizona Orphan Abduction.* Cambridge, Mass.: Harvard University Press, 1999.

Green, Sanford M. *Crime: Its Nature, Causes, Treatment and Prevention.* Philadelphia: J. B. Lippincott, 1889.

Grossberg, Michael. *A Judgment for Solomon: The d'Hauteville Case and Legal Experience in Antebellum America.* New York: Cambridge University Press, 1996.

Habermas, Jürgen. *Between Facts and Norms: Contributions to a Discourse Theory of Law and Democracy.* Translated by William Reh. Cambridge, Mass.: MIT Press, 1996.

Hale, Grace Elizabeth. *Making Whiteness: The Culture of Segregation in the South, 1890–1940.* New York: Vintage, 1998.

Hall, Kermit. *The Magic Mirror: Law in American History.* New York: Oxford University Press, 1989.

Halttunen, Karen. *Murder Most Foul.* Cambridge, Mass.: Harvard University Press, 1998.

Hariman, Robert, ed. *Popular Trials: Rhetoric, Mass Media, and the Law.* Tuscaloosa: University of Alabama Press, 1990.

Harris, Ruth. *Murder and Madness: Medicine, Law and Society in the Fin de Siècle.* Oxford: Clarendon Press, 1989.

Hart, H. L. A. *Punishment and Responsibility: Essays in the Philosophy of Law*. New York: Oxford University Press, 1968.

Hawes, Joseph M. *Children in Urban Society: Juvenile Delinquency in Nineteenth-Century America*. New York: Oxford University Press, 1971.

Herrick, Robert. *The Memoirs of an American Citizen*. New York: Macmillan, 1905.

Higginbotham, Evelyn Brooks. *Righteous Discontent: The Women's Movement in the Black Baptist Church, 1880–1920*. Cambridge, Mass.: Harvard University Press, 1993.

Holub, Renate. *Antonio Gramsci: Beyond Marxism and Postmodernism*. London: Routledge, 1992.

Horwitz, Morton J. *The Transformation of American Law, 1780–1860*. Cambridge, Mass: Harvard University Press, 1977.

Hughes, John S. *In the Law's Darkness: Isaac Ray and the Medical Jurisprudence of Insanity in Nineteenth-Century America*. New York: Oceana Press, 1986.

Hunt, Henry M. *The Crime of the Century; or, The Assassination of Dr. Patrick Henry Cronin*. [Chicago?]: H. L. & D. H. Kochersperger, 1889.

Ignatiev, Noel. *How the Irish Became White*. New York: Routledge, 1995.

Karsten, Peter. *Heart versus Head: Judge-Made Law in Nineteenth-Century America*. Chapel Hill: University of North Carolina Press, 1997.

Keller, Morton. *Affairs of State: Public Life in Late Nineteenth Century America*. Cambridge, Mass.: Belknap Press of Harvard University Press, 1977.

Knelman, Judith. *Twisting in the Wind: The Murderess and the English Press*. Toronto: University of Toronto Press, 1998.

Kohl, Lawrence Frederick. *The Politics of Individualism: Parties and the American Character in the Jacksonian Era*. New York: Oxford University Press, 1989.

Lane, Roger. *Policing the City: Boston, 1822–1885*. Cambridge, Mass.: Harvard University Press, 1967.

———. *Roots of Violence in Black Philadelphia, 1860–1900*. Cambridge, Mass.: Harvard University Press, 1986.

Levine, Lawrence W. *Highbrow/Lowbrow: The Emergence of Cultural Hierarchy in America*. Cambridge, Mass.: Harvard University Press, 1988.

Lindberg, Richard C. *To Serve and Collect: Chicago Politics and Police Corruption from the Lager Beer Riot to the Summerdale Scandal, 1855–1960*. Reprint, Carbondale: Southern Illinois University Press, 1991.

Lynching and Vigilantism in the United States: An Annotated Bibliography. Norton H. Moses, compiler. Bibliographies and Indexes in American History, no. 34. Westport, Conn.: Greenwood Press, 1997.

MacAndrew, Elizabeth. *The Gothic Tradition in Fiction*. New York: Columbia University Press, 1979.

Masters, Edgar Lee. *The Tale of Chicago*. New York: G. P. Putnam's Sons, 1933.

Masur, Louis P. *Rites of Execution: Capital Punishment and the Transformation of American Culture, 1776–1865*. New York: Oxford University Press, 1989.

Mattson, Kevin. *Creating a Democratic Republic: The Struggle for Urban Participatory Democracy during the Progressive Era*. University Park: Pennsylvania State University Press, 1998.

McCaffrey, Lawrence J., Ellen Skerrett, Michael F. Funchion, and Charles Fanning, eds. *The Irish in Chicago*. Urbana: University of Illinois Press, 1987.

McElhaney, James W. *McElhaney's Trial Notebook*. 2d ed. [Chicago]: American Bar Association, 1987.

McGerr, Michael E. *The Decline of Popular Politics: The American North, 1865–1928*. New York: Oxford University Press, 1986.

McMurry, Donald L. *The Great Burlington Strike of 1888: A Case History in Labor Relations*. Cambridge, Mass.: Harvard University Press, 1956.

Medical and Surgical Directory of Cook County, Illinois, 1888–1889. Chicago: Physician's Collective Association, [1888?].

Meranze, Michael. *Laboratories of Virtue: Punishment, Revolution and Authority in Philadelphia, 1760–1835*. Chapel Hill: University of North Carolina Press, 1996.

Merton, Robert K. *The Sociology of Science: Theoretical and Empirical Investigations*. Chicago: University of Chicago Press, 1973.

Merton, Robert K., Leonard Bloom, and Leonard S. Cottrell, Jr., eds. *Sociology Today: Problems and Prospects*. New York: Basic Books, 1959.

Meyerowitz, Joanne J. *Women Adrift: Independent Wage Earners in Chicago, 1880–1930*. Chicago: University of Chicago Press, 1988.

Miller, Donald L. *City of the Century: The Epic of Chicago and the Making of America*. New York: Simon & Schuster, 1996.

Monkkonen, Eric H. *The Local State: Public Money and American Cities*. Stanford: Stanford University Press, 1995.

Montgomery, David. *Citizen Worker: The Experience of Workers in the United States with Democracy and the Free Market during the Nineteenth Century*. New York: Cambridge University Press, 1993.

———. *The Fall of the House of Labor: The Workplace, the State, and American Labor Activism, 1865–1925*. New York: Cambridge University Press, 1987.

Mott, Frank Luther. *American Journalism, a History: 1690–1960*. 3d ed. New York: Macmillan, 1966.

Nelson, Bruce. *Beyond the Martyrs: A Social History of Chicago's Anarchists, 1870–1900*. New Brunswick, N.J.: Rutgers University Press, 1988.

Nelson, Nell [pseud.]. *The White Slave Girls of Chicago*. Chicago: Barkley Publishing Co., 1888.

Nelson, William E. *The Americanization of the Common Law: The Impact of Legal Change on Massachusetts Society, 1760–1830*. Cambridge, Mass: Harvard University Press, 1975.

Newman, Louise Michelle. *White Women's Rights: The Racial Origins of Feminism in the United States*. New York: Oxford University Press, 1999.

Novak, William J. *The People's Welfare: Law and Regulation in Nineteenth-Century America*. Chapel Hill: University of North Carolina Press, 1996.

Odem, Mary E. *Delinquent Daughters: Protecting and Policing Adolescent Female Sexuality in the United States, 1885–1920*. Chapel Hill: University of North Carolina Press, 1995.

Opinions of the Corporation Counsel and Assistants [Chicago], from January 1872 to March 1897. William G. Beale and Edward S. Day, compilers. Chicago: W. B. Conkey, n.d.

Papke, David Ray. *Framing the Criminal: Crime, Cultural Work and the Loss of Critical Perspective, 1830–1900*. Hamden, Conn.: Archon Books, 1987.

Paul, Arnold M. *Conservative Crisis and the Rule of Law: Attitudes of Bench and Bar*. Reprint, Glouchester, Mass.: Peter Smith, 1976.

Peiss, Kathy. *Cheap Amusements: Working Women and Leisure in Turn-of-the-Century New York.* Philadelphia: Temple University Press, 1989.

Pierce, Bessie Louise. *A History of Chicago,* vol. 3: *The Rise of a Modern City, 1871–1893.* Chicago: University of Chicago Press, 1957.

Pound, Roscoe. *Law and Morality.* Chapel Hill: University of North Carolina Press, 1926.

Proceedings of the Illinois State Bar Association, 1882–1887. Springfield, 1882–87.

Proceedings of the Illinois State Bar Association, 1888–1893. Springfield, 1888–93.

Pucci, Idanna. *The Trials of Maria Barbella: The True Story of a Nineteenth-Century Crime of Passion.* Translated by Stefanie Fumo. New York: Four Walls Eight Windows Press, 1996.

Roediger, David. *The Wages of Whiteness: Race and the Making of the American Working Class.* New York: Verso, 1991.

Rosenberg, Charles E. *The Trial of the Assassin Guiteau: Psychiatry and the Law in the Gilded Age.* Chicago: University of Chicago Press, 1968.

Ross, Dorothy. *The Origins of American Social Science.* New York: Cambridge University Press, 1991.

Ryan, Mary P. *Civic Wars: Democracy and Public Life in the American City during the Nineteenth Century.* Berkeley: University of California Press, 1997.

Sawislak, Karen. *Smoldering City: Chicagoans and the Great Fire, 1871–1874.* Chicago: University of Chicago Press, 1996.

Schaack, Michael J. *Anarchy and Anarchists: A History of the Red Terror and the Social Revolution in America and Europe.* Chicago: F. J. Schulte and Co., 1889.

Schiller, Dan. *Objectivity and the News: The Public and the Rise of Commercial Journalism.* Philadelphia: University of Pennsylvania Press, 1981.

Schneirov, Richard. *Labor and Urban Politics: Class Conflict and the Origins of Modern Liberalism.* Urbana: University of Illinois Press, 1998.

Scull, Andrew, ed. *Madhouses, Mad-Doctors, and Madmen: The Social History of Psychiatry in the Victorian Era.* Philadelphia: University of Pennsylvania Press, 1981.

Sellers, Charles. *The Market Revolution: Jacksonian America, 1815–1846.* New York: Oxford University Press, 1991.

Skocpol, Theda. *Protecting Soldiers and Mothers: The Political Origins of Social Policy in the United States.* Cambridge, Mass.: Belknap Press of the Harvard University Press, 1992.

Skultans, Vieda, comp. *Madness and Morals: Ideas on Insanity in the Nineteenth Century.* Boston: Routledge and Kegan Paul, 1975.

Smith, Carl S. *Chicago and the Literary Imagination, 1880–1920.* Chicago: University of Chicago Press, 1984.

———. *Urban Disorder and the Shape of Disbelief: The Great Chicago Fire, the Haymarket Riot, and the Model Town of Pullman.* Chicago: University of Chicago Press, 1995.

Smith, Roger. *Trial by Medicine: Insanity and Responsibility in Victorian Trials.* Edinburgh: Edinburgh University Press, 1981.

Spear, Allan H. *Black Chicago: The Making of a Negro Ghetto, 1890–1920.* Chicago: University of Chicago Press, 1967.

Stanley, Amy Dru. *From Bondage to Contract: Wage Labor, Marriage, and the Market in the Age of Slave Emancipation.* New York: Cambridge University Press, 1998.

Steinberg, Allen. *The Transformation of Criminal Justice: Philadelphia, 1800–1880.* Chapel Hill: University of North Carolina Press, 1989.

Sugrue, Thomas J. *The Origins of the Urban Crisis: Race and Inequality in Postwar Detroit.* Princeton: Princeton University Press, 1996.

Teaford, Jon C. *The Unheralded Triumph: City Government in America, 1870–1900.* Baltimore: Johns Hopkins University Press, 1984.

Terdiman, Richard. *Discourse/Counter-Discourse: The Theory and Practice of Symbolic Resistance in Nineteenth-Century France.* Ithaca, N.Y.: Cornell University Press, 1985.

Tocqueville, Alexis de. *Democracy in America.* Edited by J. P. Mayer. Translated by George Lawrence. 2 vols. in 1. New York: Harper and Row, 1966.

Tomlins, Christopher L. *Law, Labor, and Ideology in the Early American Republic.* New York: Cambridge University Press, 1993.

Tourgee, Albion W. *Appeal to Caesar.* New York: Ford, Howard & Hulbert, 1884.

Tuchman, Gaye. *Making News: A Study in the Construction of Reality.* New York: Free Press, 1980.

Wade, Louise Carol. *Chicago's Pride: The Stockyards, Packingtown, and Environs in the Nineteenth Century.* Urbana: University of Illinois Press, 1987.

Waldrep, Christopher. *Roots of Disorder: Race and Criminal Justice in the American South, 1817–1880.* Urbana: University of Illinois Press, 1998.

Walker, Samuel. *Popular Justice: A History of American Criminal Justice.* 2d ed. New York: Oxford University Press, 1998.

Weibe, Robert H. *The Search for Order, 1877–1920.* New York: Hill and Wang, 1967.

Wellman, Francis L. *The Art of Cross-Examination.* New York: Macmillan, 1903; New York: Collier Books, 1962.

Wharton, Francis. *Treatise on Criminal Law.* 8th ed. 2 vols. Philadelphia: Kay and Brothers, 1880.

Wiecek, William M. *The Lost World of Classical Legal Thought: Law and Ideology in America, 1886–1937.* New York: Oxford University Press, 1998.

Wilentz, Sean. *Chants Democratic: New York City and the Rise of the American Working Class, 1788–1850.* New York: Oxford University Press, 1984.

Williams, Daniel E. *Pillars of Salt: An Anthology of Early American Criminal Narratives.* Madison, Wis.: Madison House, 1993.

Williamson, Joel. *The Crucible of Race: Black/White Relations in the American South since Emancipation.* New York: Oxford University Press, 1984.

Winslow, L. Forbes. *Recollections of Forty Years: Being an Account at First Hand of Some Famous Criminal Lunacy Cases, English and American.* London: J. Ouseley, 1910.

INDEX

The History of Crime and Criminal Justice Series
David R. Johnson and Jeffrey S. Adler, Series Editors

The series explores the history of crime and criminality, violence, criminal justice, and legal systems without restriction as to chronological scope, geographic focus, or methodological approach.